Kudzu

by Doug Marlette

BALLANTINE BOOKS • NEW YORK

Copyright © 1982 by Jefferson Communications, Inc.

All rights reserved under International and Pan-American Copyright Conventions. Published in the United States by Ballantine Books, a division of Random House, Inc., New York, and simultaneously in Canada by Random House of Canada Limited, Toronto, Canada.

Library of Congress Catalogue Card Number: 82-90225

ISBN: 0-345-30573-6

Manufactured in United States of America

First Edition: August 1982

1 2 3 4 5 6 7 8 9 10

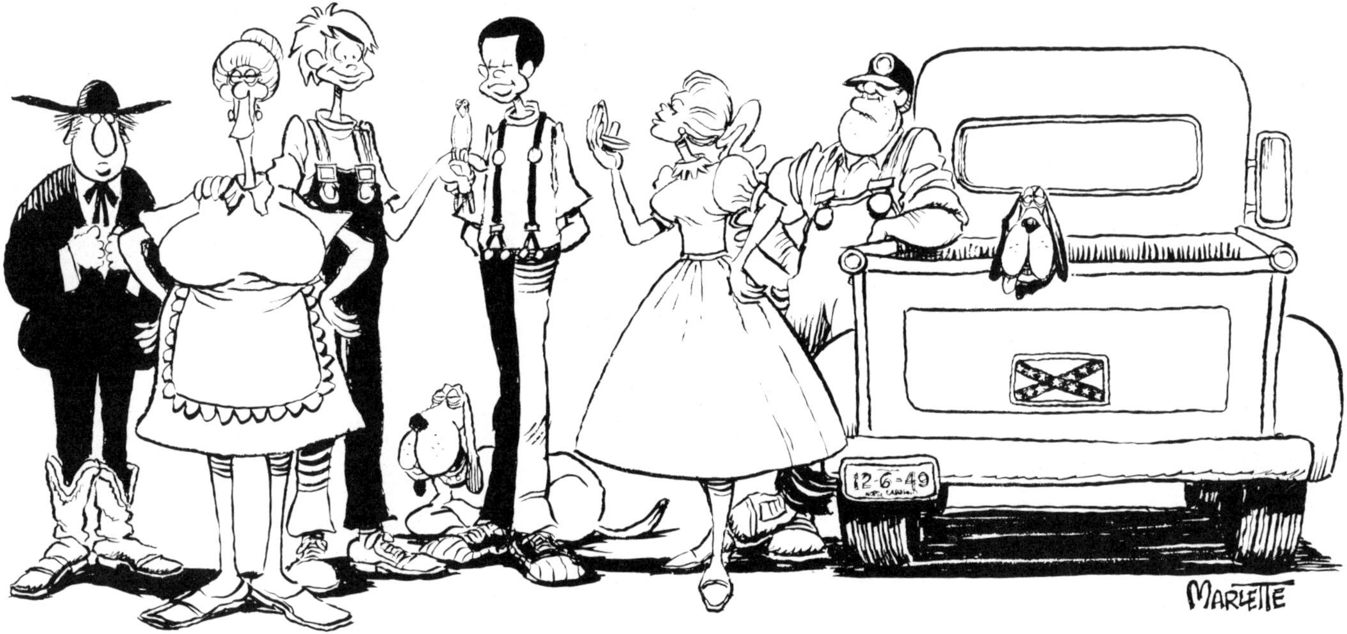
12-6-49
MARLETTE

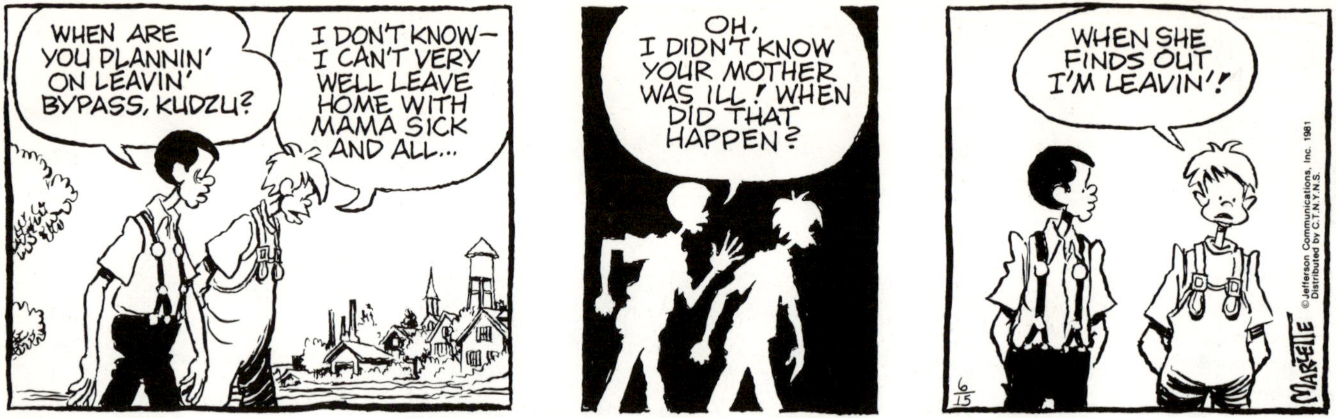
WHEN ARE YOU PLANNIN' ON LEAVIN' BYPASS, KUDZU?
I DON'T KNOW— I CAN'T VERY WELL LEAVE HOME WITH MAMA SICK AND ALL...
OH, I DIDN'T KNOW YOUR MOTHER WAS ILL! WHEN DID THAT HAPPEN?
WHEN SHE FINDS OUT I'M LEAVIN'!
6/15
MARLETTE
© Jefferson Communications, Inc. 1981
Distributed by C.T.N.Y.N.S.

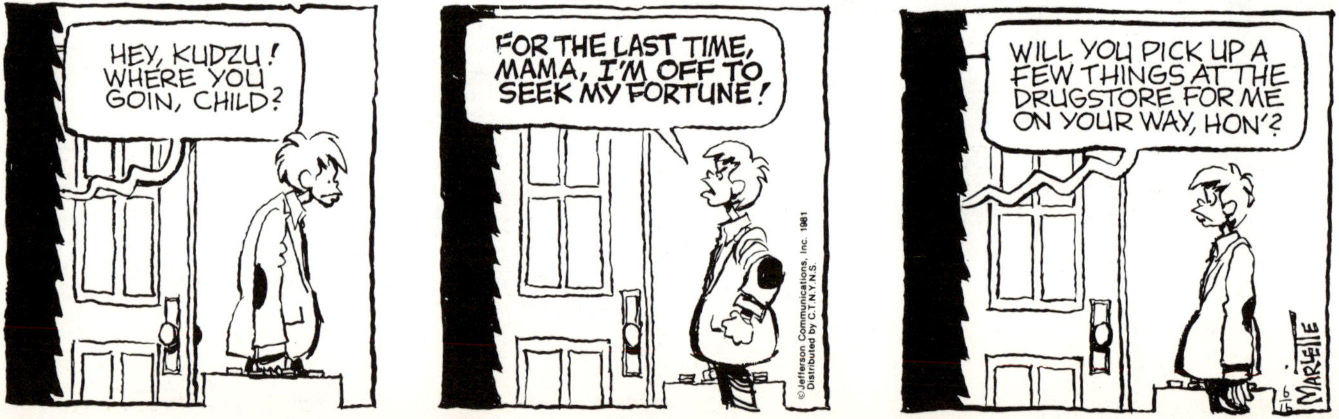
HEY, KUDZU! WHERE YOU GOIN, CHILD?
FOR THE LAST TIME, MAMA, I'M OFF TO SEEK MY FORTUNE!
© Jefferson Communications, Inc. 1981
Distributed by C.T.N.Y.N.S.
WILL YOU PICK UP A FEW THINGS AT THE DRUGSTORE FOR ME ON YOUR WAY, HON'?
6/16
MARLETTE

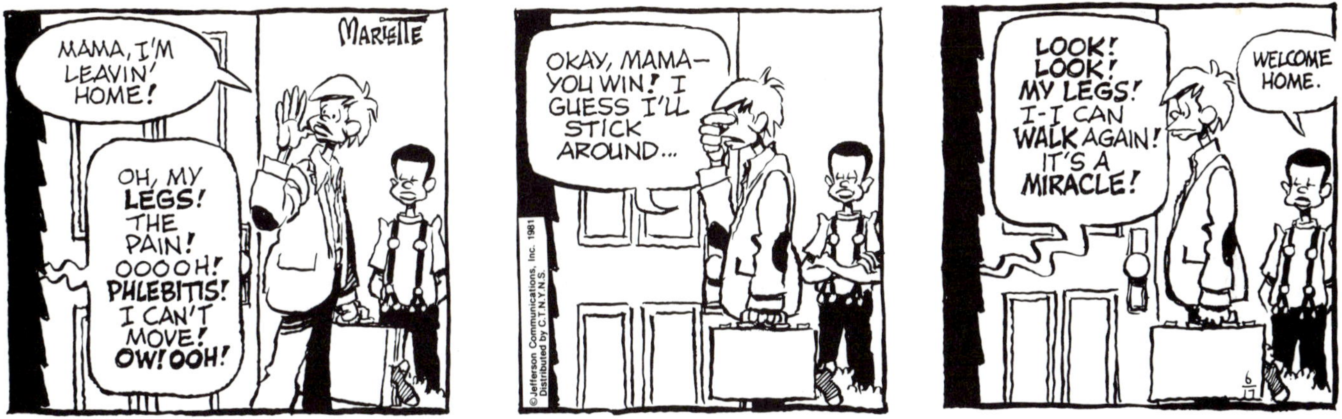
MARLETTE
MAMA, I'M LEAVIN' HOME!
OH, MY LEGS! THE PAIN! OOOOH! PHLEBITIS! I CAN'T MOVE! OW! OOH!
OKAY, MAMA— YOU WIN! I GUESS I'LL STICK AROUND...
© Jefferson Communications, Inc. 1981 Distributed by C.T.N.Y.N.S.
LOOK! LOOK! MY LEGS! I-I CAN WALK AGAIN! IT'S A MIRACLE!
WELCOME HOME.
6/17

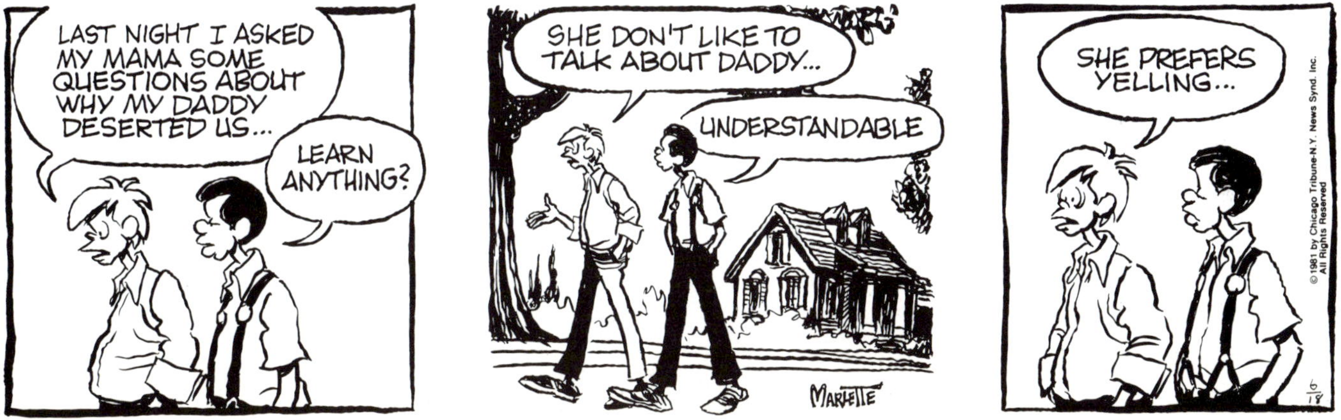
LAST NIGHT I ASKED MY MAMA SOME QUESTIONS ABOUT WHY MY DADDY DESERTED US...
LEARN ANYTHING?
SHE DON'T LIKE TO TALK ABOUT DADDY...
UNDERSTANDABLE
MARLETTE
SHE PREFERS YELLING...
© 1981 by Chicago Tribune-N.Y. News Synd. Inc. All Rights Reserved
6/18

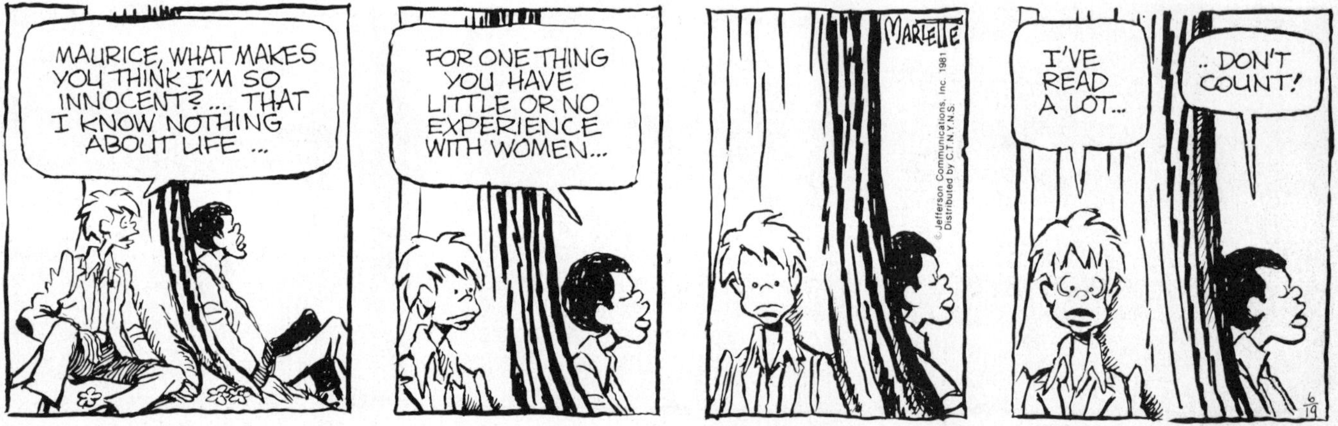
MAURICE, WHAT MAKES YOU THINK I'M SO INNOCENT?... THAT I KNOW NOTHING ABOUT LIFE ...
FOR ONE THING YOU HAVE LITTLE OR NO EXPERIENCE WITH WOMEN...
MARLETTE
© Jefferson Communications, Inc. 1981 Distributed by C.T.N.Y.N.S.
I'VE READ A LOT...
.. DON'T COUNT!
6/19

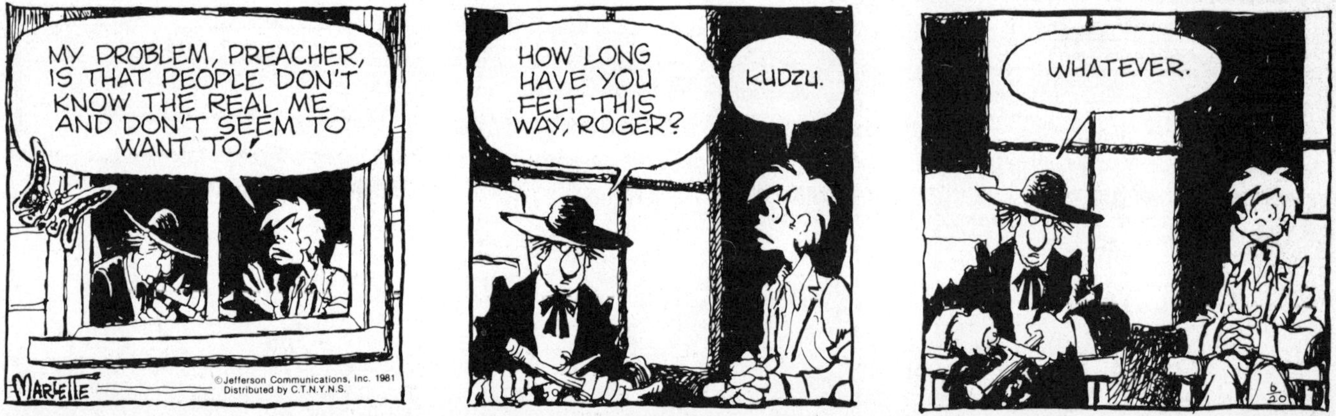
MY PROBLEM, PREACHER, IS THAT PEOPLE DON'T KNOW THE REAL ME AND DON'T SEEM TO WANT TO!
MARLETTE
©Jefferson Communications, Inc. 1981 Distributed by C.T.N.Y.N.S.
HOW LONG HAVE YOU FELT THIS WAY, ROGER?
KUDZU.
WHATEVER.
6/20

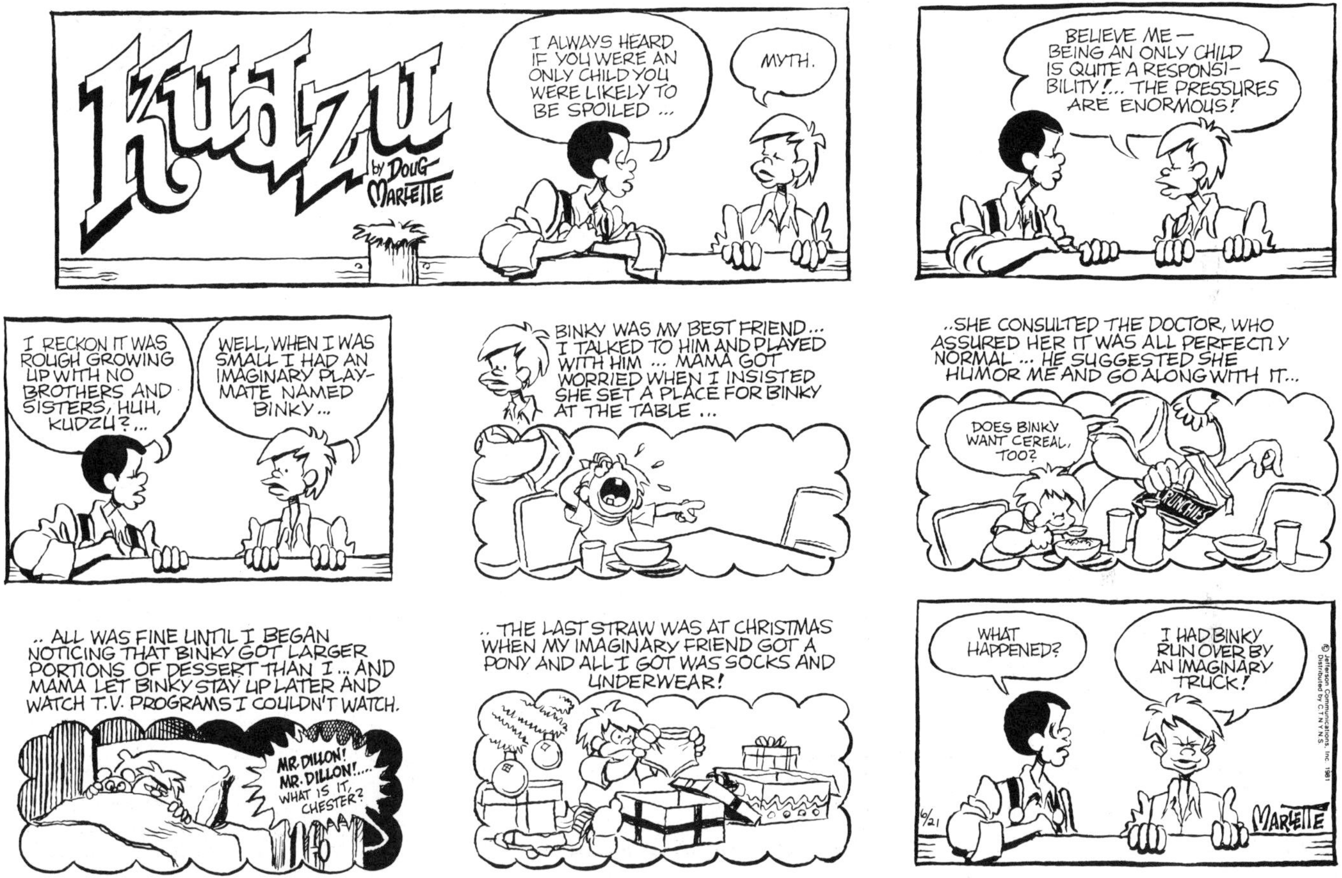

KUDZU
by DOUG MARLETTE
I ALWAYS HEARD IF YOU WERE AN ONLY CHILD YOU WERE LIKELY TO BE SPOILED ...
MYTH.
BELIEVE ME — BEING AN ONLY CHILD IS QUITE A RESPONSIBILITY!... THE PRESSURES ARE ENORMOUS!
I RECKON IT WAS ROUGH GROWING UP WITH NO BROTHERS AND SISTERS, HUH, KUDZU?...
WELL, WHEN I WAS SMALL I HAD AN IMAGINARY PLAYMATE NAMED BINKY...
BINKY WAS MY BEST FRIEND... I TALKED TO HIM AND PLAYED WITH HIM ... MAMA GOT WORRIED WHEN I INSISTED SHE SET A PLACE FOR BINKY AT THE TABLE ...
..SHE CONSULTED THE DOCTOR, WHO ASSURED HER IT WAS ALL PERFECTLY NORMAL ... HE SUGGESTED SHE HUMOR ME AND GO ALONG WITH IT...
DOES BINKY WANT CEREAL, TOO?
CRUNCHIES
.. ALL WAS FINE UNTIL I BEGAN NOTICING THAT BINKY GOT LARGER PORTIONS OF DESSERT THAN I... AND MAMA LET BINKY STAY UP LATER AND WATCH T.V. PROGRAMS I COULDN'T WATCH.
MR. DILLON! MR. DILLON!... WHAT IS IT, CHESTER?
.. THE LAST STRAW WAS AT CHRISTMAS WHEN MY IMAGINARY FRIEND GOT A PONY AND ALL I GOT WAS SOCKS AND UNDERWEAR!
WHAT HAPPENED?
I HAD BINKY RUN OVER BY AN IMAGINARY TRUCK!
© Jefferson Communications, Inc. 1981 Distributed by C.T.N.Y.N.S.
6/21
MARLETTE

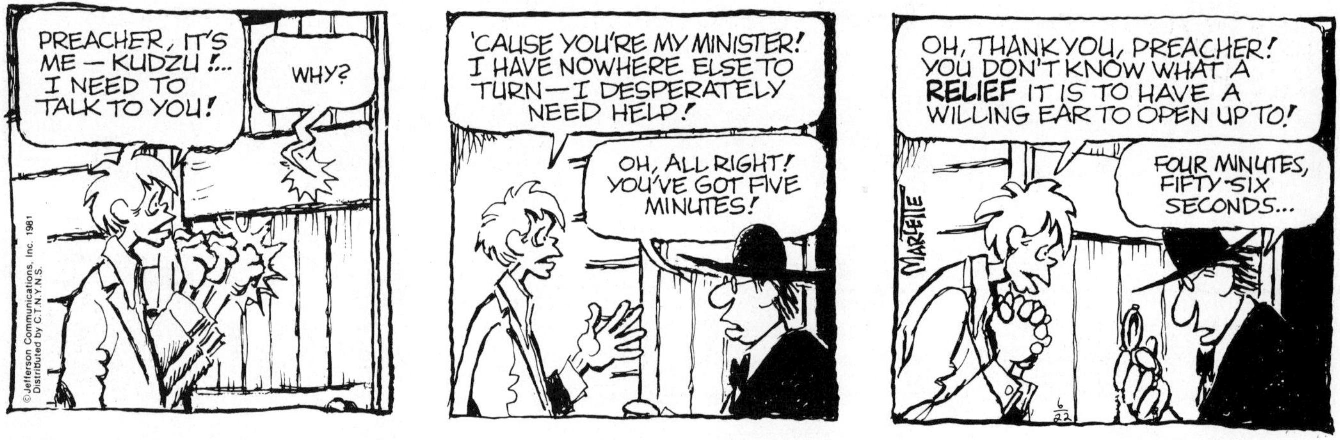

PREACHER, IT'S ME — KUDZU!... I NEED TO TALK TO YOU!
WHY?
© Jefferson Communications, Inc. 1981 Distributed by C.T.N.Y.N.S.
'CAUSE YOU'RE MY MINISTER! I HAVE NOWHERE ELSE TO TURN—I DESPERATELY NEED HELP!
OH, ALL RIGHT! YOU'VE GOT FIVE MINUTES!
OH, THANK YOU, PREACHER! YOU DON'T KNOW WHAT A **RELIEF** IT IS TO HAVE A WILLING EAR TO OPEN UP TO!
FOUR MINUTES, FIFTY-SIX SECONDS...
MARLETTE
6/22

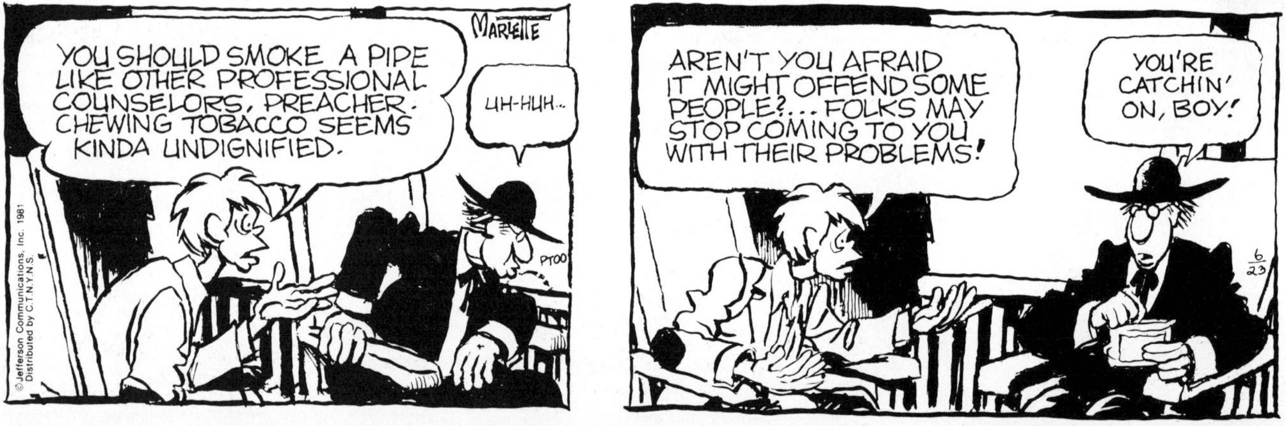

MARLETTE
YOU SHOULD SMOKE A PIPE LIKE OTHER PROFESSIONAL COUNSELORS, PREACHER. CHEWING TOBACCO SEEMS KINDA UNDIGNIFIED.
UH-HUH...
PTOO
© Jefferson Communications, Inc. 1981 Distributed by C.T.N.Y.N.S.
AREN'T YOU AFRAID IT MIGHT OFFEND SOME PEOPLE?... FOLKS MAY STOP COMING TO YOU WITH THEIR PROBLEMS!
YOU'RE CATCHIN' ON, BOY!
6/23

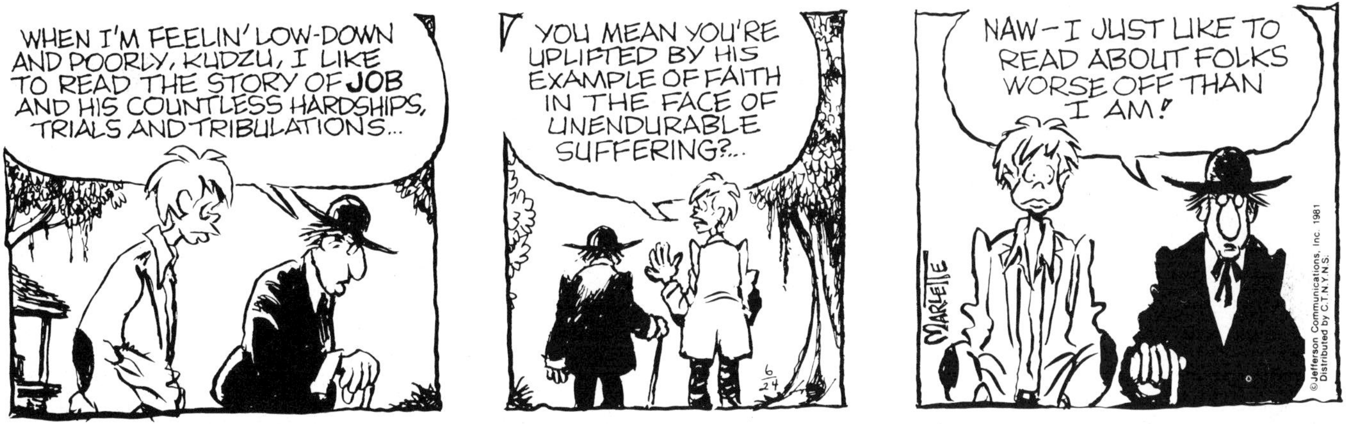
WHEN I'M FEELIN' LOW-DOWN AND POORLY, KUDZU, I LIKE TO READ THE STORY OF **JOB** AND HIS COUNTLESS HARDSHIPS, TRIALS AND TRIBULATIONS...
YOU MEAN YOU'RE UPLIFTED BY HIS EXAMPLE OF FAITH IN THE FACE OF UNENDURABLE SUFFERING?...
6/24
NAW—I JUST LIKE TO READ ABOUT FOLKS WORSE OFF THAN I AM!
MARLETTE
©Jefferson Communications, Inc. 1981
Distributed by C.T.N.Y.N.S.

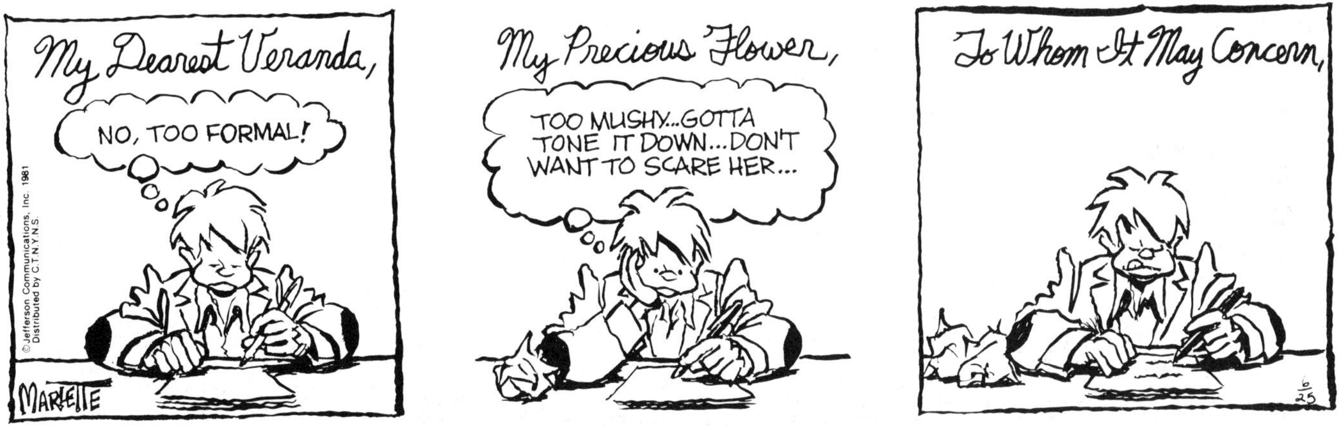
My Dearest Veranda,
NO, TOO FORMAL!
©Jefferson Communications, Inc. 1981
Distributed by C.T.N.Y.N.S.
MARLETTE
My Precious Flower,
TOO MUSHY...GOTTA TONE IT DOWN...DON'T WANT TO SCARE HER...
To Whom It May Concern,
2/6
25

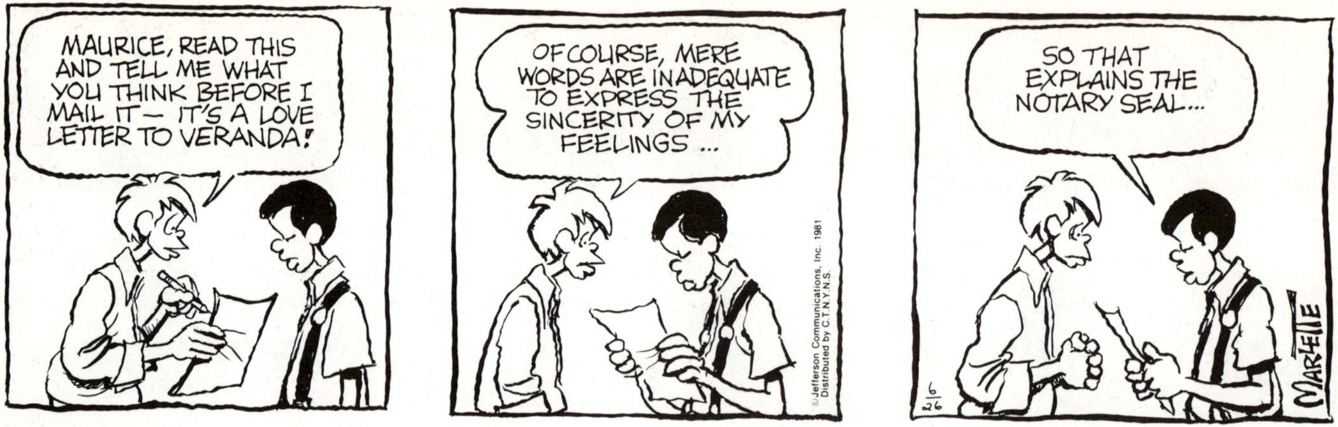
MAURICE, READ THIS AND TELL ME WHAT YOU THINK BEFORE I MAIL IT— IT'S A LOVE LETTER TO VERANDA!
OF COURSE, MERE WORDS ARE INADEQUATE TO EXPRESS THE SINCERITY OF MY FEELINGS ...
© Jefferson Communications, Inc. 1981
Distributed by C.T.N.Y.N.S.
SO THAT EXPLAINS THE NOTARY SEAL...
6/26
MARLETTE

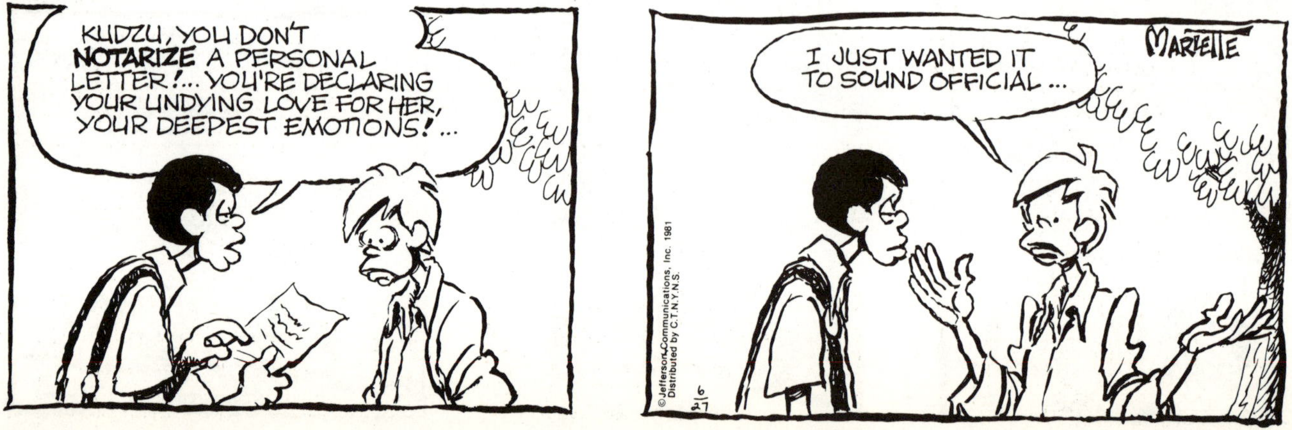
KUDZU, YOU DON'T **NOTARIZE** A PERSONAL LETTER!... YOU'RE DECLARING YOUR UNDYING LOVE FOR HER, YOUR DEEPEST EMOTIONS!...
© Jefferson Communications, Inc. 1981
Distributed by C.T.N.Y.N.S.
6/27
MARLETTE
I JUST WANTED IT TO SOUND OFFICIAL ...

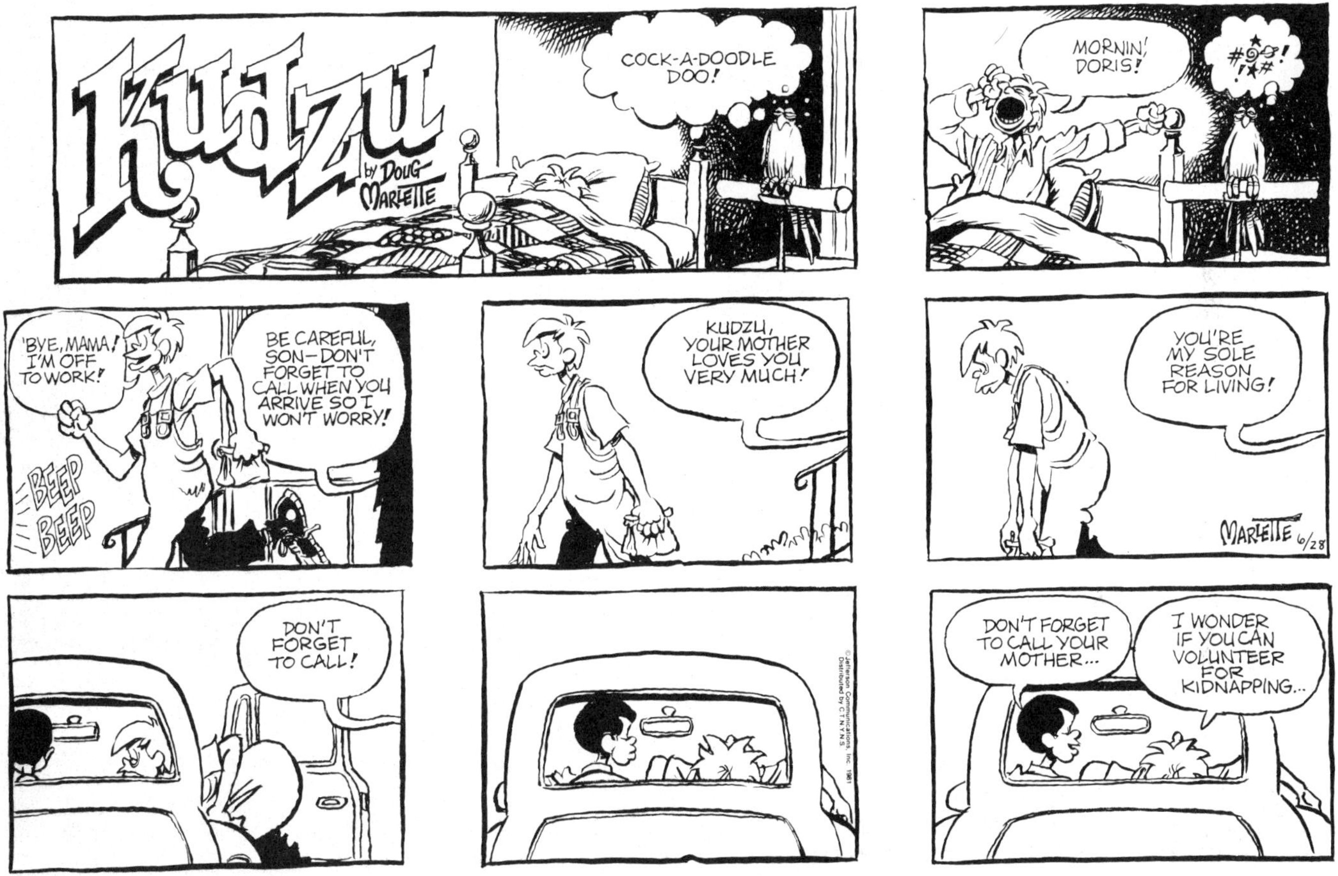
KUDZU
by DOUG MARLETTE
COCK-A-DOODLE DOO!
MORNIN' DORIS!
#@*! !*#
'BYE, MAMA! I'M OFF TO WORK!
BE CAREFUL, SON—DON'T FORGET TO CALL WHEN YOU ARRIVE SO I WON'T WORRY!
BEEP BEEP
KUDZU, YOUR MOTHER LOVES YOU VERY MUCH!
YOU'RE MY SOLE REASON FOR LIVING!
MARLETTE 6/28
DON'T FORGET TO CALL!
©Jefferson Communications, Inc. 1981 Distributed by C.T.N.Y.N.S.
DON'T FORGET TO CALL YOUR MOTHER...
I WONDER IF YOU CAN VOLUNTEER FOR KIDNAPPING...

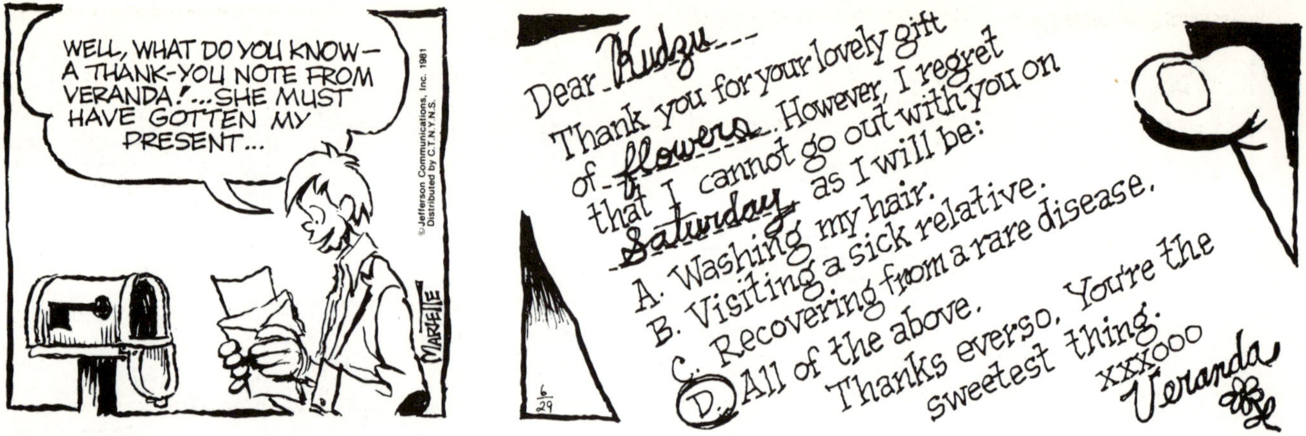
WELL, WHAT DO YOU KNOW— A THANK-YOU NOTE FROM VERANDA!...SHE MUST HAVE GOTTEN MY PRESENT...
© Jefferson Communications, Inc. 1981 Distributed by C.T.N.Y.N.S.
MARLETTE
Dear Kudzu---
Thank you for your lovely gift of flowers. However, I regret that I cannot go out with you on Saturday as I will be:
A. Washing my hair.
B. Visiting a sick relative.
C. Recovering from a rare disease.
D. All of the above.
Thanks everso. You're the sweetest thing.
XXXOOO
Veranda
6/29

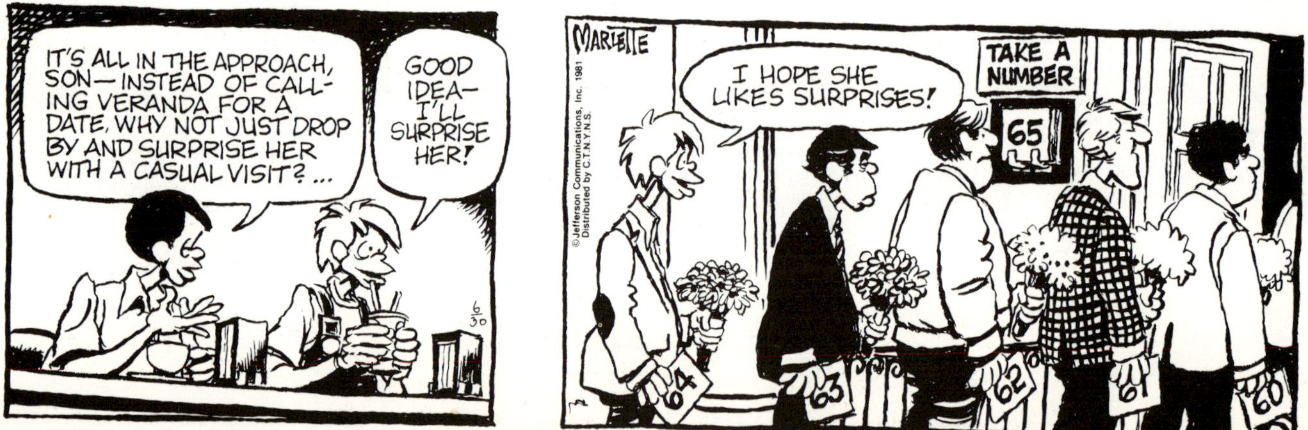
IT'S ALL IN THE APPROACH, SON—INSTEAD OF CALLING VERANDA FOR A DATE, WHY NOT JUST DROP BY AND SURPRISE HER WITH A CASUAL VISIT?...
GOOD IDEA—I'LL SURPRISE HER!
6/30
MARLETTE
© Jefferson Communications, Inc. 1981 Distributed by C.T.N.Y.N.S.
I HOPE SHE LIKES SURPRISES!
TAKE A NUMBER
65
64
63
62
61
60

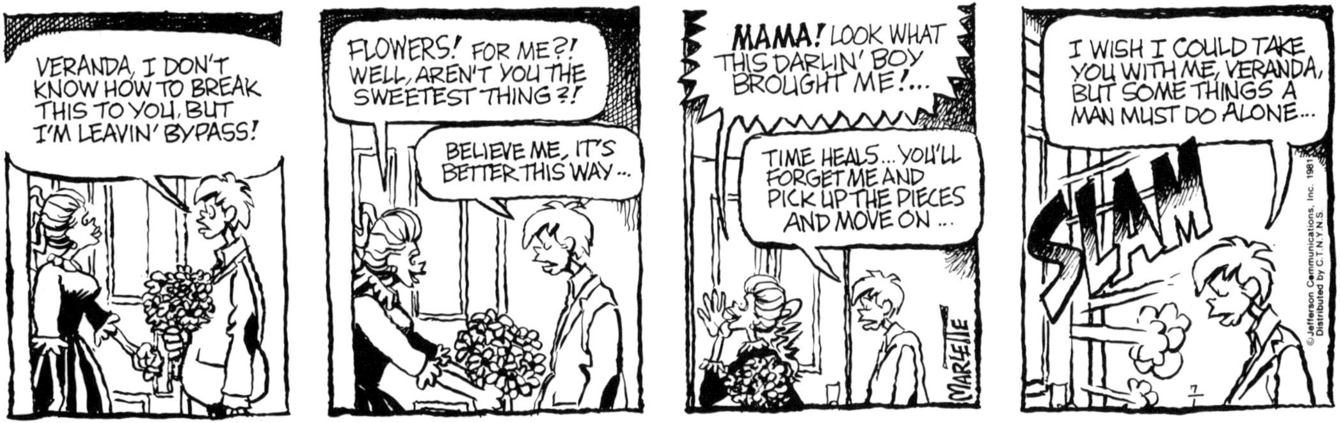
VERANDA, I DON'T KNOW HOW TO BREAK THIS TO YOU, BUT I'M LEAVIN' BYPASS!
FLOWERS! FOR ME?! WELL, AREN'T YOU THE SWEETEST THING?!
BELIEVE ME, IT'S BETTER THIS WAY...
MAMA! LOOK WHAT THIS DARLIN' BOY BROUGHT ME!...
TIME HEALS... YOU'LL FORGET ME AND PICK UP THE PIECES AND MOVE ON...
MARLETTE
I WISH I COULD TAKE YOU WITH ME, VERANDA, BUT SOME THINGS A MAN MUST DO ALONE...
SLAM
7/1
© Jefferson Communications, Inc. 1981
Distributed by C.T.N.Y.N.S.

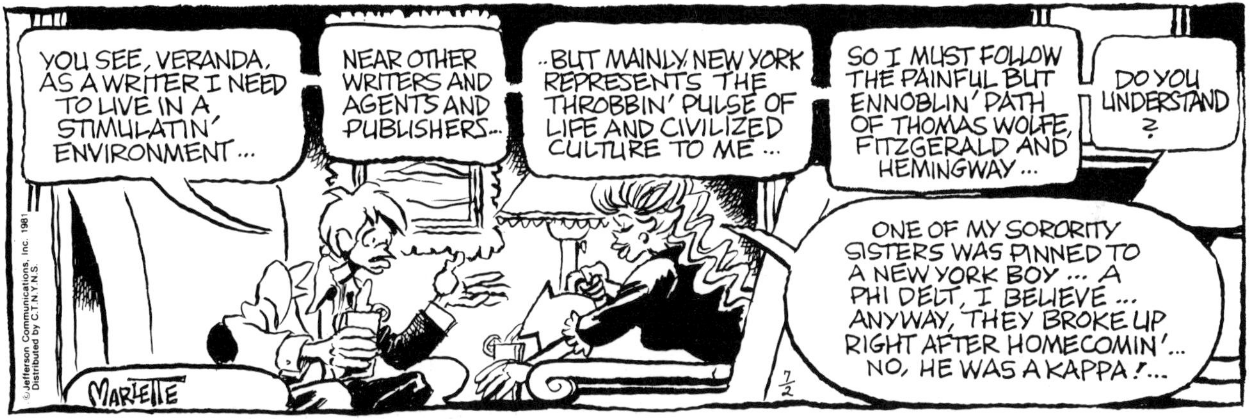
YOU SEE, VERANDA, AS A WRITER I NEED TO LIVE IN A STIMULATIN' ENVIRONMENT...
NEAR OTHER WRITERS AND AGENTS AND PUBLISHERS...
..BUT MAINLY NEW YORK REPRESENTS THE THROBBIN' PULSE OF LIFE AND CIVILIZED CULTURE TO ME...
SO I MUST FOLLOW THE PAINFUL BUT ENNOBLIN' PATH OF THOMAS WOLFE, FITZGERALD AND HEMINGWAY...
DO YOU UNDERSTAND?
ONE OF MY SORORITY SISTERS WAS PINNED TO A NEW YORK BOY... A PHI DELT, I BELIEVE... ANYWAY, THEY BROKE UP RIGHT AFTER HOMECOMIN'... NO, HE WAS A KAPPA!...
© Jefferson Communications, Inc. 1981
Distributed by C.T.N.Y.N.S.
MARLETTE
7/2

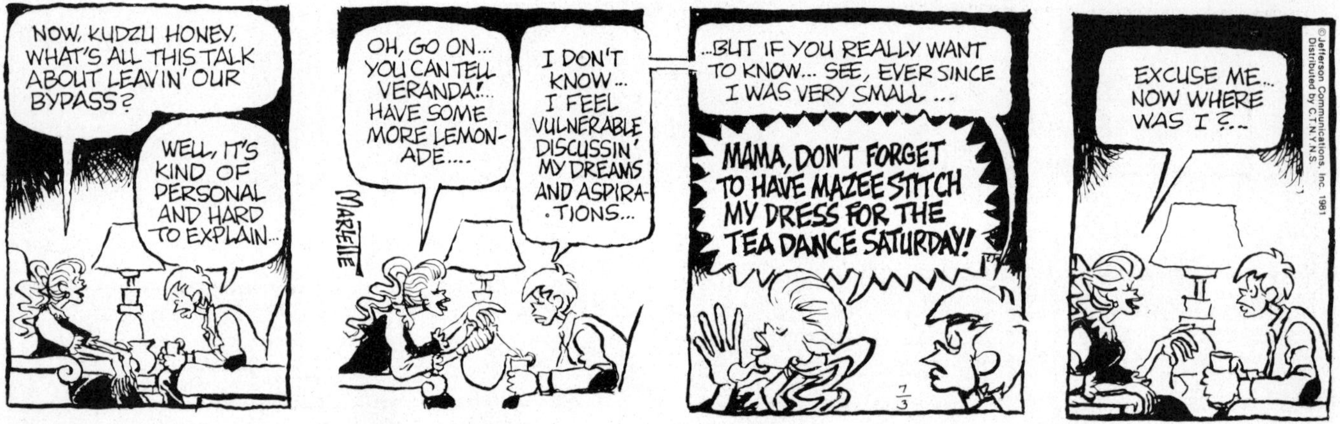
NOW, KUDZU HONEY, WHAT'S ALL THIS TALK ABOUT LEAVIN' OUR BYPASS?
WELL, IT'S KIND OF PERSONAL AND HARD TO EXPLAIN...
MARLETTE
OH, GO ON... YOU CAN TELL VERANDA!... HAVE SOME MORE LEMON-ADE....
I DON'T KNOW... I FEEL VULNERABLE DISCUSSIN' MY DREAMS AND ASPIRA-TIONS...
...BUT IF YOU REALLY WANT TO KNOW... SEE, EVER SINCE I WAS VERY SMALL ...
MAMA, DON'T FORGET TO HAVE MAZEE STITCH MY DRESS FOR THE TEA DANCE SATURDAY!
7/3
EXCUSE ME... NOW WHERE WAS I?...
© Jefferson Communications, Inc. 1981 Distributed by C.T.N.Y.N.S.

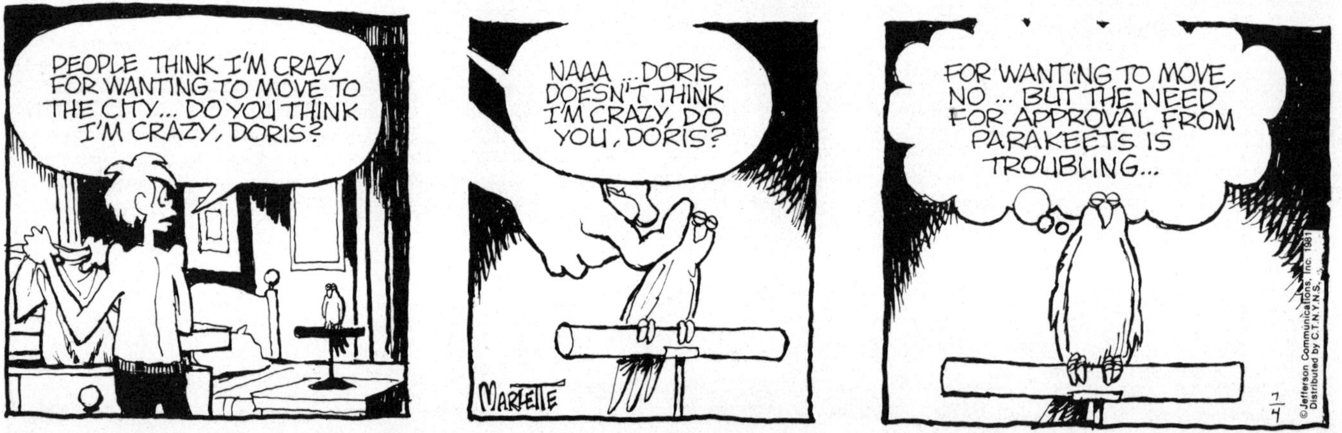
PEOPLE THINK I'M CRAZY FOR WANTING TO MOVE TO THE CITY... DO YOU THINK I'M CRAZY, DORIS?
NAAA ...DORIS DOESN'T THINK I'M CRAZY, DO YOU, DORIS?
MARLETTE
FOR WANTING TO MOVE, NO ... BUT THE NEED FOR APPROVAL FROM PARAKEETS IS TROUBLING...
7/4
© Jefferson Communications, Inc. 1981 Distributed by C.T.N.Y.N.S.

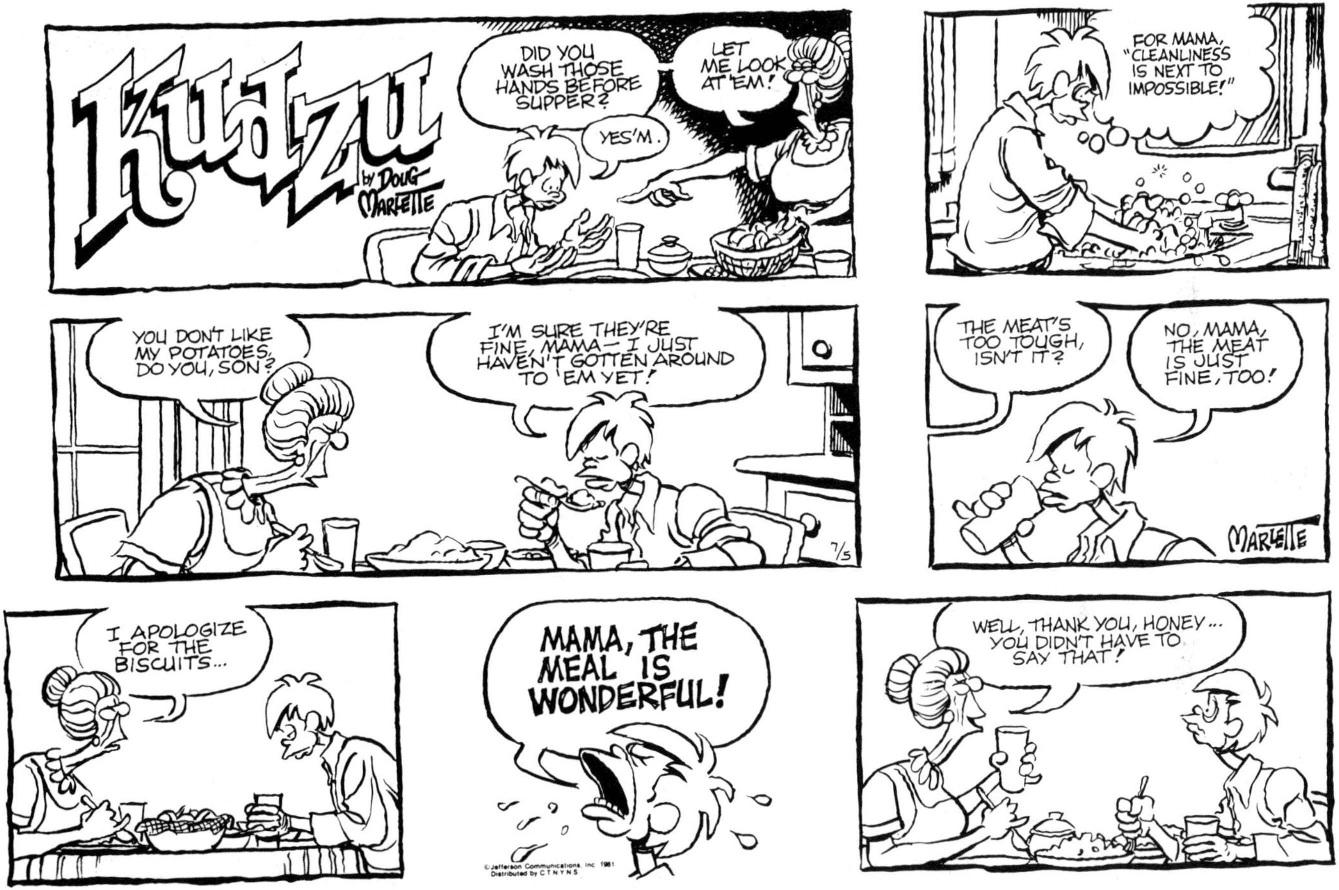

Kudzu
by DOUG MARLETTE
DID YOU WASH THOSE HANDS BEFORE SUPPER?
YES'M.
LET ME LOOK AT 'EM!
FOR MAMA, "CLEANLINESS IS NEXT TO IMPOSSIBLE!"
YOU DON'T LIKE MY POTATOES, DO YOU, SON?
I'M SURE THEY'RE FINE, MAMA— I JUST HAVEN'T GOTTEN AROUND TO 'EM YET!
7/5
THE MEAT'S TOO TOUGH, ISN'T IT?
NO, MAMA, THE MEAT IS JUST FINE, TOO!
MARLETTE
I APOLOGIZE FOR THE BISCUITS...
MAMA, THE MEAL IS WONDERFUL!
WELL, THANK YOU, HONEY... YOU DIDN'T HAVE TO SAY THAT!

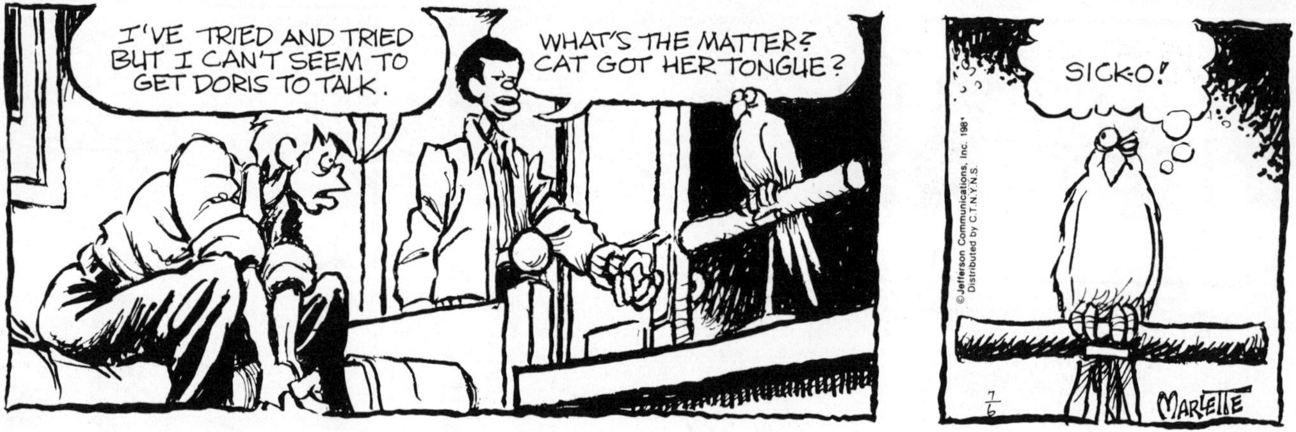
I'VE TRIED AND TRIED BUT I CAN'T SEEM TO GET DORIS TO TALK.
WHAT'S THE MATTER? CAT GOT HER TONGUE?
SICK-O!
© Jefferson Communications, Inc. 1981 Distributed by C.T.N.Y.N.S.
7/6
MARLETTE

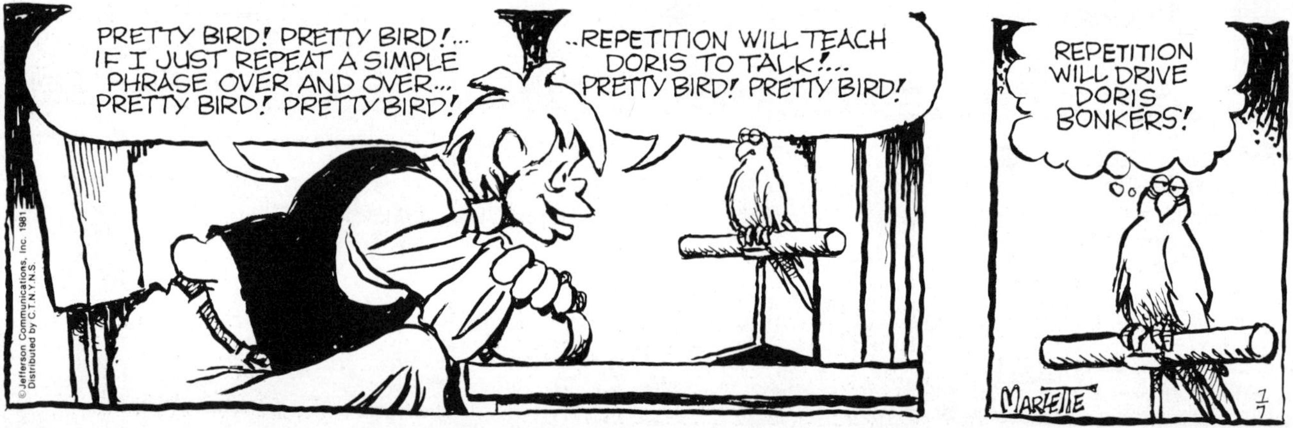
PRETTY BIRD! PRETTY BIRD!... IF I JUST REPEAT A SIMPLE PHRASE OVER AND OVER... PRETTY BIRD! PRETTY BIRD!
..REPETITION WILL TEACH DORIS TO TALK!... PRETTY BIRD! PRETTY BIRD!
REPETITION WILL DRIVE DORIS BONKERS!
© Jefferson Communications, Inc. 1981 Distributed by C.T.N.Y.N.S.
MARLETTE
7/7

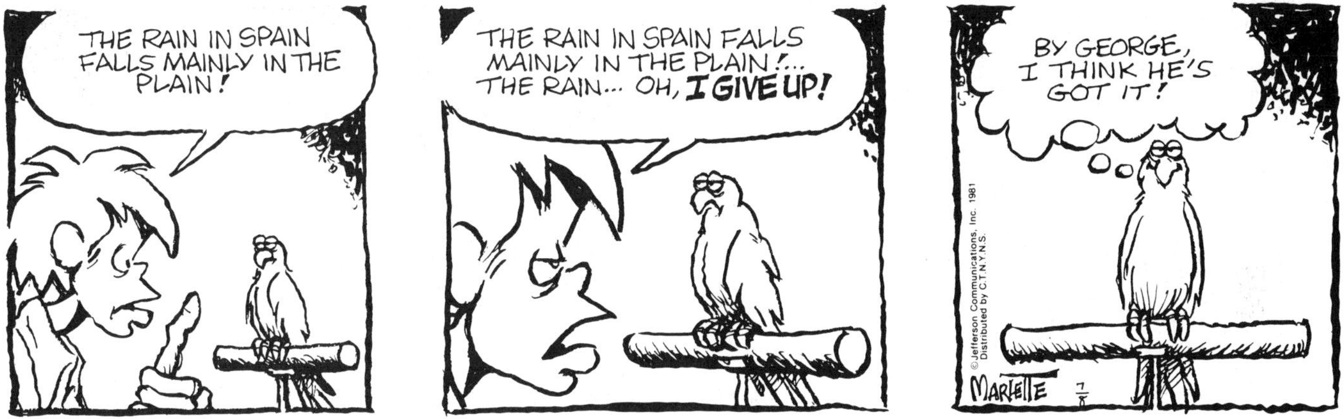
THE RAIN IN SPAIN FALLS MAINLY IN THE PLAIN!
THE RAIN IN SPAIN FALLS MAINLY IN THE PLAIN!... THE RAIN... OH, **I GIVE UP!**
BY GEORGE, I THINK HE'S GOT IT!
© Jefferson Communications, Inc. 1981
Distributed by C.T.N.Y.N.S.
MARLETTE 7/8

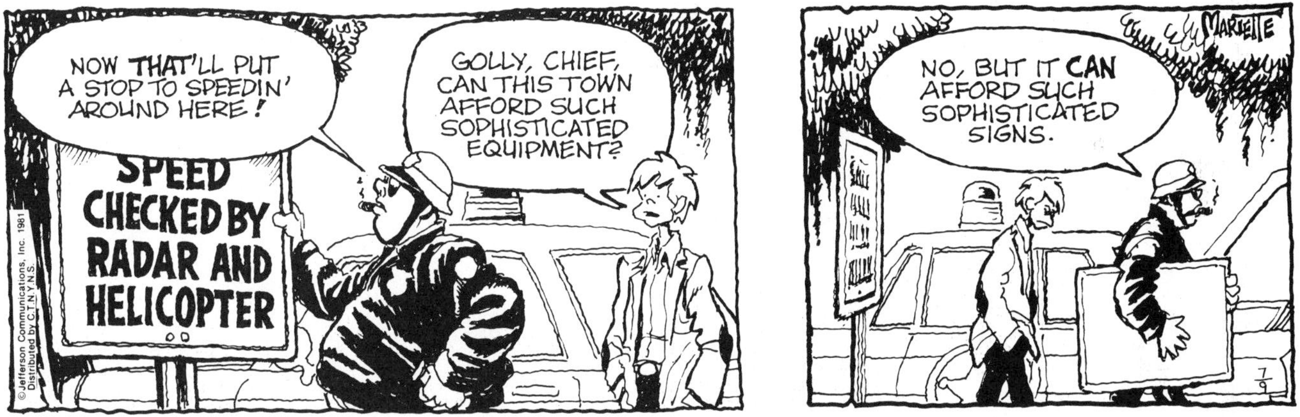
NOW **THAT**'LL PUT A STOP TO SPEEDIN' AROUND HERE!
SPEED CHECKED BY RADAR AND HELICOPTER
GOLLY, CHIEF, CAN THIS TOWN AFFORD SUCH SOPHISTICATED EQUIPMENT?
© Jefferson Communications, Inc. 1981
Distributed by C.T.N.Y.N.S.
MARLETTE
NO, BUT IT **CAN** AFFORD SUCH SOPHISTICATED SIGNS.
7/9

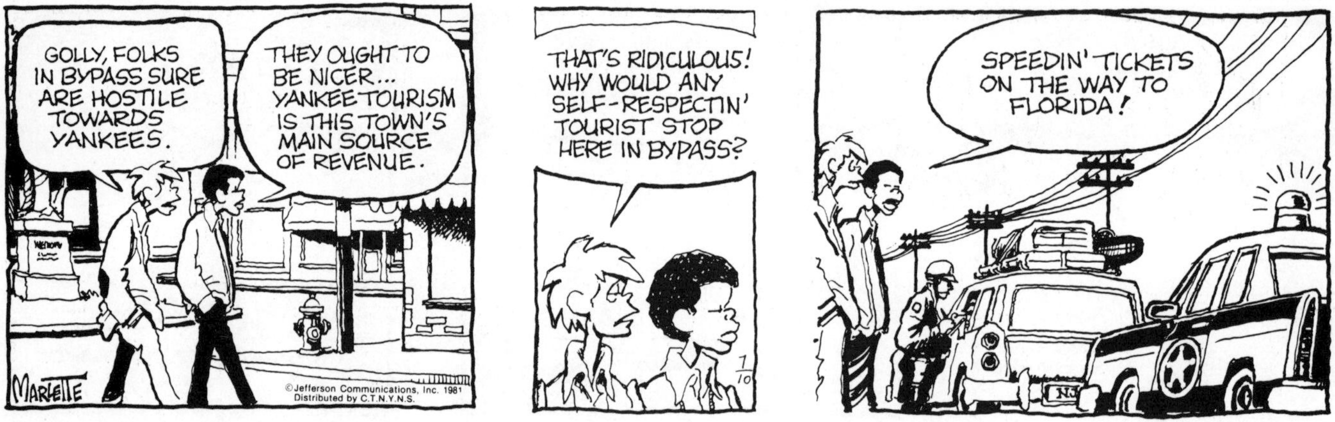
GOLLY, FOLKS IN BYPASS SURE ARE HOSTILE TOWARDS YANKEES.
THEY OUGHT TO BE NICER... YANKEE TOURISM IS THIS TOWN'S MAIN SOURCE OF REVENUE.
MARLETTE
©Jefferson Communications, Inc. 1981 Distributed by C.T.N.Y.N.S.
THAT'S RIDICULOUS! WHY WOULD ANY SELF-RESPECTIN' TOURIST STOP HERE IN BYPASS?
7/10
SPEEDIN' TICKETS ON THE WAY TO FLORIDA!
NJ

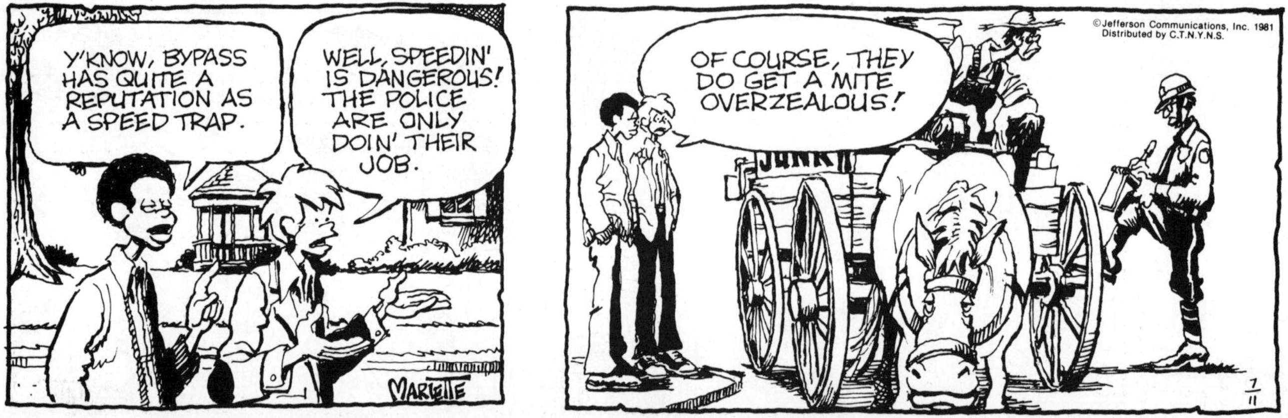
Y'KNOW, BYPASS HAS QUITE A REPUTATION AS A SPEED TRAP.
WELL, SPEEDIN' IS DANGEROUS! THE POLICE ARE ONLY DOIN' THEIR JOB.
MARLETTE
©Jefferson Communications, Inc. 1981 Distributed by C.T.N.Y.N.S.
OF COURSE, THEY DO GET A MITE OVERZEALOUS!
7/11

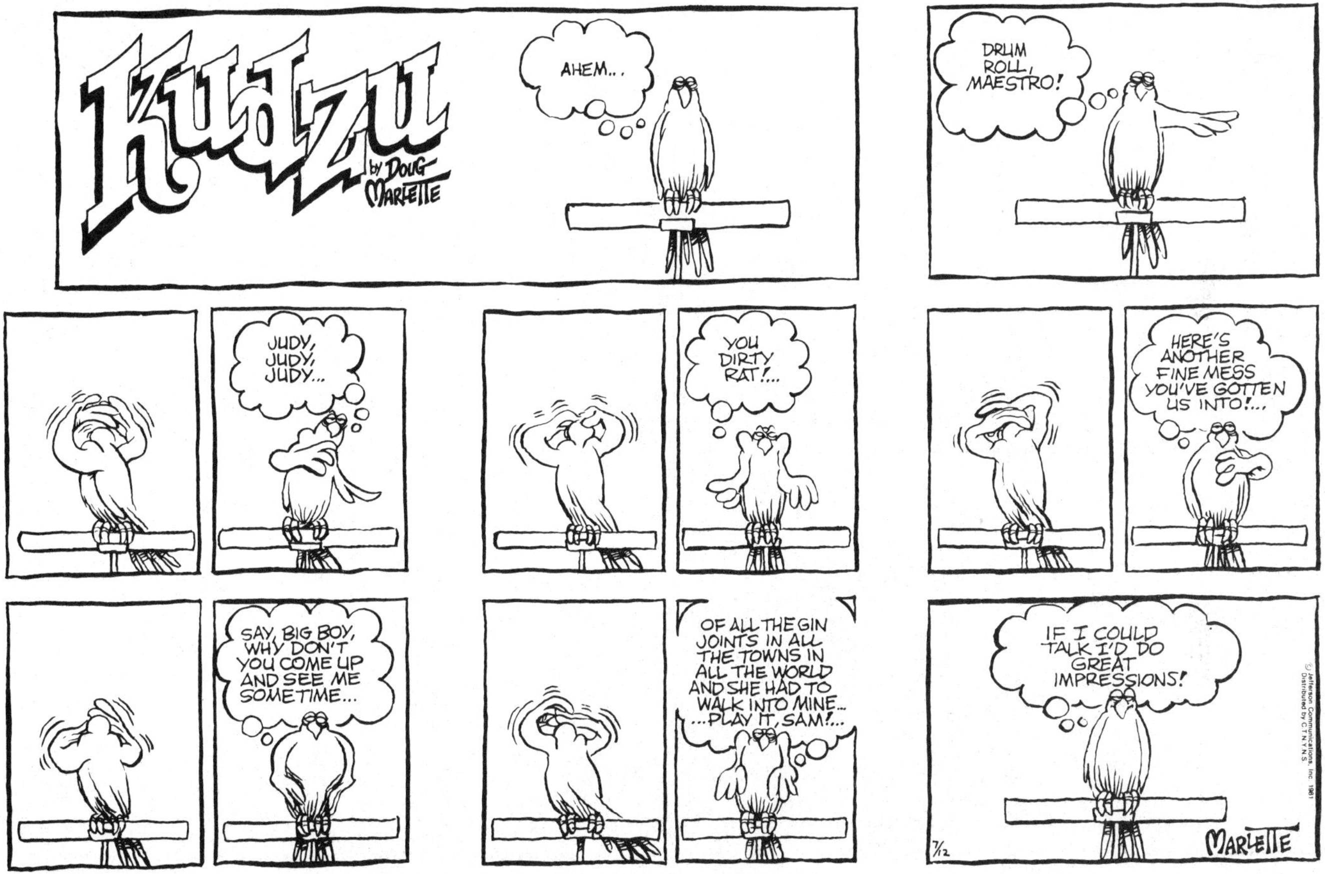
Kudzu
by Doug Marlette
AHEM...
DRUM ROLL, MAESTRO!
JUDY, JUDY, JUDY...
YOU DIRTY RAT!...
HERE'S ANOTHER FINE MESS YOU'VE GOTTEN US INTO!...
SAY, BIG BOY, WHY DON'T YOU COME UP AND SEE ME SOMETIME...
OF ALL THE GIN JOINTS IN ALL THE TOWNS IN ALL THE WORLD AND SHE HAD TO WALK INTO MINE... ...PLAY IT, SAM!...
IF I COULD TALK I'D DO GREAT IMPRESSIONS!
© Jefferson Communications, Inc. 1981 Distributed by C.T.N.Y.N.S.
7/12
MARLETTE

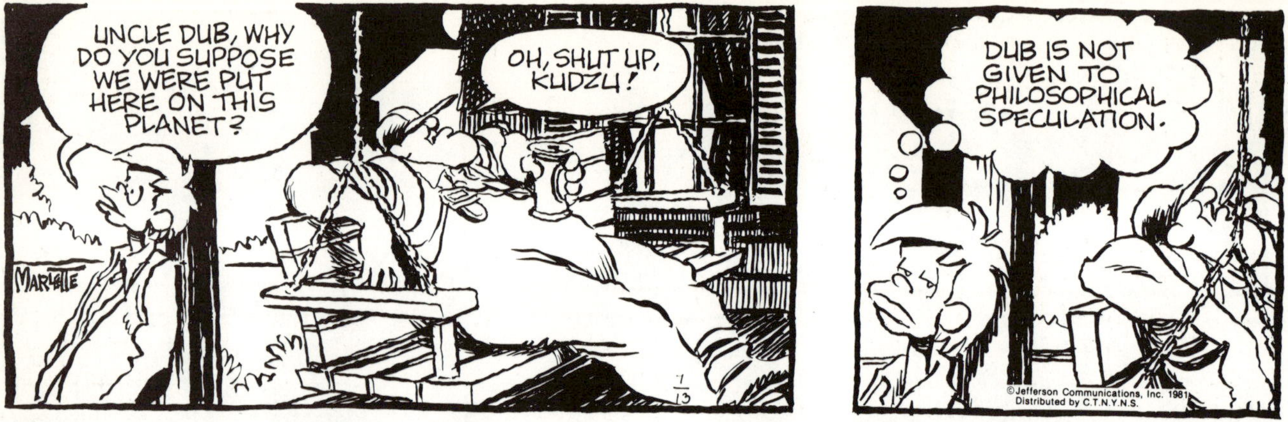
UNCLE DUB, WHY DO YOU SUPPOSE WE WERE PUT HERE ON THIS PLANET?
OH, SHUT UP, KUDZU!
MARLETTE
7/13
DUB IS NOT GIVEN TO PHILOSOPHICAL SPECULATION.
©Jefferson Communications, Inc. 1981
Distributed by C.T.N.Y.N.S.

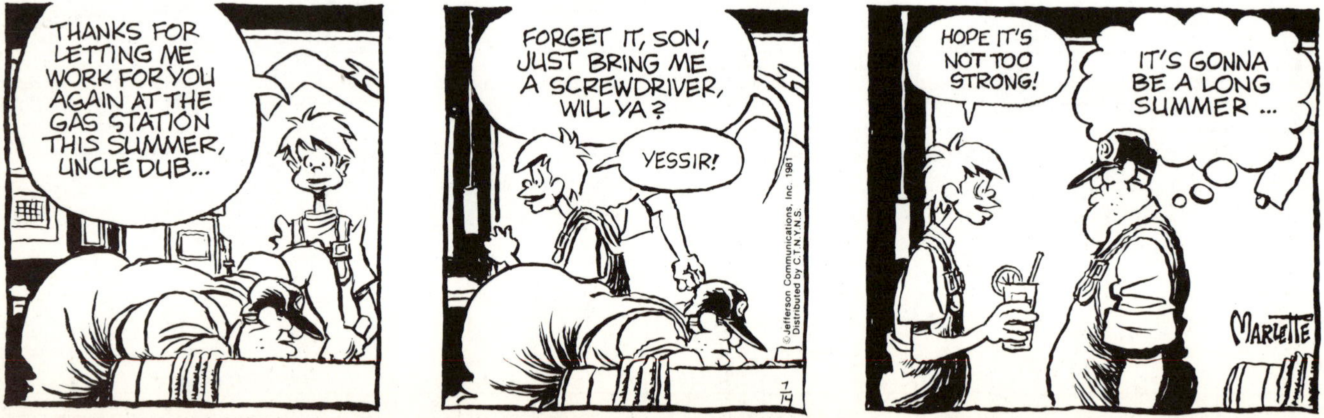
THANKS FOR LETTING ME WORK FOR YOU AGAIN AT THE GAS STATION THIS SUMMER, UNCLE DUB...
FORGET IT, SON, JUST BRING ME A SCREWDRIVER, WILL YA?
YESSIR!
©Jefferson Communications, Inc. 1981
Distributed by C.T.N.Y.N.S.
7/14
HOPE IT'S NOT TOO STRONG!
IT'S GONNA BE A LONG SUMMER ...
MARLETTE

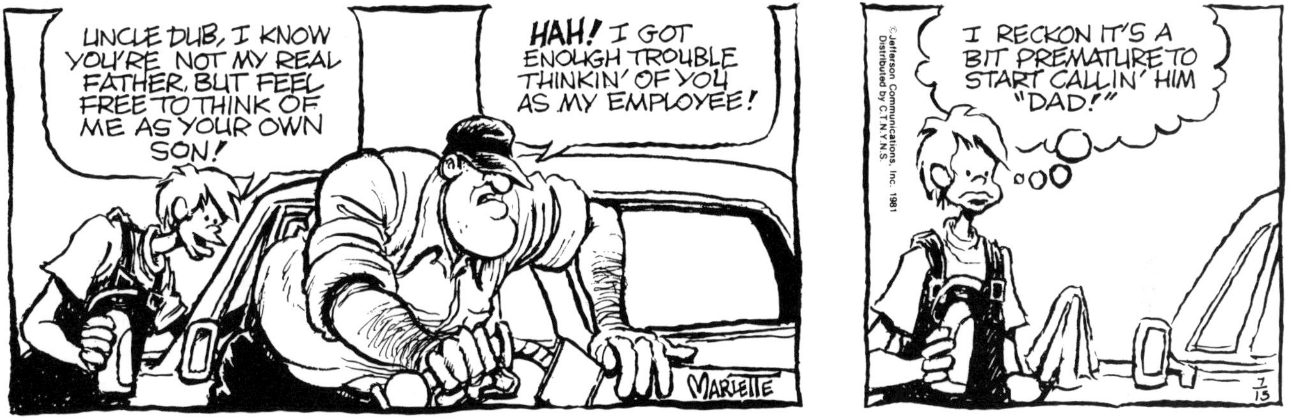
UNCLE DUB, I KNOW YOU'RE NOT MY REAL FATHER, BUT FEEL FREE TO THINK OF ME AS YOUR OWN SON!
HAH! I GOT ENOUGH TROUBLE THINKIN' OF YOU AS MY EMPLOYEE!
MARLETTE
© Jefferson Communications, Inc. 1981
Distributed by C.T.N.Y.N.S.
I RECKON IT'S A BIT PREMATURE TO START CALLIN' HIM "DAD!"
7/15

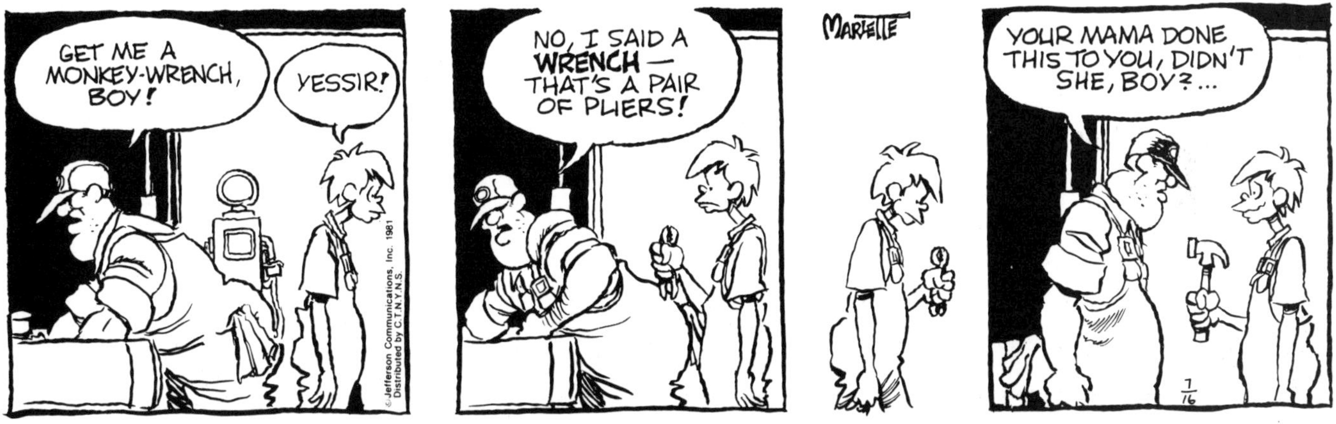
GET ME A MONKEY-WRENCH, BOY!
YESSIR!
© Jefferson Communications, Inc. 1981
Distributed by C.T.N.Y.N.S.
NO, I SAID A WRENCH — THAT'S A PAIR OF PLIERS!
MARLETTE
YOUR MAMA DONE THIS TO YOU, DIDN'T SHE, BOY?...
7/16

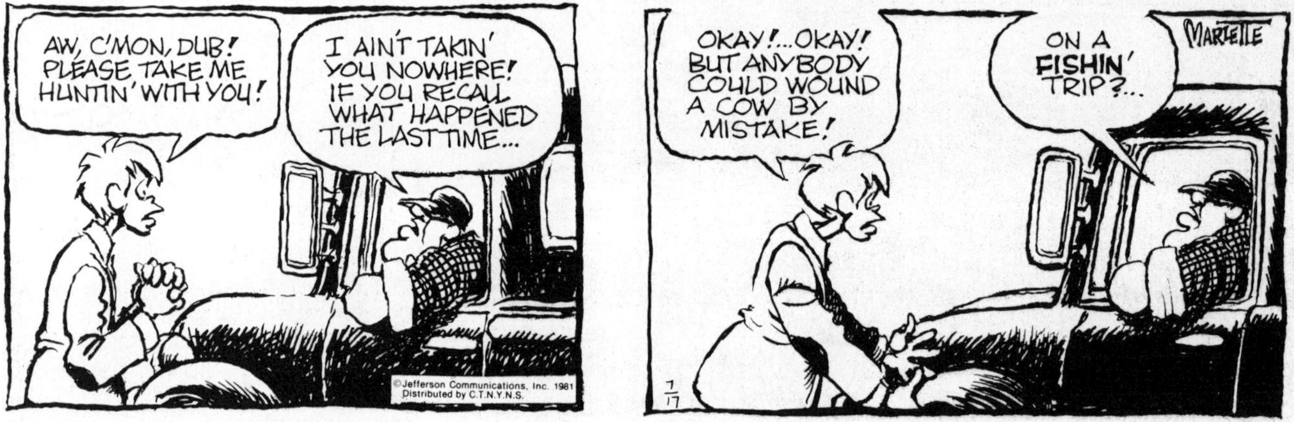
AW, C'MON, DUB! PLEASE TAKE ME HUNTIN' WITH YOU!
I AIN'T TAKIN' YOU NOWHERE! IF YOU RECALL WHAT HAPPENED THE LAST TIME...
©Jefferson Communications, Inc. 1981 Distributed by C.T.N.Y.N.S.
OKAY!...OKAY! BUT ANYBODY COULD WOUND A COW BY MISTAKE!
MARLETTE
ON A **FISHIN'** TRIP?...
7/17

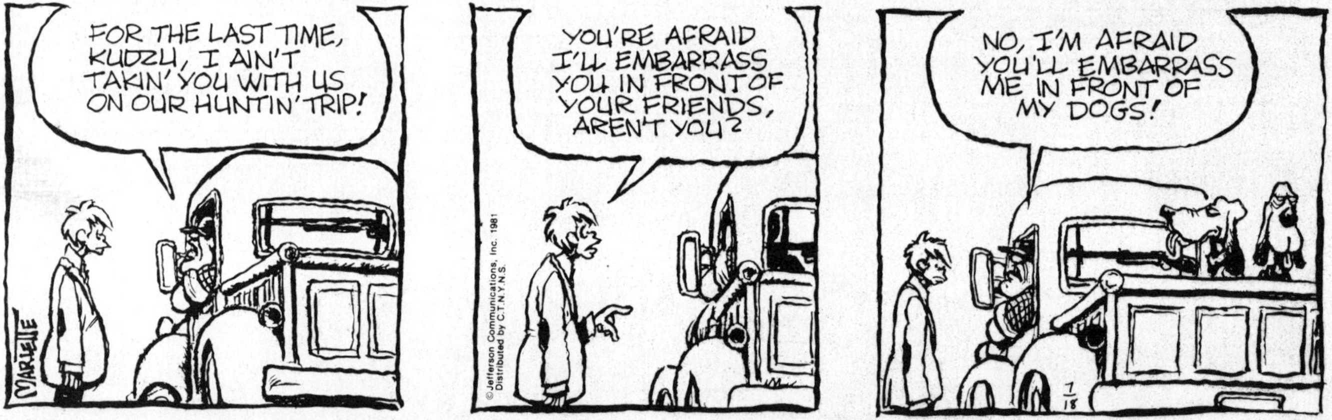
FOR THE LAST TIME, KUDZU, I AIN'T TAKIN' YOU WITH US ON OUR HUNTIN' TRIP!
MARLETTE
YOU'RE AFRAID I'LL EMBARRASS YOU IN FRONT OF YOUR FRIENDS, AREN'T YOU?
© Jefferson Communications, Inc. 1981 Distributed by C.T.N.Y.N.S.
NO, I'M AFRAID YOU'LL EMBARRASS ME IN FRONT OF MY DOGS!
7/18

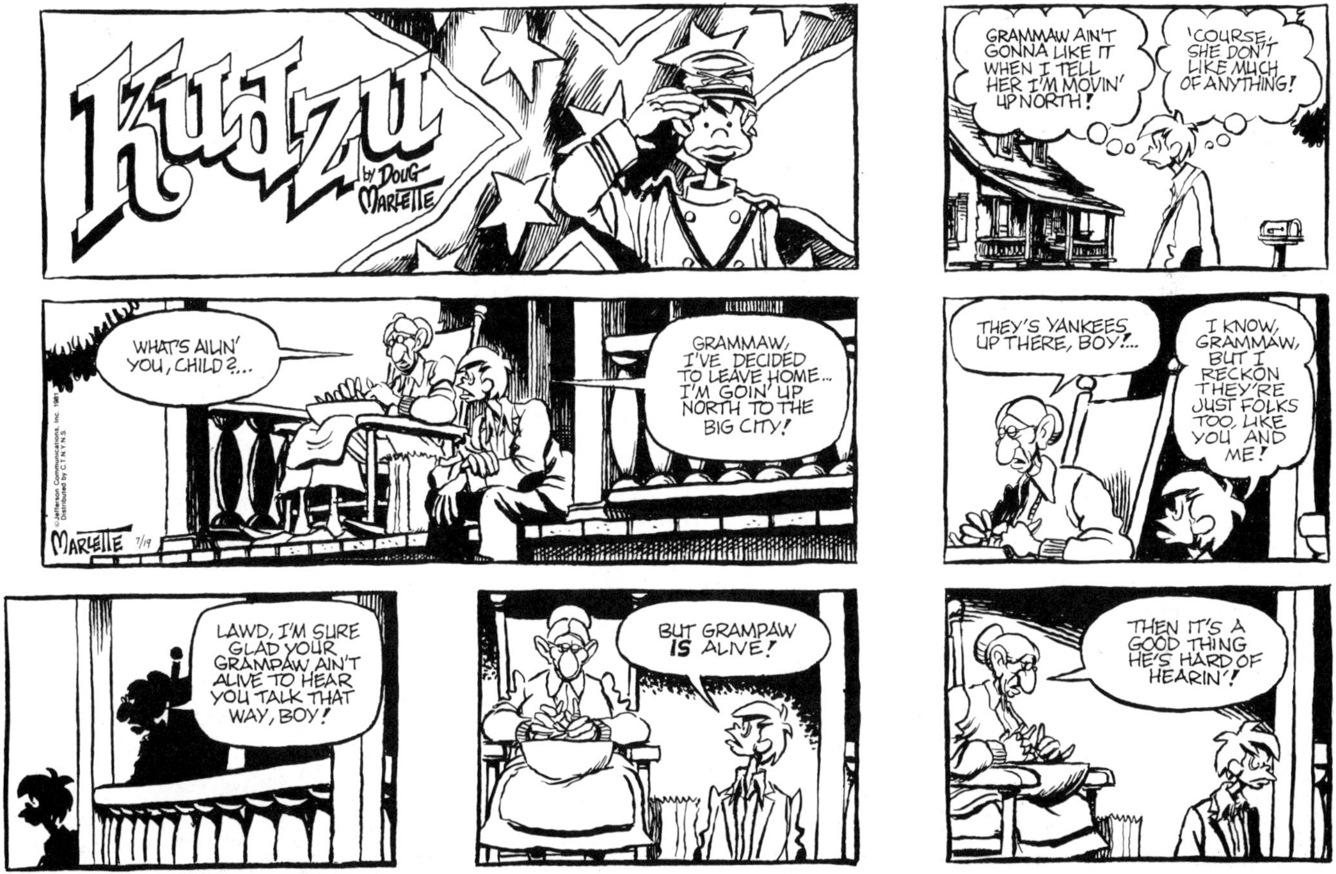
Kudzu
by Doug Marlette
GRAMMAW AIN'T GONNA LIKE IT WHEN I TELL HER I'M MOVIN' UP NORTH!
'COURSE, SHE DON'T LIKE MUCH OF ANYTHING!
WHAT'S AILIN' YOU, CHILD?...
GRAMMAW, I'VE DECIDED TO LEAVE HOME... I'M GOIN' UP NORTH TO THE BIG CITY!
© Jefferson Communications, Inc. 1981 Distributed by C.T.N.Y.N.S.
MARLETTE 7/19
THEY'S YANKEES UP THERE, BOY!...
I KNOW, GRAMMAW, BUT I RECKON THEY'RE JUST FOLKS TOO, LIKE YOU AND ME!
LAWD, I'M SURE GLAD YOUR GRAMPAW AIN'T ALIVE TO HEAR YOU TALK THAT WAY, BOY!
BUT GRAMPAW IS ALIVE!
THEN IT'S A GOOD THING HE'S HARD OF HEARIN'!

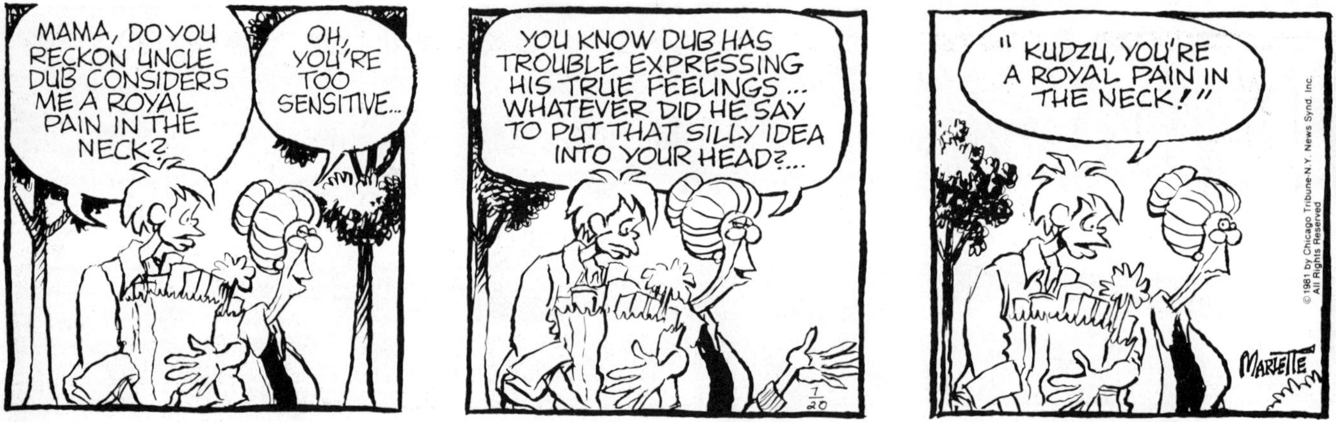
MAMA, DO YOU RECKON UNCLE DUB CONSIDERS ME A ROYAL PAIN IN THE NECK?
OH, YOU'RE TOO SENSITIVE...
YOU KNOW DUB HAS TROUBLE EXPRESSING HIS TRUE FEELINGS ... WHATEVER DID HE SAY TO PUT THAT SILLY IDEA INTO YOUR HEAD?...
7/20
"KUDZU, YOU'RE A ROYAL PAIN IN THE NECK!"
© 1981 by Chicago Tribune-N.Y. News Synd. Inc. All Rights Reserved
MARLETTE

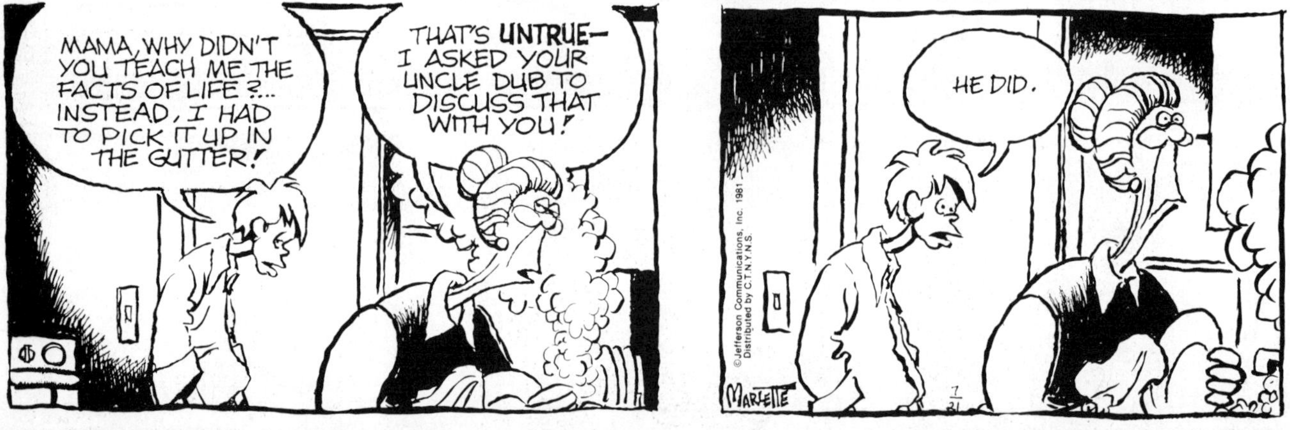
MAMA, WHY DIDN'T YOU TEACH ME THE FACTS OF LIFE?... INSTEAD, I HAD TO PICK IT UP IN THE GUTTER!
THAT'S **UNTRUE**— I ASKED YOUR UNCLE DUB TO DISCUSS THAT WITH YOU!
HE DID.
© Jefferson Communications, Inc. 1981 Distributed by C.T.N.Y.N.S.
MARLETTE
7/21

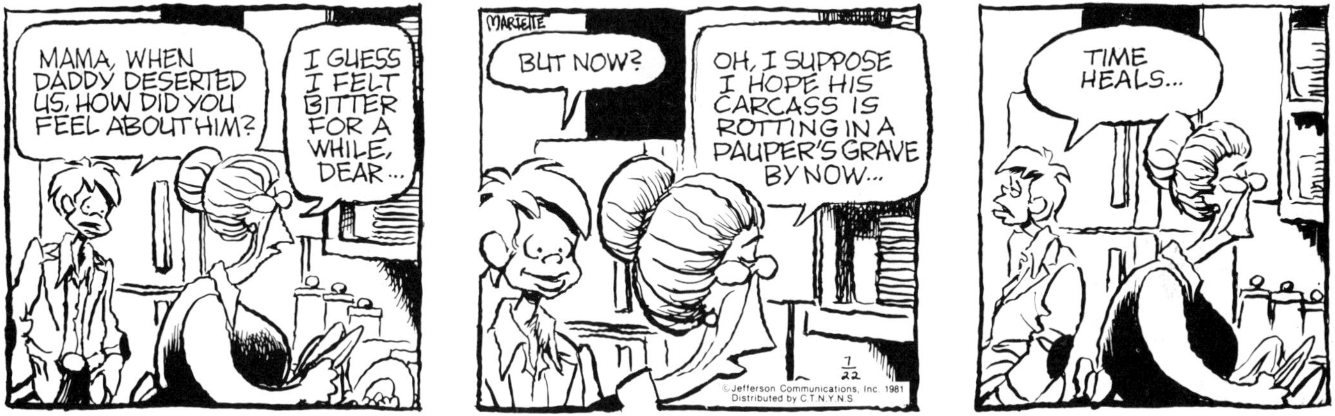
MAMA, WHEN DADDY DESERTED US, HOW DID YOU FEEL ABOUT HIM?
I GUESS I FELT BITTER FOR A WHILE, DEAR...
MARLETTE
BUT NOW?
OH, I SUPPOSE I HOPE HIS CARCASS IS ROTTING IN A PAUPER'S GRAVE BY NOW...
7/22
© Jefferson Communications, Inc. 1981
Distributed by C.T.N.Y.N.S.
TIME HEALS...

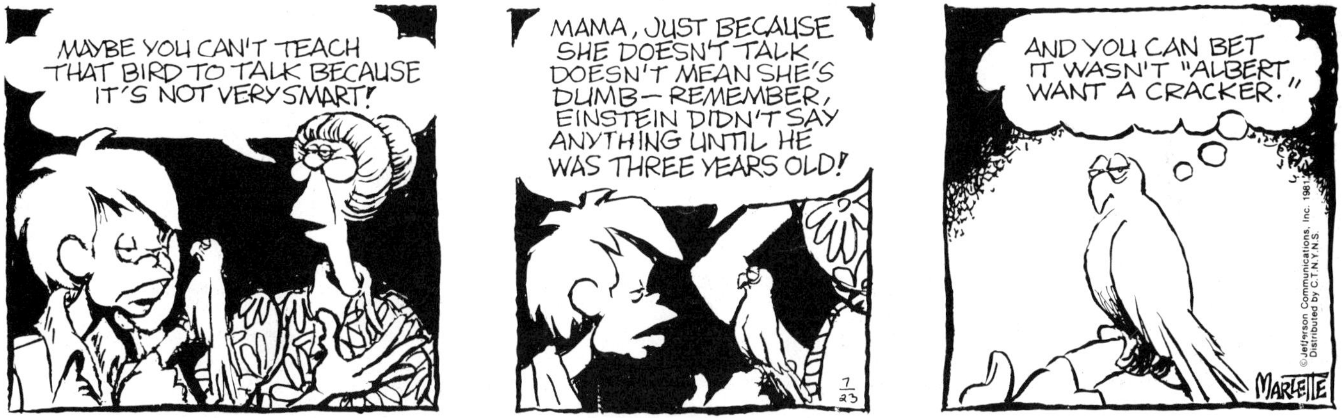
MAYBE YOU CAN'T TEACH THAT BIRD TO TALK BECAUSE IT'S NOT VERY SMART!
MAMA, JUST BECAUSE SHE DOESN'T TALK DOESN'T MEAN SHE'S DUMB— REMEMBER, EINSTEIN DIDN'T SAY ANYTHING UNTIL HE WAS THREE YEARS OLD!
7/23
AND YOU CAN BET IT WASN'T "ALBERT WANT A CRACKER."
© Jefferson Communications, Inc. 1981
Distributed by C.T.N.Y.N.S.
MARLETTE

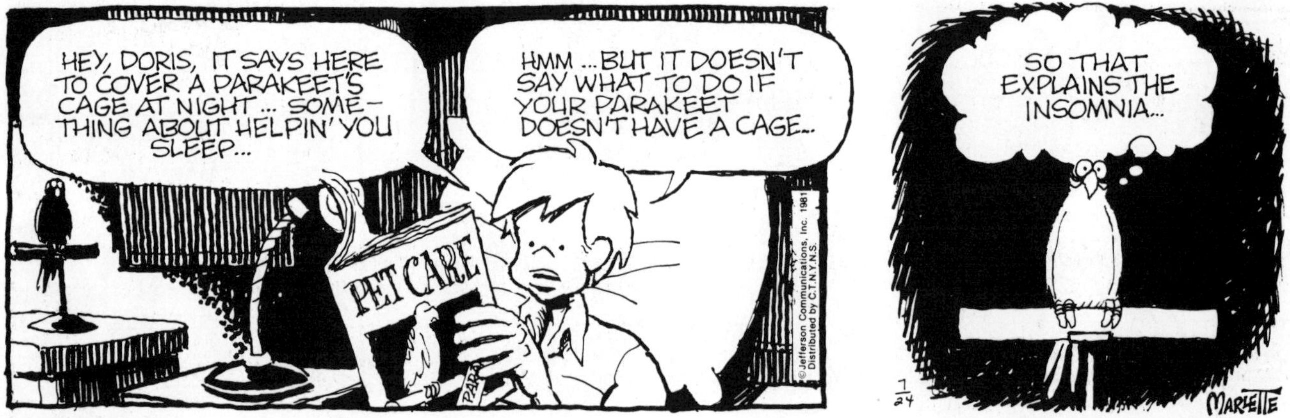
HEY, DORIS, IT SAYS HERE TO COVER A PARAKEET'S CAGE AT NIGHT ... SOME-THING ABOUT HELPIN' YOU SLEEP...
HMM ... BUT IT DOESN'T SAY WHAT TO DO IF YOUR PARAKEET DOESN'T HAVE A CAGE...
PET CARE
© Jefferson Communications, Inc. 1981
Distributed by C.T.N.Y.N.S.
SO THAT EXPLAINS THE INSOMNIA...
7/24
MARLETTE

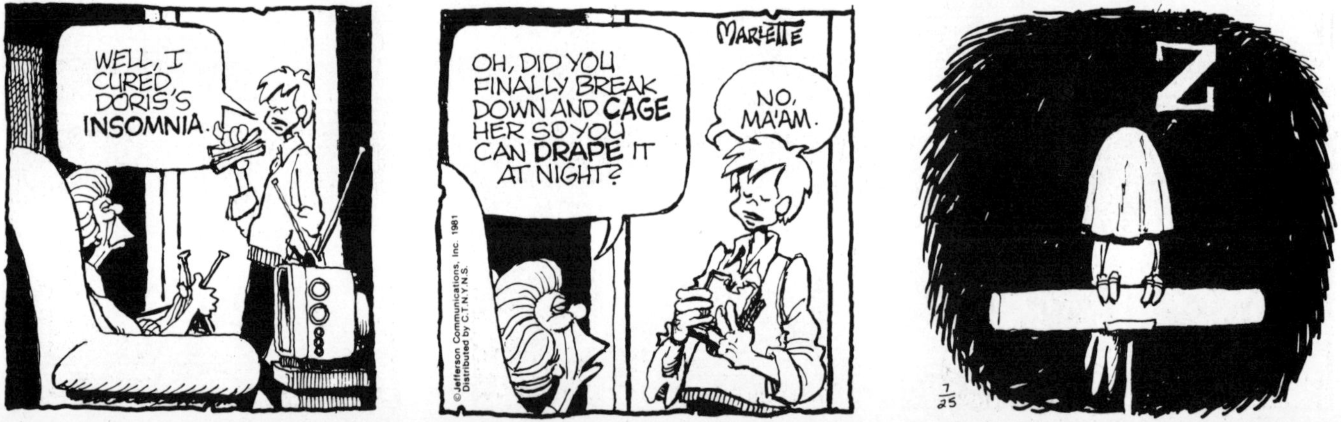
WELL, I CURED DORIS'S **INSOMNIA**.
© Jefferson Communications, Inc. 1981
Distributed by C.T.N.Y.N.S.
MARLETTE
OH, DID YOU FINALLY BREAK DOWN AND **CAGE** HER SO YOU CAN **DRAPE** IT AT NIGHT?
NO, MA'AM.
Z
7/25

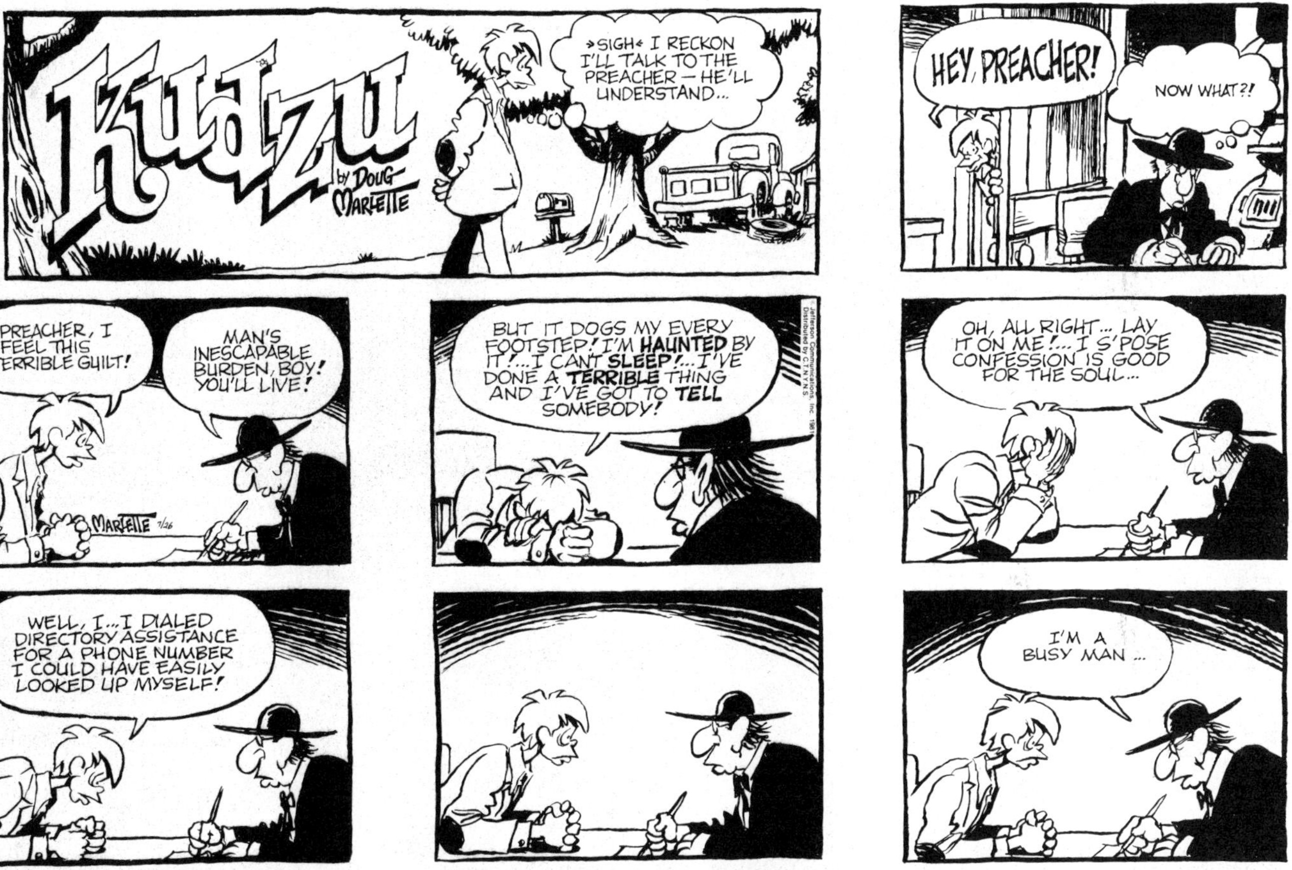
Kudzu
by DOUG MARLETTE
»SIGH« I RECKON I'LL TALK TO THE PREACHER — HE'LL UNDERSTAND...
HEY, PREACHER!
NOW WHAT?!
PREACHER, I FEEL THIS TERRIBLE GUILT!
MAN'S INESCAPABLE BURDEN, BOY! YOU'LL LIVE!
MARLETTE 7/26
BUT IT DOGS MY EVERY FOOTSTEP! I'M HAUNTED BY IT!... I CAN'T SLEEP!... I'VE DONE A TERRIBLE THING AND I'VE GOT TO TELL SOMEBODY!
© Jefferson Communications, Inc. 1981
Distributed by C.T.N.Y.N.S.
OH, ALL RIGHT... LAY IT ON ME!... I S'POSE CONFESSION IS GOOD FOR THE SOUL...
WELL, I... I DIALED DIRECTORY ASSISTANCE FOR A PHONE NUMBER I COULD HAVE EASILY LOOKED UP MYSELF!
I'M A BUSY MAN ...

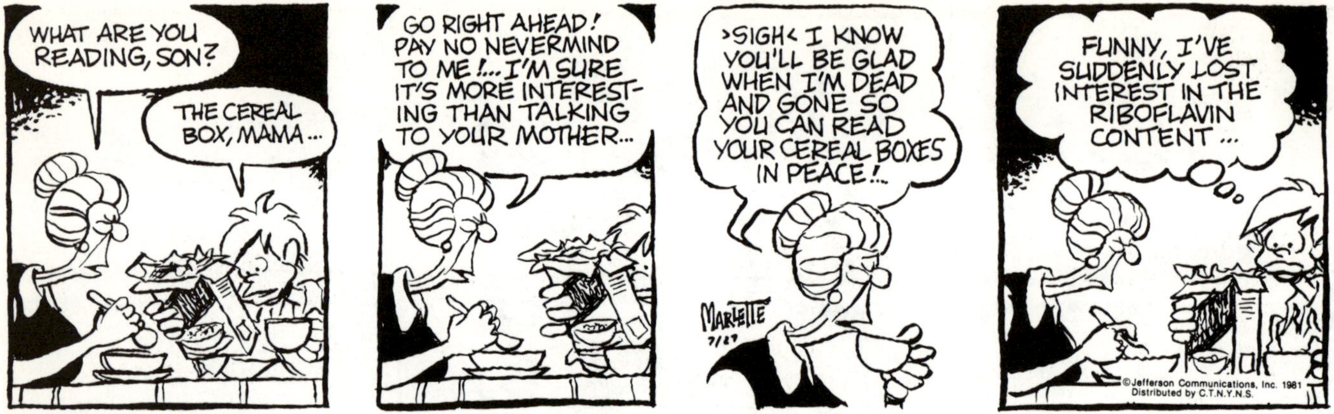
WHAT ARE YOU READING, SON?
THE CEREAL BOX, MAMA ...
GO RIGHT AHEAD! PAY NO NEVERMIND TO ME!... I'M SURE IT'S MORE INTEREST-ING THAN TALKING TO YOUR MOTHER...
>SIGH< I KNOW YOU'LL BE GLAD WHEN I'M DEAD AND GONE SO YOU CAN READ YOUR CEREAL BOXES IN PEACE!...
MARLETTE 7/27
FUNNY, I'VE SUDDENLY LOST INTEREST IN THE RIBOFLAVIN CONTENT ...
©Jefferson Communications, Inc. 1981 Distributed by C.T.N.Y.N.S.

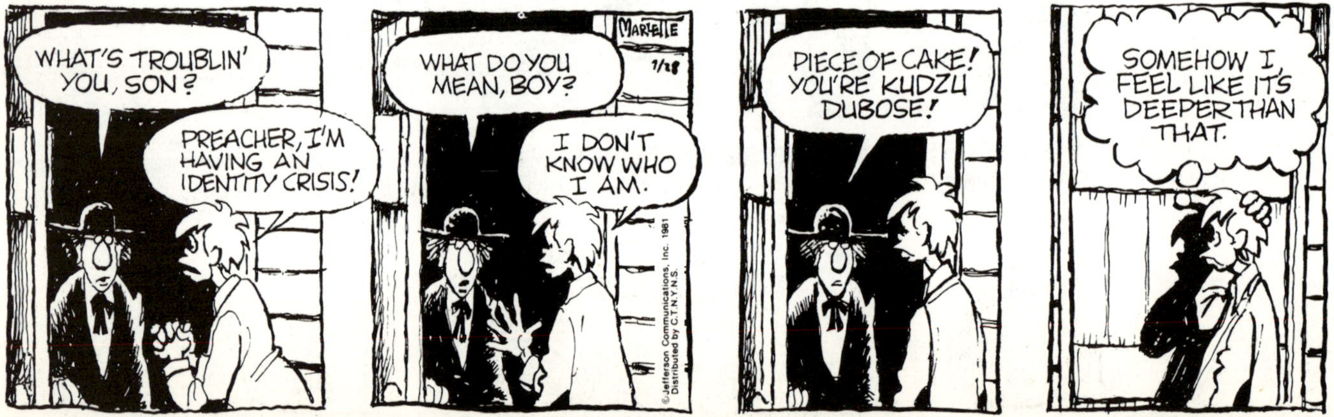
WHAT'S TROUBLIN' YOU, SON?
PREACHER, I'M HAVING AN IDENTITY CRISIS!
MARLETTE 7/28
WHAT DO YOU MEAN, BOY?
I DON'T KNOW WHO I AM.
©Jefferson Communications, Inc. 1981 Distributed by C.T.N.Y.N.S.
PIECE OF CAKE! YOU'RE KUDZU DUBOSE!
SOMEHOW I, FEEL LIKE IT'S DEEPER THAN THAT.

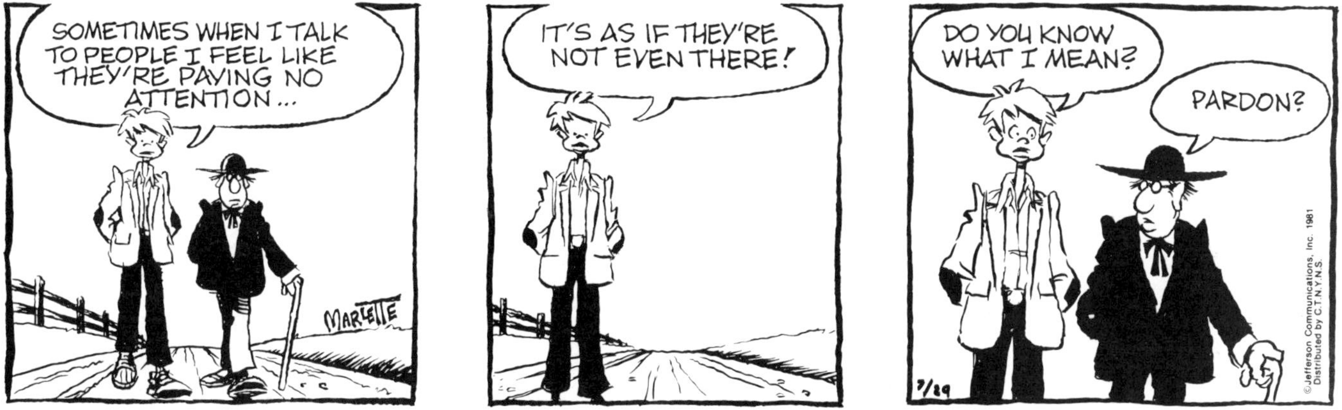
SOMETIMES WHEN I TALK TO PEOPLE I FEEL LIKE THEY'RE PAYING NO ATTENTION...
MARLETTE
IT'S AS IF THEY'RE NOT EVEN THERE!
DO YOU KNOW WHAT I MEAN?
PARDON?
7/29
© Jefferson Communications, Inc. 1981
Distributed by C.T.N.Y.N.S.

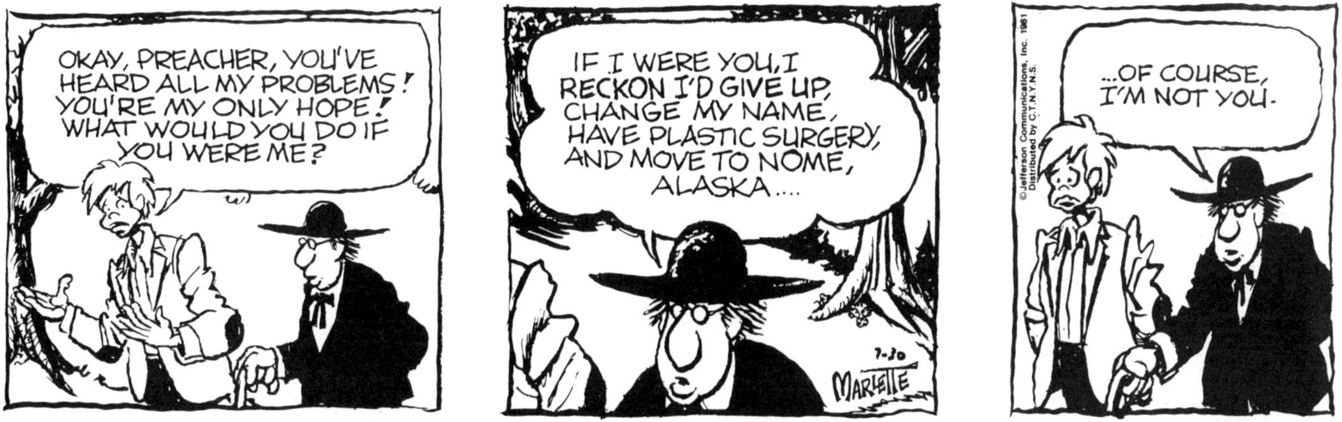
OKAY, PREACHER, YOU'VE HEARD ALL MY PROBLEMS! YOU'RE MY ONLY HOPE! WHAT WOULD YOU DO IF YOU WERE ME?
IF I WERE YOU, I RECKON I'D GIVE UP, CHANGE MY NAME, HAVE PLASTIC SURGERY, AND MOVE TO NOME, ALASKA....
7-30
MARLETTE
© Jefferson Communications, Inc. 1981
Distributed by C.T.N.Y.N.S.
...OF COURSE, I'M NOT YOU.

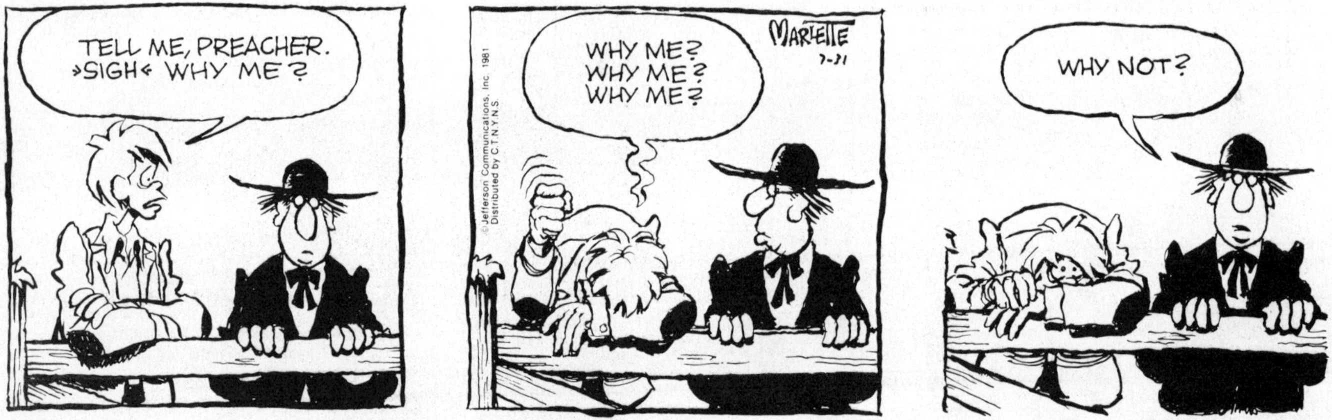
TELL ME, PREACHER. >SIGH< WHY ME?
© Jefferson Communications, Inc. 1981
Distributed by C.T.N.Y.N.S.
MARLETTE
7-31
WHY ME? WHY ME? WHY ME?
WHY NOT?

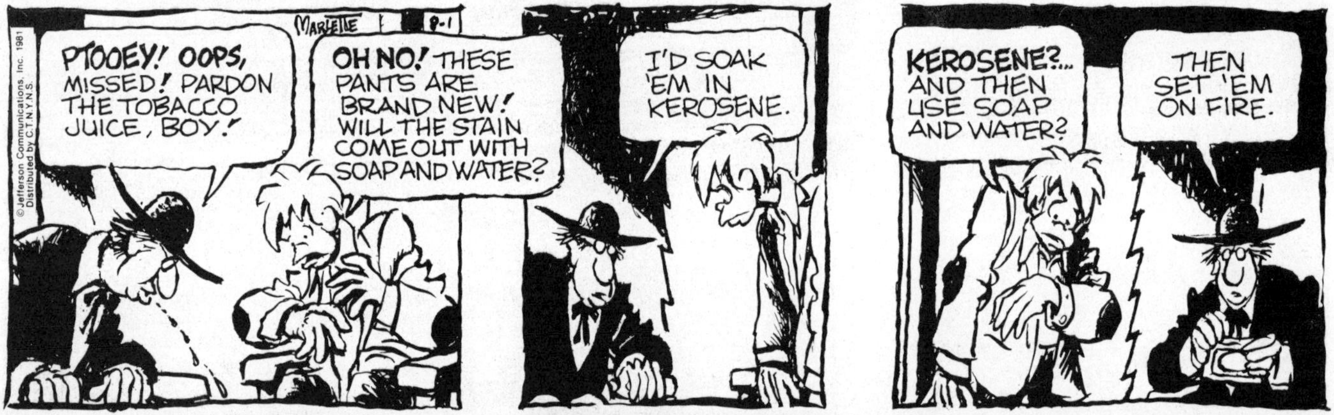
MARLETTE
8-1
© Jefferson Communications, Inc. 1981
Distributed by C.T.N.Y.N.S.
PTOOEY! OOPS, MISSED! PARDON THE TOBACCO JUICE, BOY!
OH NO! THESE PANTS ARE BRAND NEW! WILL THE STAIN COME OUT WITH SOAP AND WATER?
I'D SOAK 'EM IN KEROSENE.
KEROSENE?... AND THEN USE SOAP AND WATER?
THEN SET 'EM ON FIRE.

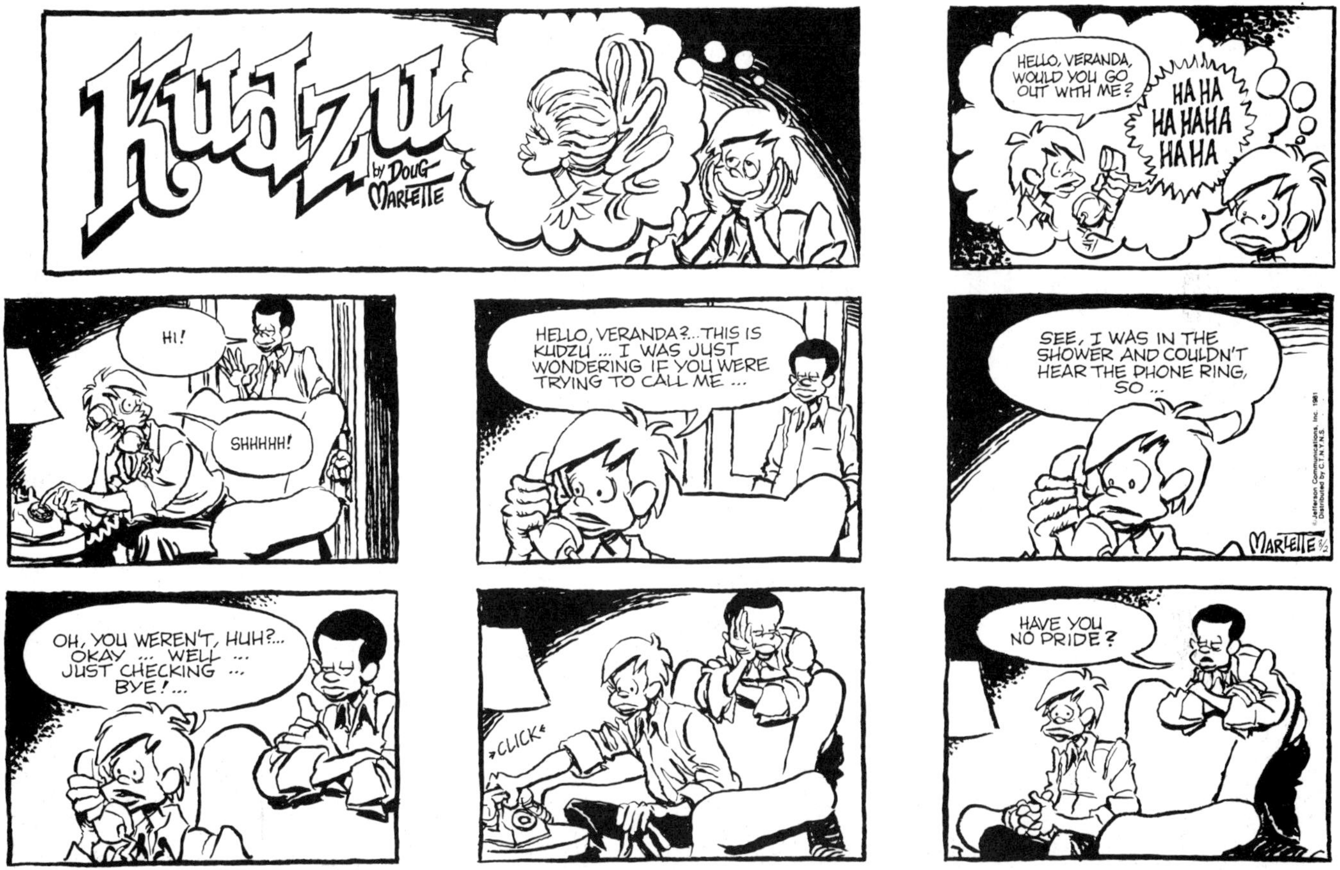
Kudzu
by Doug Marlette
HELLO, VERANDA, WOULD YOU GO OUT WITH ME?
HA HA HA HAHA HA HA
HI!
SHHHHH!
HELLO, VERANDA?...THIS IS KUDZU ... I WAS JUST WONDERING IF YOU WERE TRYING TO CALL ME ...
SEE, I WAS IN THE SHOWER AND COULDN'T HEAR THE PHONE RING, SO ...
MARLETTE 8/2
OH, YOU WEREN'T, HUH?... OKAY ... WELL ... JUST CHECKING ... BYE!...
CLICK
HAVE YOU NO PRIDE?

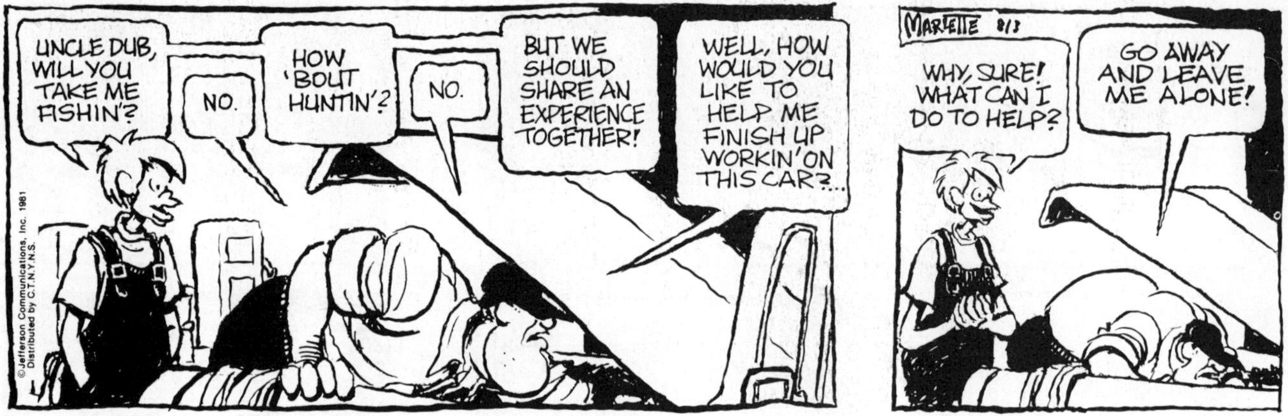
MARLETTE 8/3
© Jefferson Communications, Inc. 1981
Distributed by C.T.N.Y.N.S.
UNCLE DUB, WILL YOU TAKE ME FISHIN'?
NO.
HOW 'BOUT HUNTIN'?
NO.
BUT WE SHOULD SHARE AN EXPERIENCE TOGETHER!
WELL, HOW WOULD YOU LIKE TO HELP ME FINISH UP WORKIN' ON THIS CAR?...
WHY, SURE! WHAT CAN I DO TO HELP?
GO AWAY AND LEAVE ME ALONE!

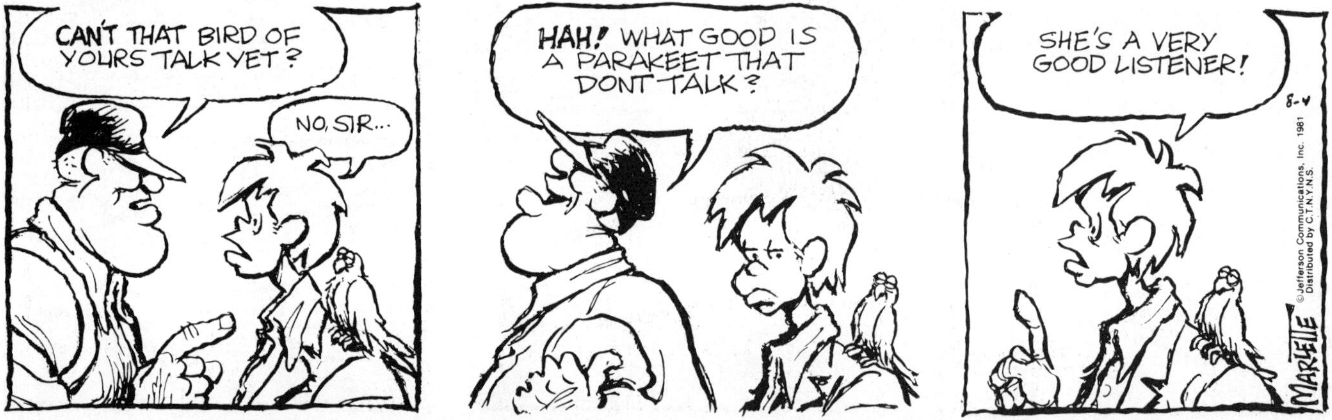
CAN'T THAT BIRD OF YOURS TALK YET?
NO, SIR...
HAH! WHAT GOOD IS A PARAKEET THAT DONT TALK?
SHE'S A VERY GOOD LISTENER!
8-4
© Jefferson Communications, Inc. 1981
Distributed by C.T.N.Y.N.S.
MARLETTE

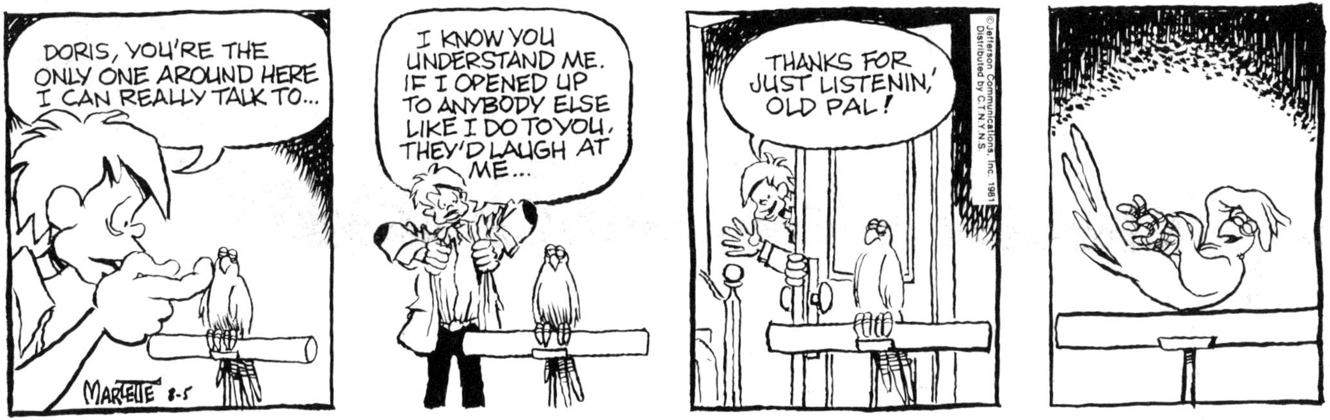
DORIS, YOU'RE THE ONLY ONE AROUND HERE I CAN REALLY TALK TO...
MARLETTE 8-5
I KNOW YOU UNDERSTAND ME. IF I OPENED UP TO ANYBODY ELSE LIKE I DO TO YOU, THEY'D LAUGH AT ME...
THANKS FOR JUST LISTENIN,' OLD PAL!
© Jefferson Communications, Inc. 1981
Distributed by C.T.N.Y.N.S.

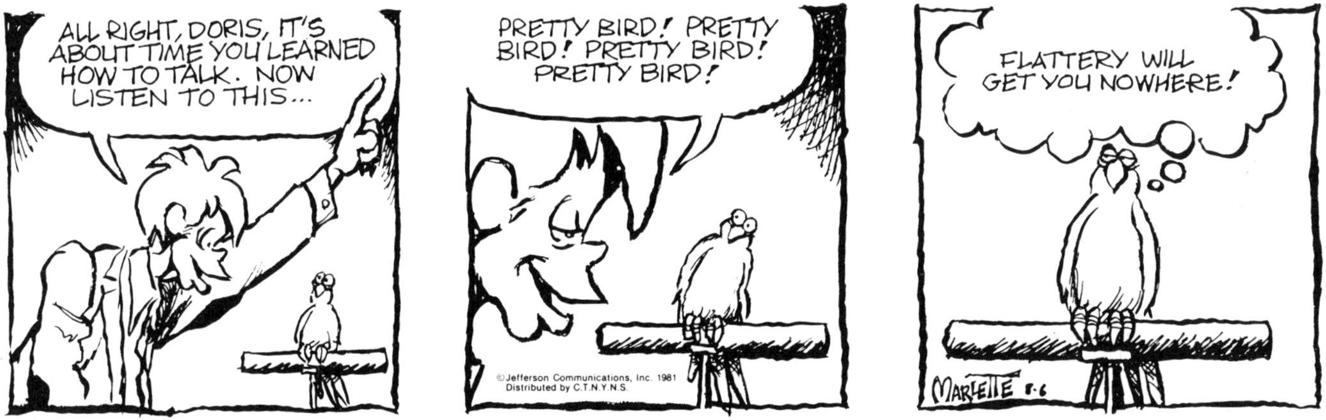
ALL RIGHT, DORIS, IT'S ABOUT TIME YOU LEARNED HOW TO TALK. NOW LISTEN TO THIS...
PRETTY BIRD! PRETTY BIRD! PRETTY BIRD! PRETTY BIRD!
©Jefferson Communications, Inc. 1981
Distributed by C.T.N.Y.N.S.
FLATTERY WILL GET YOU NOWHERE!
MARLETTE 8-6

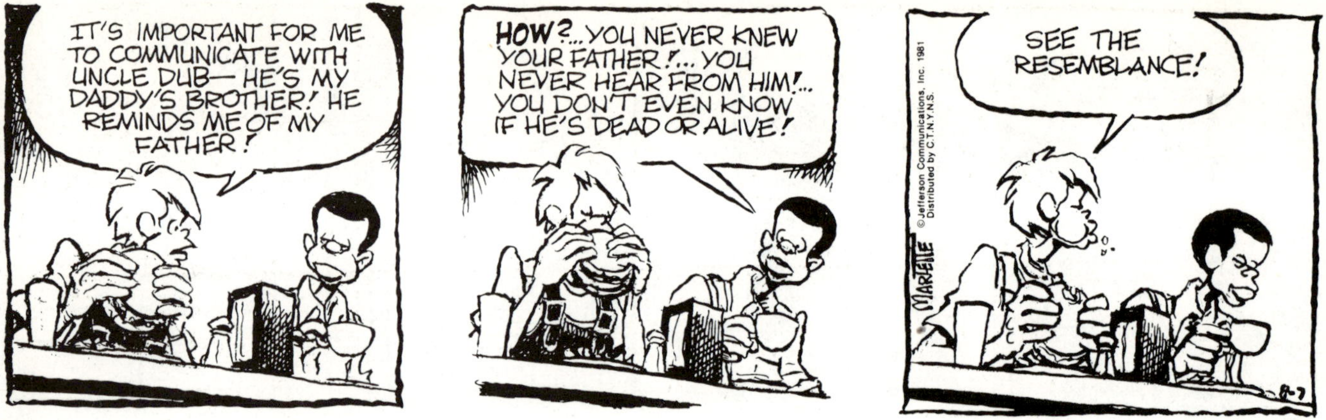
IT'S IMPORTANT FOR ME TO COMMUNICATE WITH UNCLE DUB— HE'S MY DADDY'S BROTHER! HE REMINDS ME OF MY FATHER!
HOW?... YOU NEVER KNEW YOUR FATHER!... YOU NEVER HEAR FROM HIM!... YOU DON'T EVEN KNOW IF HE'S DEAD OR ALIVE!
SEE THE RESEMBLANCE!
MARLETTE
© Jefferson Communications, Inc. 1981
Distributed by C.T.N.Y.N.S.
8-7

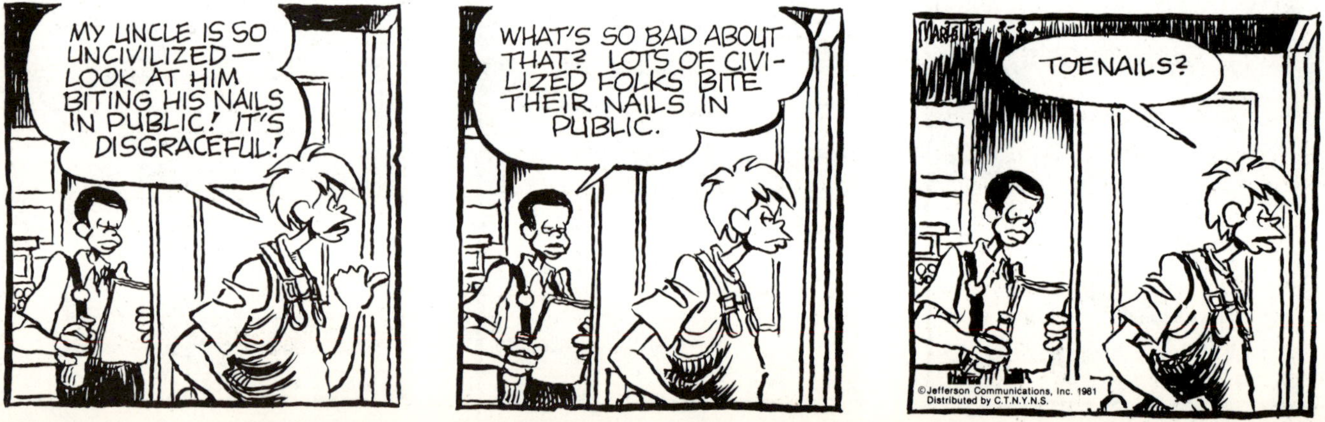
MY UNCLE IS SO UNCIVILIZED— LOOK AT HIM BITING HIS NAILS IN PUBLIC! IT'S DISGRACEFUL!
WHAT'S SO BAD ABOUT THAT? LOTS OF CIVILIZED FOLKS BITE THEIR NAILS IN PUBLIC.
MARLETTE
TOENAILS?
©Jefferson Communications, Inc. 1981
Distributed by C.T.N.Y.N.S.

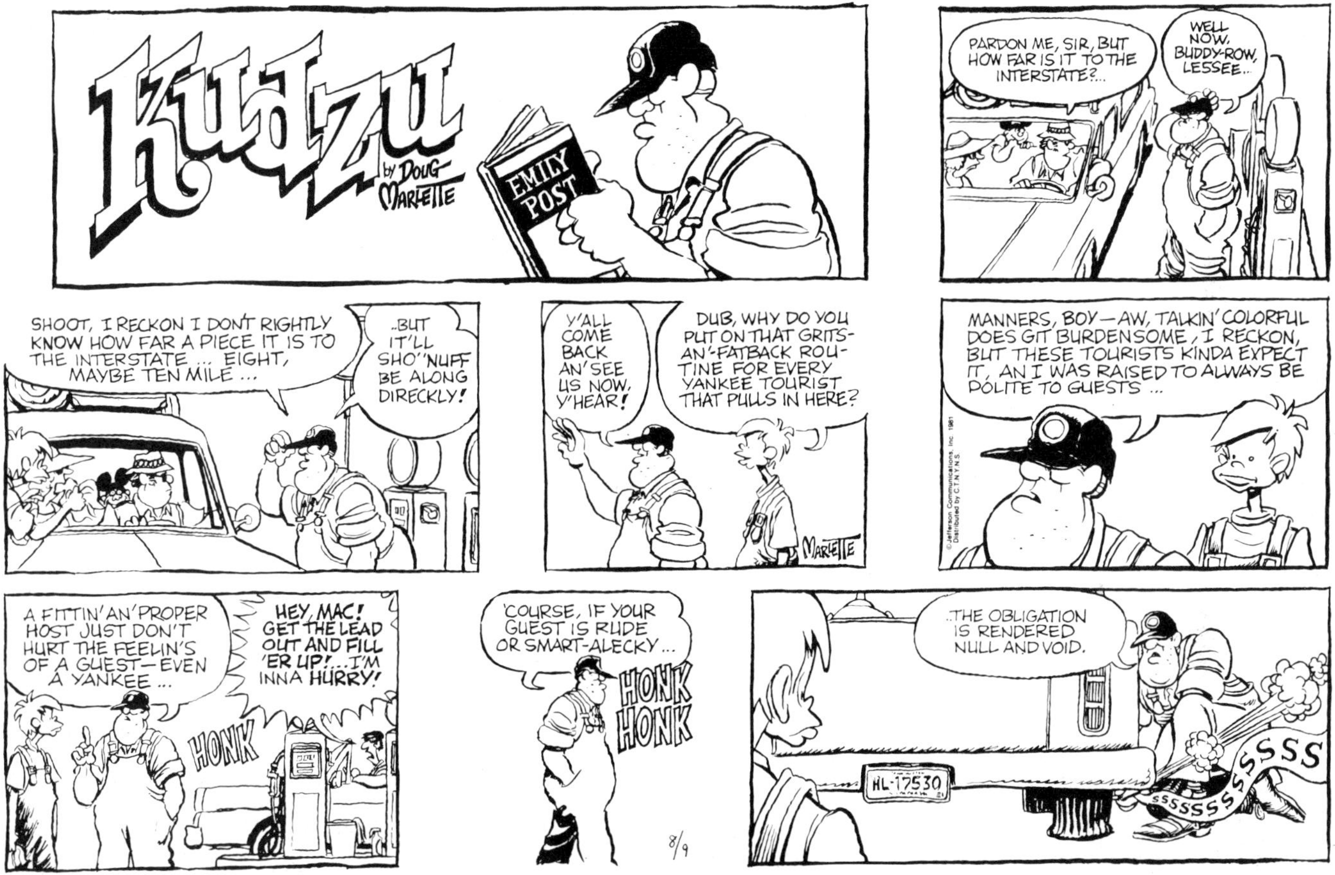
Kudzu
by Doug Marlette
EMILY POST
PARDON ME, SIR, BUT HOW FAR IS IT TO THE INTERSTATE?...
WELL NOW, BUDDY-ROW, LESSEE...
SHOOT, I RECKON I DON'T RIGHTLY KNOW HOW FAR A PIECE IT IS TO THE INTERSTATE ... EIGHT, MAYBE TEN MILE ...
..BUT IT'LL SHO' 'NUFF BE ALONG DIRECKLY!
Y'ALL COME BACK AN' SEE US NOW, Y'HEAR!
DUB, WHY DO YOU PUT ON THAT GRITS-AN'-FATBACK ROUTINE FOR EVERY YANKEE TOURIST THAT PULLS IN HERE?
MARLETTE
MANNERS, BOY—AW, TALKIN' COLORFUL DOES GIT BURDENSOME, I RECKON, BUT THESE TOURISTS KINDA EXPECT IT, AN I WAS RAISED TO ALWAYS BE POLITE TO GUESTS ...
© Jefferson Communications, Inc. 1981
Distributed by C.T.N.Y.N.S.
A FITTIN' AN' PROPER HOST JUST DON'T HURT THE FEELIN'S OF A GUEST—EVEN A YANKEE ...
HEY, MAC! GET THE LEAD OUT AND FILL 'ER UP!...I'M INNA HURRY!
HONK
'COURSE, IF YOUR GUEST IS RUDE OR SMART-ALECKY ...
HONK HONK
8/9
..THE OBLIGATION IS RENDERED NULL AND VOID.
HL-17530
SSSSSSSSSSSSSSS

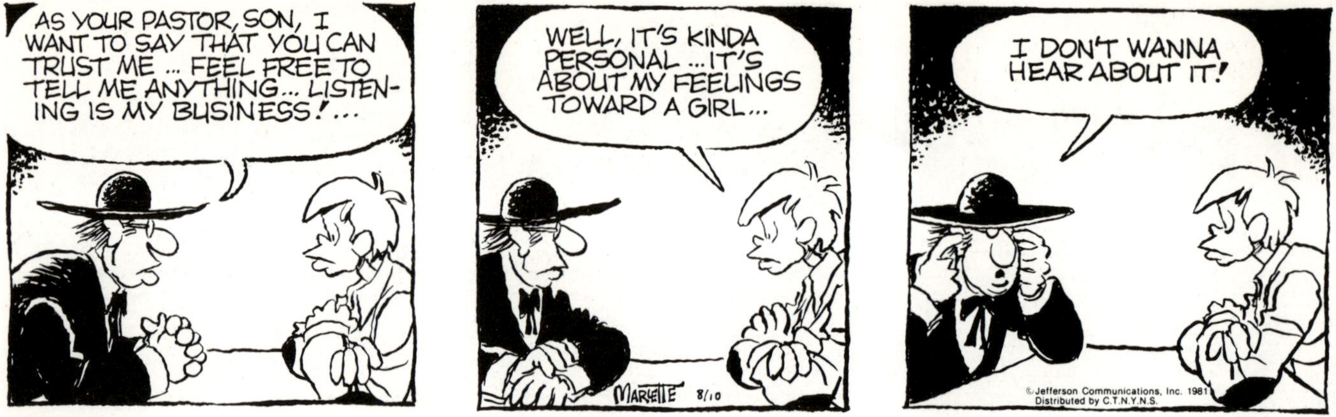
AS YOUR PASTOR, SON, I WANT TO SAY THAT YOU CAN TRUST ME ... FEEL FREE TO TELL ME ANYTHING... LISTENING IS MY BUSINESS!...
WELL, IT'S KINDA PERSONAL ...IT'S ABOUT MY FEELINGS TOWARD A GIRL...
MARLETTE 8/10
I DON'T WANNA HEAR ABOUT IT!
©Jefferson Communications, Inc. 1981
Distributed by C.T.N.Y.N.S.

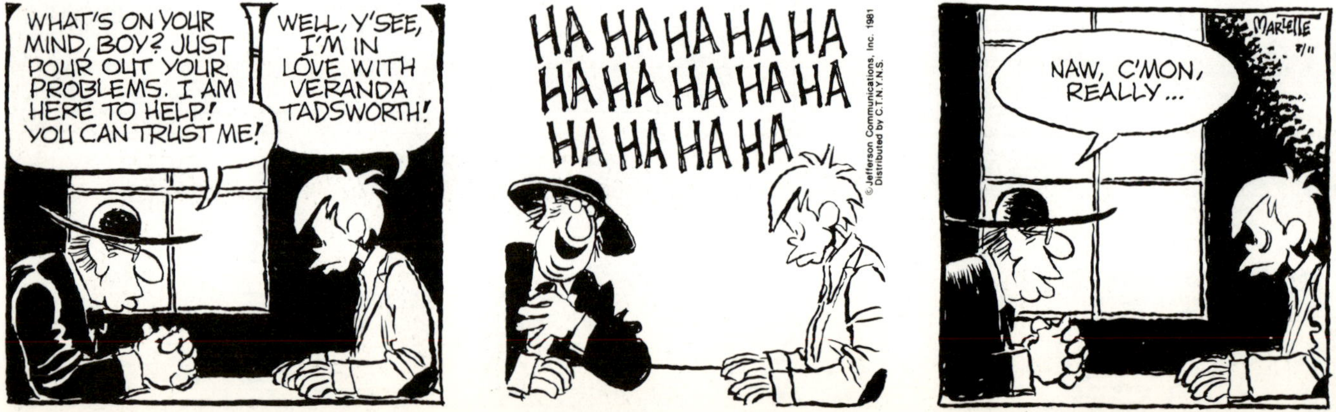
WHAT'S ON YOUR MIND, BOY? JUST POUR OUT YOUR PROBLEMS. I AM HERE TO HELP! YOU CAN TRUST ME!
WELL, Y'SEE, I'M IN LOVE WITH VERANDA TADSWORTH!
HA HA HA HA HA HA HA HA HA HA HA HA HA HA HA HA
© Jefferson Communications, Inc. 1981
Distributed by C.T.N.Y.N.S.
MARLETTE 8/11
NAW, C'MON, REALLY...

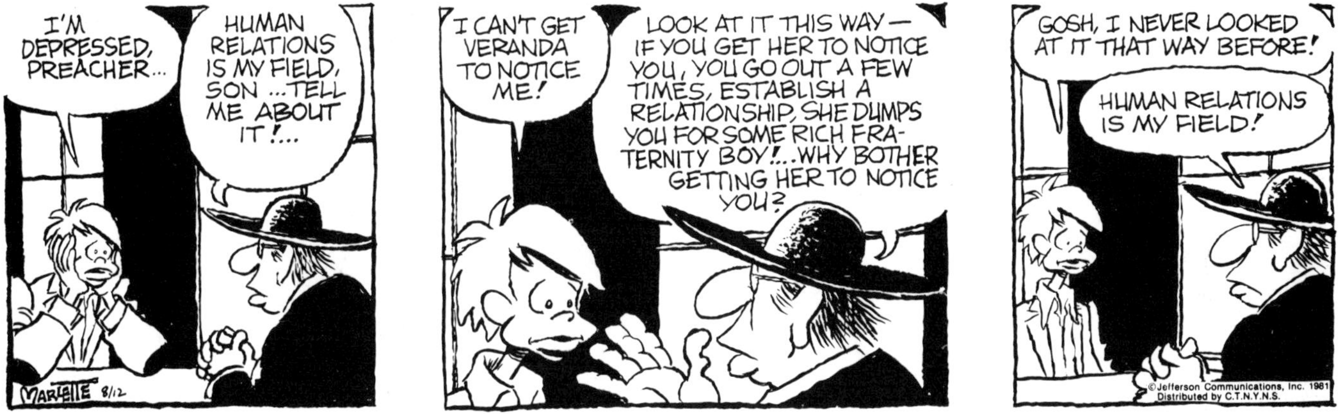
I'M DEPRESSED, PREACHER...
HUMAN RELATIONS IS MY FIELD, SON ...TELL ME ABOUT IT!...
MARLETTE 8/12
I CAN'T GET VERANDA TO NOTICE ME!
LOOK AT IT THIS WAY— IF YOU GET HER TO NOTICE YOU, YOU GO OUT A FEW TIMES, ESTABLISH A RELATIONSHIP, SHE DUMPS YOU FOR SOME RICH FRATERNITY BOY!...WHY BOTHER GETTING HER TO NOTICE YOU?
GOSH, I NEVER LOOKED AT IT THAT WAY BEFORE!
HUMAN RELATIONS IS MY FIELD!
©Jefferson Communications, Inc. 1981
Distributed by C.T.N.Y.N.S.

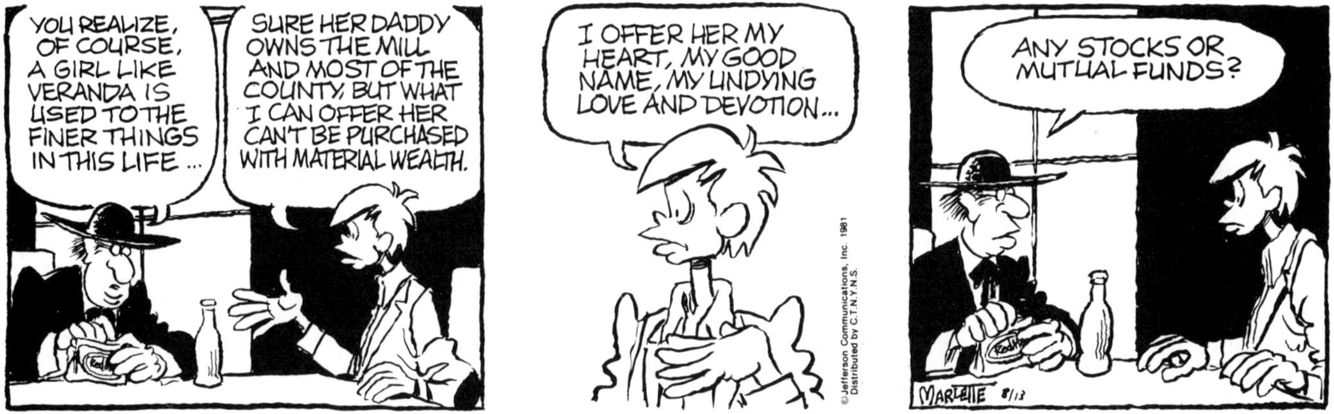
YOU REALIZE, OF COURSE, A GIRL LIKE VERANDA IS USED TO THE FINER THINGS IN THIS LIFE ...
SURE HER DADDY OWNS THE MILL AND MOST OF THE COUNTY, BUT WHAT I CAN OFFER HER CAN'T BE PURCHASED WITH MATERIAL WEALTH.
I OFFER HER MY HEART, MY GOOD NAME, MY UNDYING LOVE AND DEVOTION...
© Jefferson Communications, Inc. 1981
Distributed by C.T.N.Y.N.S.
ANY STOCKS OR MUTUAL FUNDS?
MARLETTE 8/13

I'M IN LOVE WITH VERANDA TADSWORTH AND I DON'T KNOW WHAT TO DO!...
FORGET HER, BOY! THERE ARE PLENTY MORE FISH IN THE SEA!
©Jefferson Communications, Inc. 1981 Distributed by C.T.N.Y.N.S.
PREACHER, I WOULD APPRECIATE IT IF YOU WOULDN'T CALL MY VERANDA A **FISH**!
YOU GOT IT BAD, AIN'TCHA, BOY?
UH-HUH...
8/14
MARLETTE

THANKS FOR ALL THE ENCOURAGEMENT, PREACHER!
AND WHAT DID YOU LEARN, BOY?
8/15
MARLETTE
THAT I SHOULD GET IN THERE AND FIGHT FOR VERANDA'S LOVE.
NO MATTER THE REJECTION...
NO MATTER THE REJECTION AND NO MATTER HOW HUMILIATIN' AND NO MATTER HOW MUCH I MAKE A FOOL OF MYSELF!
'ATTABOY!
I SHOULD BE ASHAMED OF MYSELF!
©Jefferson Communications, Inc. 1981 Distributed by C.T.N.Y.N.S.

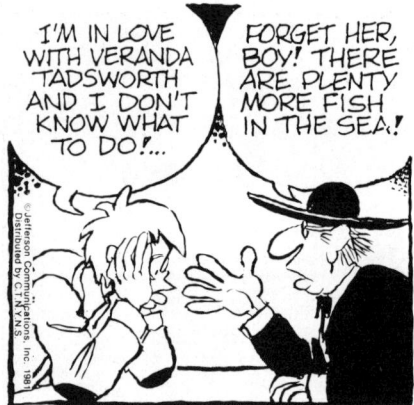

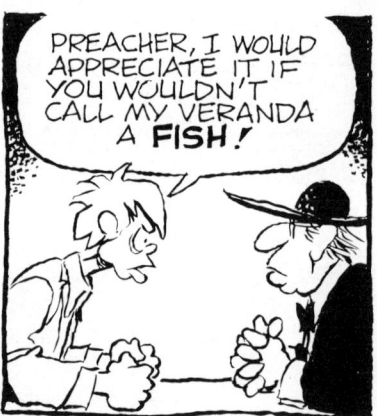

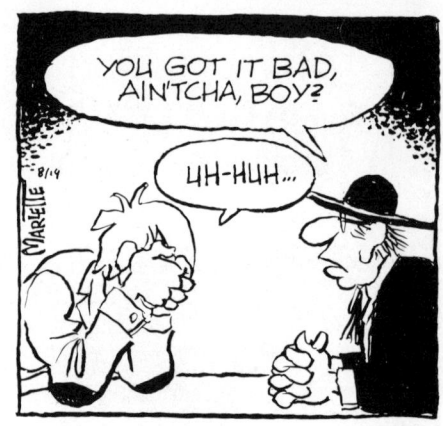

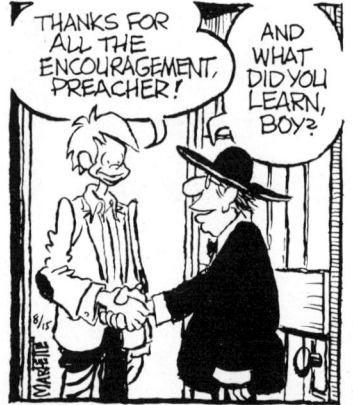

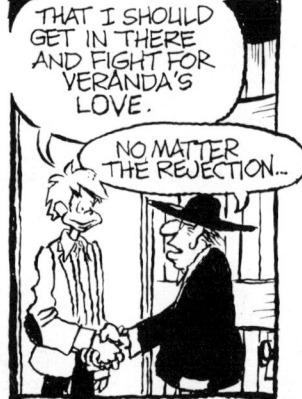

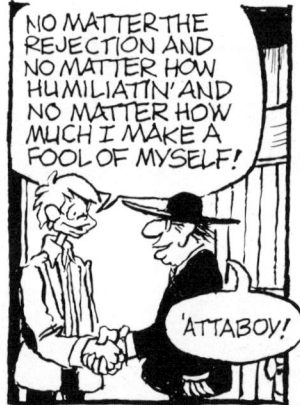

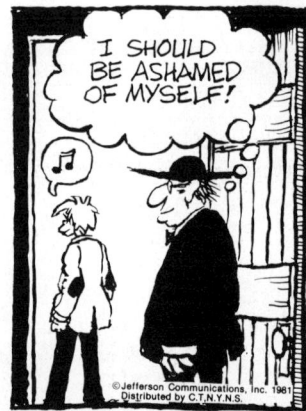

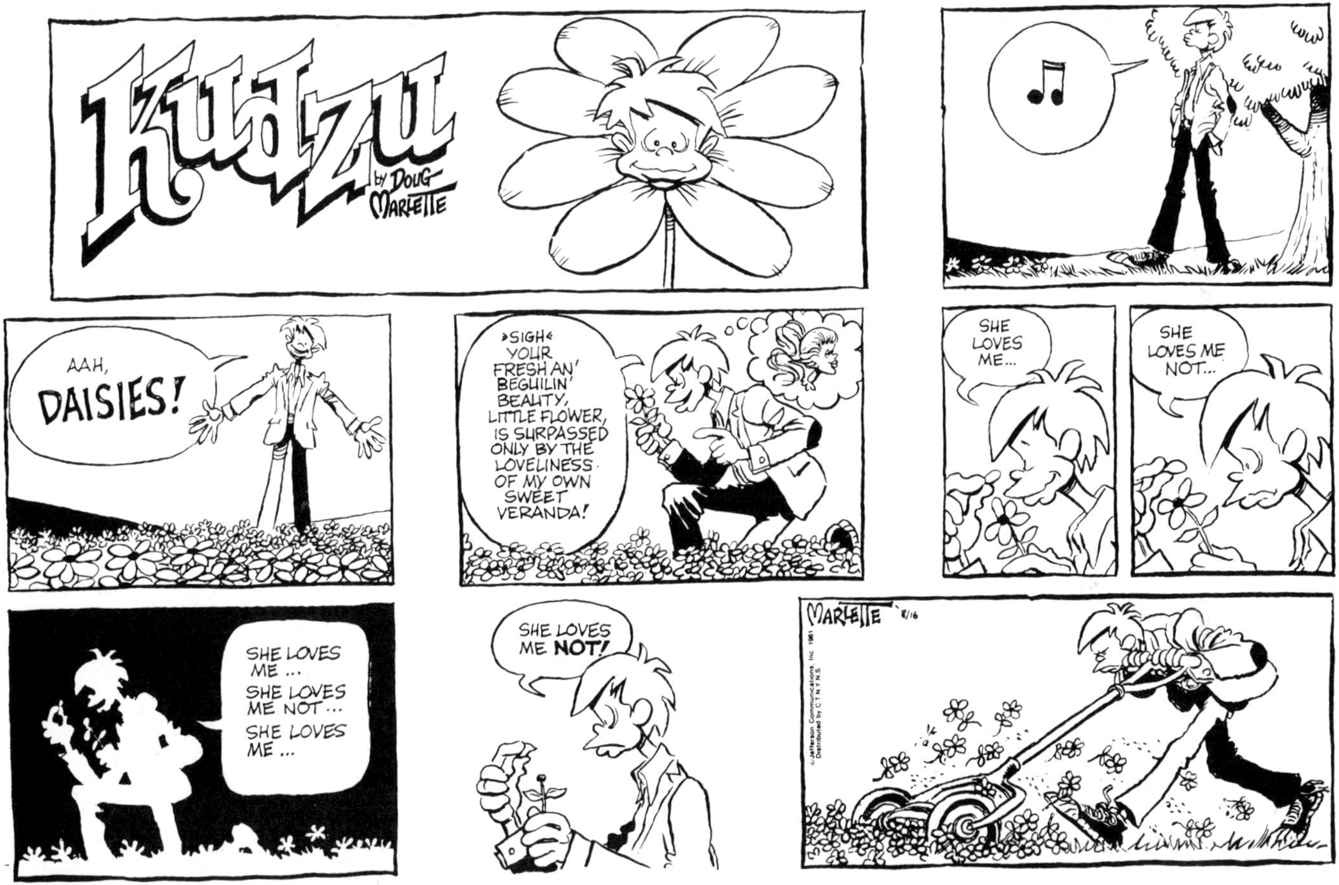
Kudzu
by Doug Marlette
♫
AAH, DAISIES!
»SIGH« YOUR FRESH AN' BEGUILIN' BEAUTY, LITTLE FLOWER, IS SURPASSED ONLY BY THE LOVELINESS OF MY OWN SWEET VERANDA!
SHE LOVES ME...
SHE LOVES ME NOT...
SHE LOVES ME ... SHE LOVES ME NOT ... SHE LOVES ME ...
SHE LOVES ME **NOT!**
MARLETTE 8/16
© Jefferson Communications, Inc 1981
Distributed by C.T.N.Y.N.S.

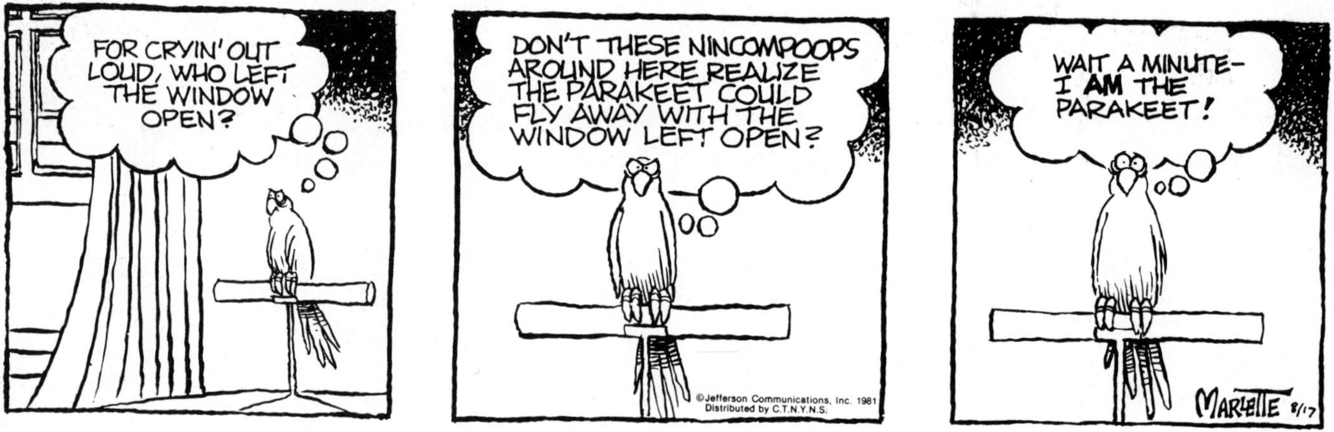
FOR CRYIN' OUT LOUD, WHO LEFT THE WINDOW OPEN?
DON'T THESE NINCOMPOOPS AROUND HERE REALIZE THE PARAKEET COULD FLY AWAY WITH THE WINDOW LEFT OPEN?
©Jefferson Communications, Inc. 1981
Distributed by C.T.N.Y.N.S.
WAIT A MINUTE- I **AM** THE PARAKEET!
MARLETTE 8/17

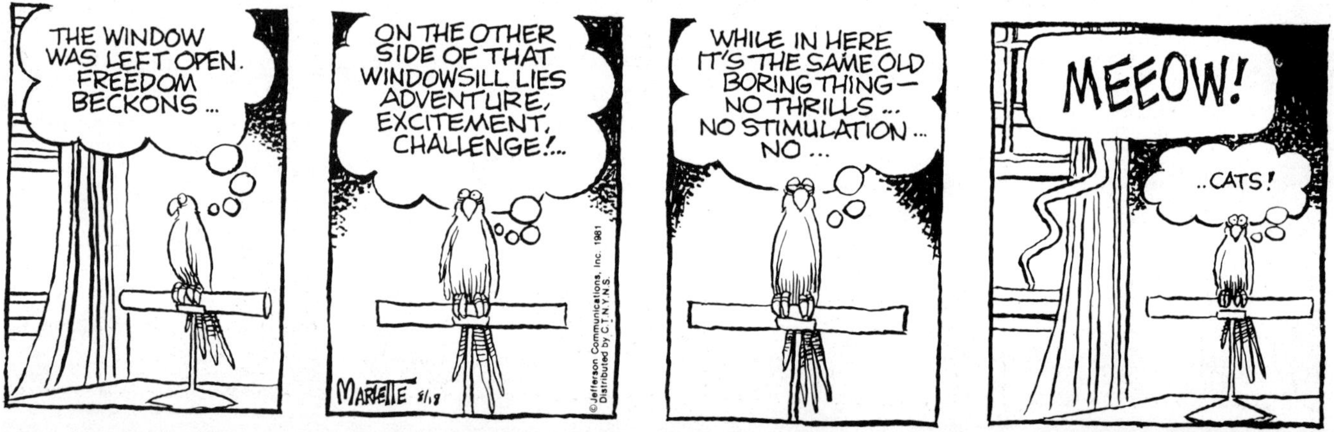
THE WINDOW WAS LEFT OPEN. FREEDOM BECKONS ...
ON THE OTHER SIDE OF THAT WINDOWSILL LIES ADVENTURE, EXCITEMENT, CHALLENGE!...
MARLETTE 8/18
©Jefferson Communications, Inc. 1981
Distributed by C.T.N.Y.N.S.
WHILE IN HERE IT'S THE SAME OLD BORING THING— NO THRILLS ... NO STIMULATION ... NO ...
MEEOW!
..CATS!

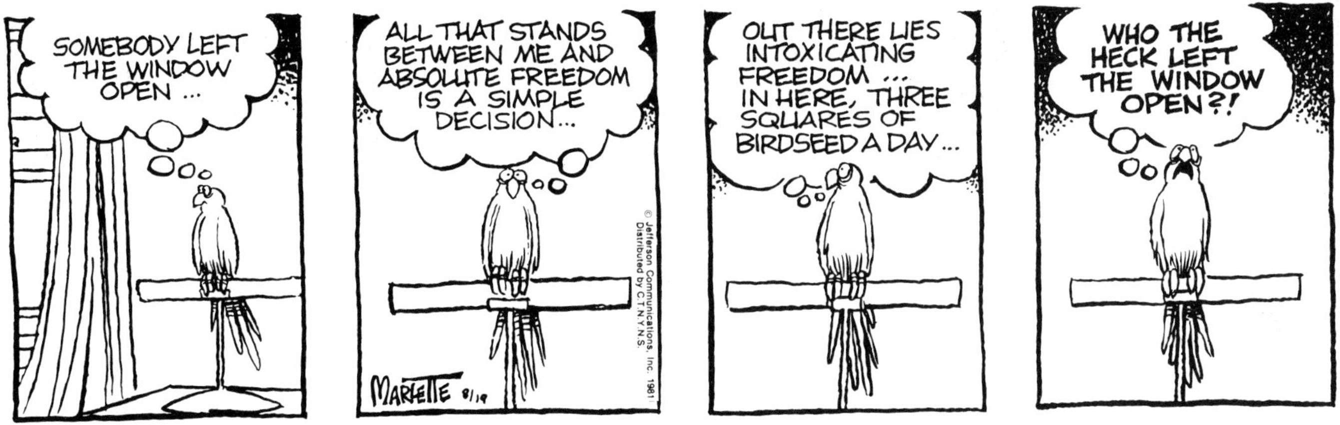
SOMEBODY LEFT THE WINDOW OPEN ...
ALL THAT STANDS BETWEEN ME AND ABSOLUTE FREEDOM IS A SIMPLE DECISION...
MARLETTE 8/19
© Jefferson Communications, Inc. 1981
Distributed by C.T.N.Y.N.S.
OUT THERE LIES INTOXICATING FREEDOM ... IN HERE, THREE SQUARES OF BIRDSEED A DAY...
WHO THE HECK LEFT THE WINDOW OPEN?!

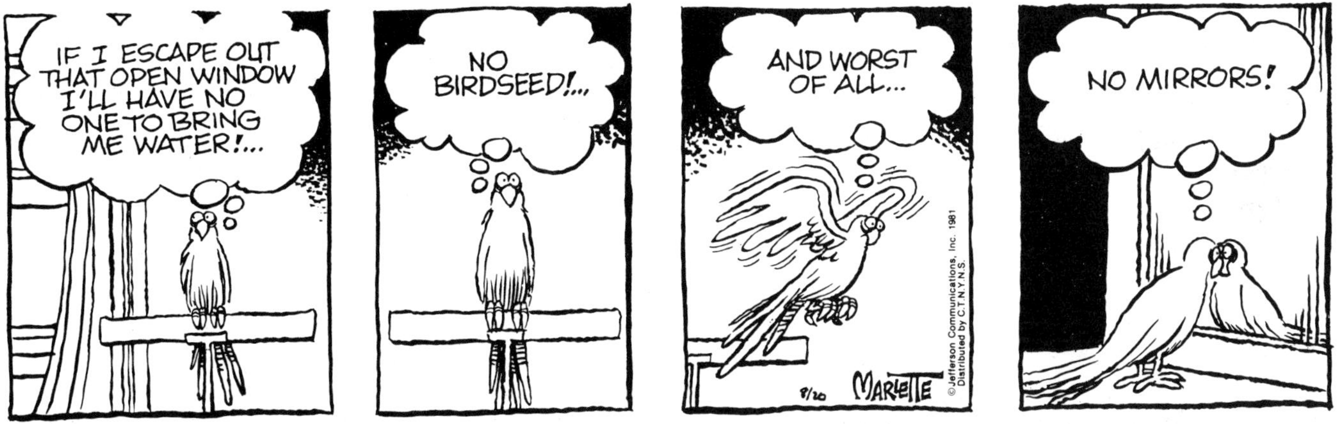
IF I ESCAPE OUT THAT OPEN WINDOW I'LL HAVE NO ONE TO BRING ME WATER!...
NO BIRDSEED!...
AND WORST OF ALL...
8/20
MARLETTE
© Jefferson Communications, Inc. 1981
Distributed by C.T.N.Y.N.S.
NO MIRRORS!

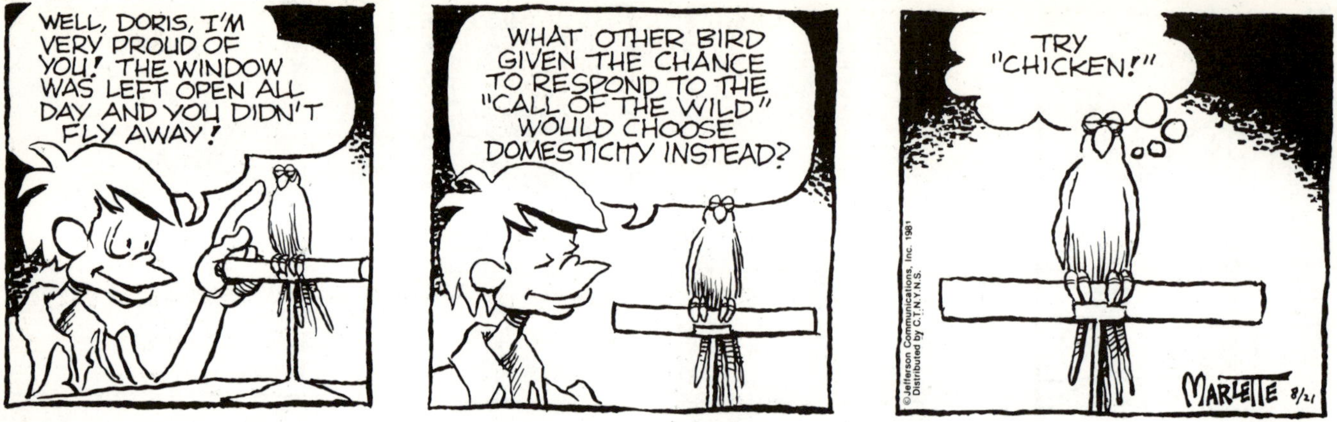
WELL, DORIS, I'M VERY PROUD OF YOU! THE WINDOW WAS LEFT OPEN ALL DAY AND YOU DIDN'T FLY AWAY!
WHAT OTHER BIRD GIVEN THE CHANCE TO RESPOND TO THE "CALL OF THE WILD" WOULD CHOOSE DOMESTICITY INSTEAD?
TRY "CHICKEN!"
© Jefferson Communications, Inc. 1981
Distributed by C.T.N.Y.N.S.
MARLETTE 8/21

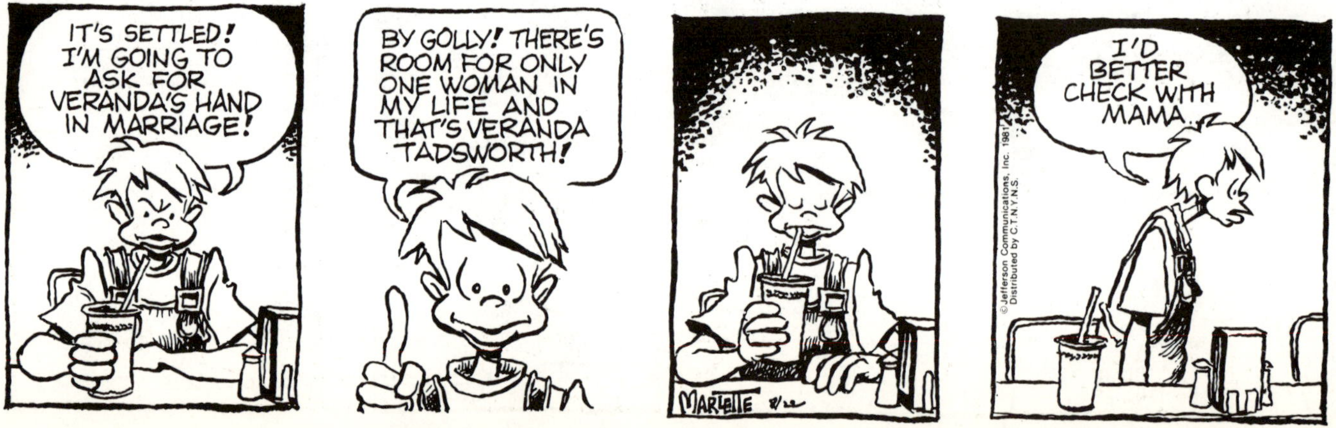
IT'S SETTLED! I'M GOING TO ASK FOR VERANDA'S HAND IN MARRIAGE!
BY GOLLY! THERE'S ROOM FOR ONLY ONE WOMAN IN MY LIFE AND THAT'S VERANDA TADSWORTH!
MARLETTE 8/22
© Jefferson Communications, Inc. 1981
Distributed by C.T.N.Y.N.S.
I'D BETTER CHECK WITH MAMA.

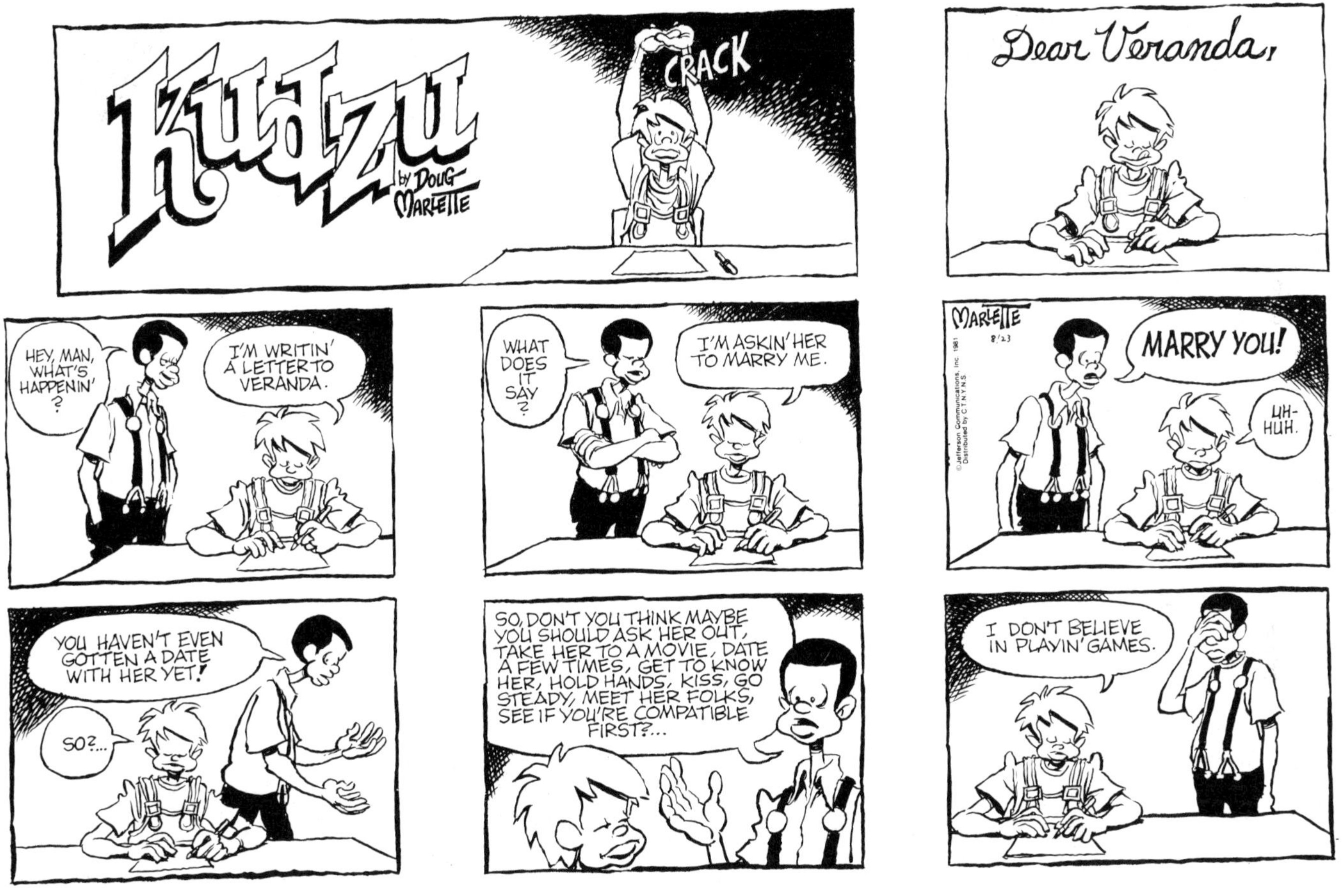
Kudzu
by Doug Marlette
CRACK
Dear Veranda,
HEY, MAN, WHAT'S HAPPENIN' ?
I'M WRITIN' A LETTER TO VERANDA.
WHAT DOES IT SAY ?
I'M ASKIN' HER TO MARRY ME.
MARLETTE 8/23
©Jefferson Communications, Inc. 1981
Distributed by C.T.N.Y.N.S.
MARRY YOU!
UH-HUH.
YOU HAVEN'T EVEN GOTTEN A DATE WITH HER YET!
SO?...
SO, DON'T YOU THINK MAYBE YOU SHOULD ASK HER OUT, TAKE HER TO A MOVIE, DATE A FEW TIMES, GET TO KNOW HER, HOLD HANDS, KISS, GO STEADY, MEET HER FOLKS, SEE IF YOU'RE COMPATIBLE FIRST?...
I DON'T BELIEVE IN PLAYIN' GAMES.

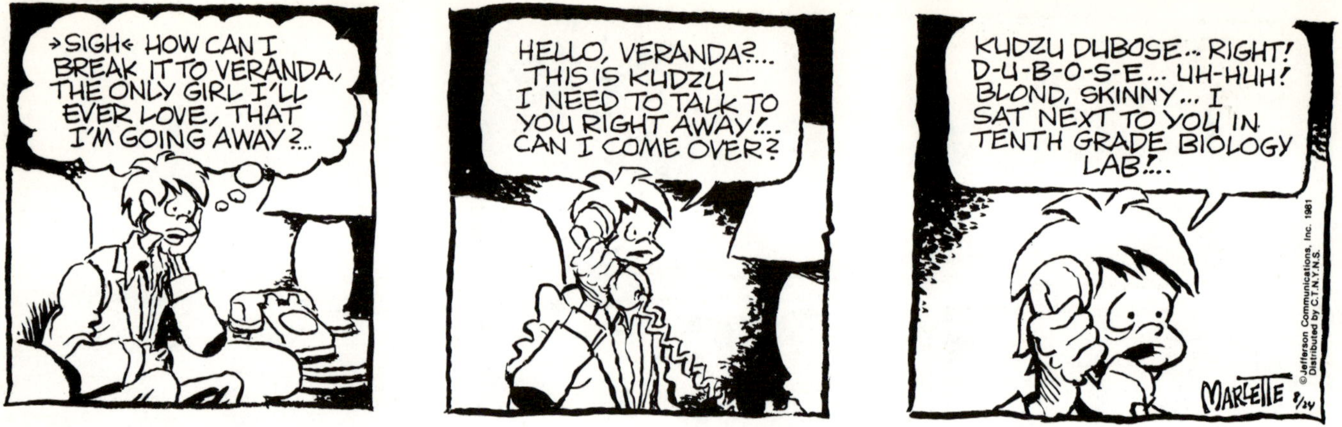
>SIGH< HOW CAN I BREAK IT TO VERANDA, THE ONLY GIRL I'LL EVER LOVE, THAT I'M GOING AWAY?...
HELLO, VERANDA?... THIS IS KUDZU— I NEED TO TALK TO YOU RIGHT AWAY!... CAN I COME OVER?
KUDZU DUBOSE... RIGHT! D-U-B-O-S-E... UH-HUH! BLOND, SKINNY... I SAT NEXT TO YOU IN TENTH GRADE BIOLOGY LAB!...
© Jefferson Communications, Inc. 1981 Distributed by C.T.N.Y.N.S.
MARLETTE 8/24

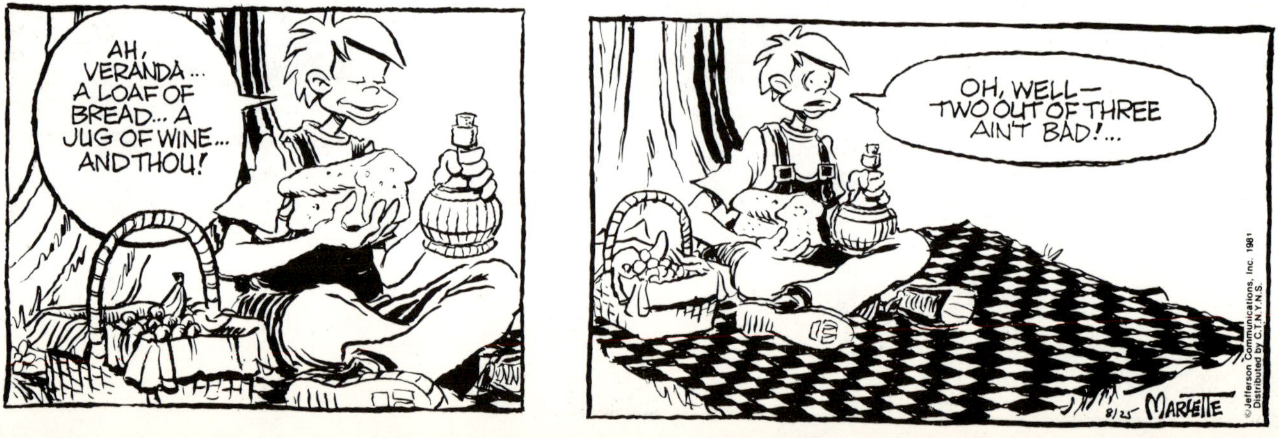
AH, VERANDA... A LOAF OF BREAD... A JUG OF WINE... AND THOU!
OH, WELL— TWO OUT OF THREE AIN'T BAD!...
© Jefferson Communications, Inc. 1981 Distributed by C.T.N.Y.N.S.
8/25 MARLETTE

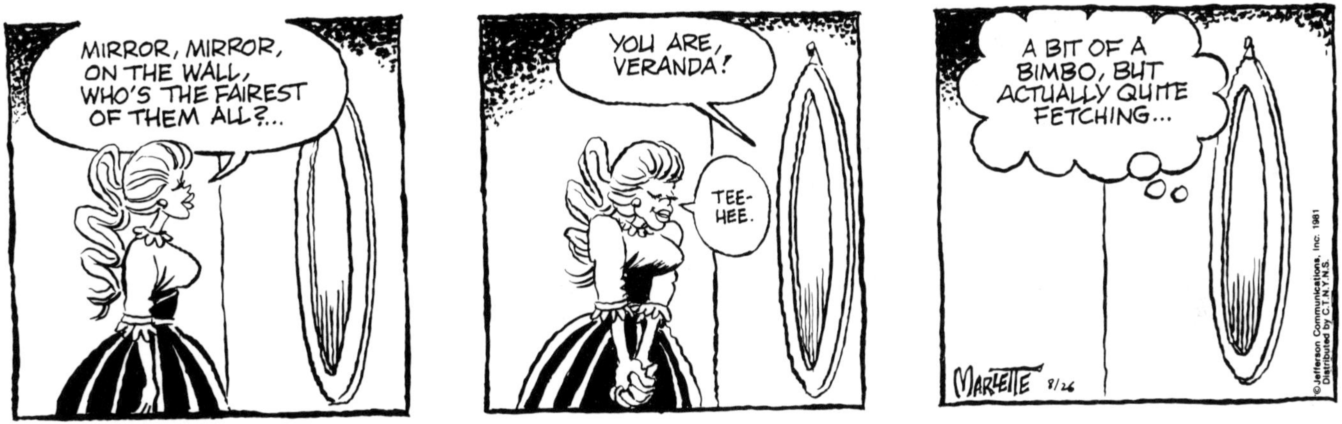
MIRROR, MIRROR, ON THE WALL, WHO'S THE FAIREST OF THEM ALL?...
YOU ARE, VERANDA!
TEE-HEE.
A BIT OF A BIMBO, BUT ACTUALLY QUITE FETCHING...
MARLETTE 8/26
© Jefferson Communications, Inc. 1981
Distributed by C.T.N.Y.N.S.

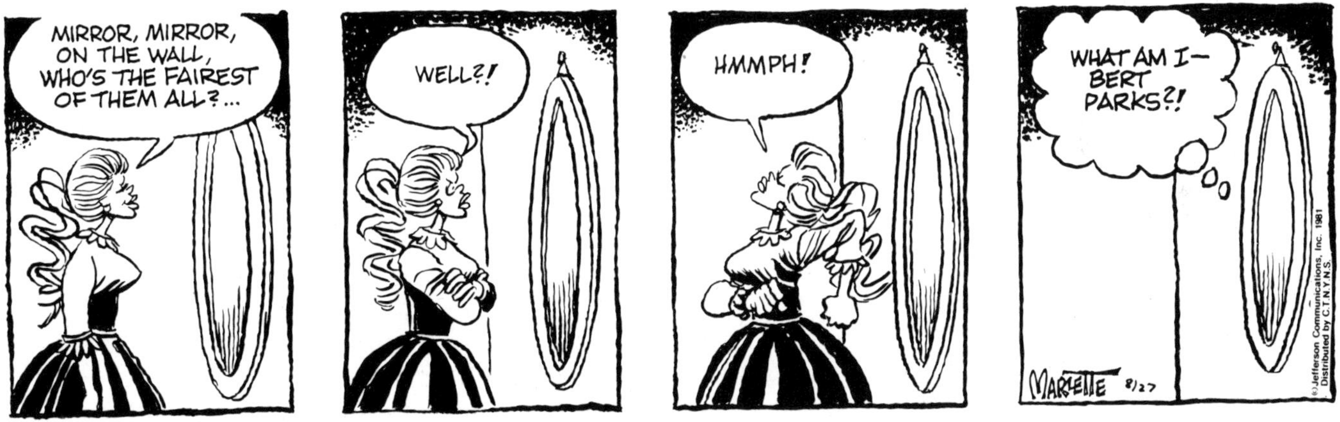
MIRROR, MIRROR, ON THE WALL, WHO'S THE FAIREST OF THEM ALL?...
WELL?!
HMMPH!
WHAT AM I— BERT PARKS?!
MARLETTE 8/27
© Jefferson Communications, Inc. 1981
Distributed by C.T.N.Y.N.S.

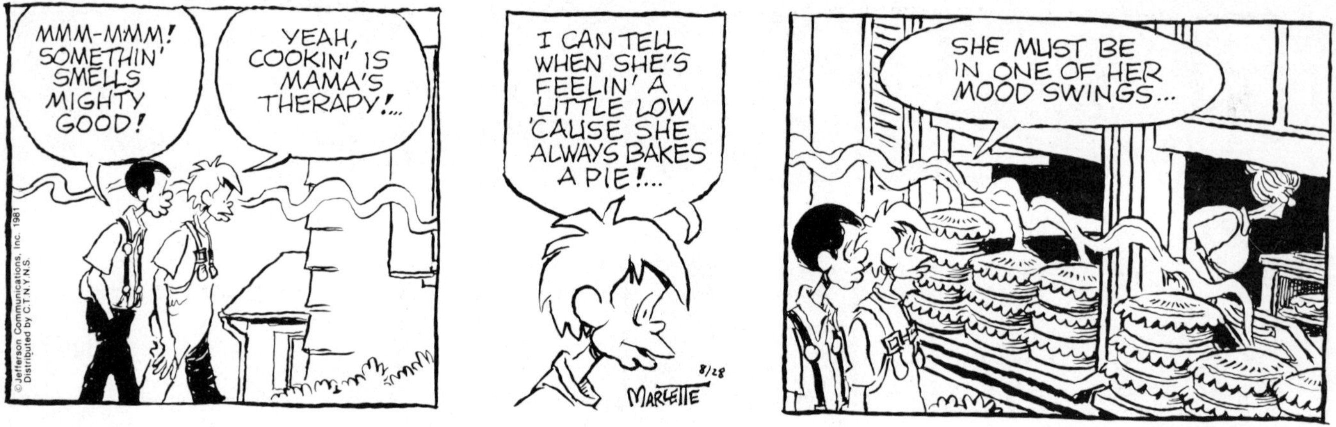
MMM-MMM! SOMETHIN' SMELLS MIGHTY GOOD!
YEAH, COOKIN' IS MAMA'S THERAPY!...
© Jefferson Communications, Inc. 1981
Distributed by C.T.N.Y.N.S.
I CAN TELL WHEN SHE'S FEELIN' A LITTLE LOW 'CAUSE SHE ALWAYS BAKES A PIE!...
8/28
MARLETTE
SHE MUST BE IN ONE OF HER MOOD SWINGS...

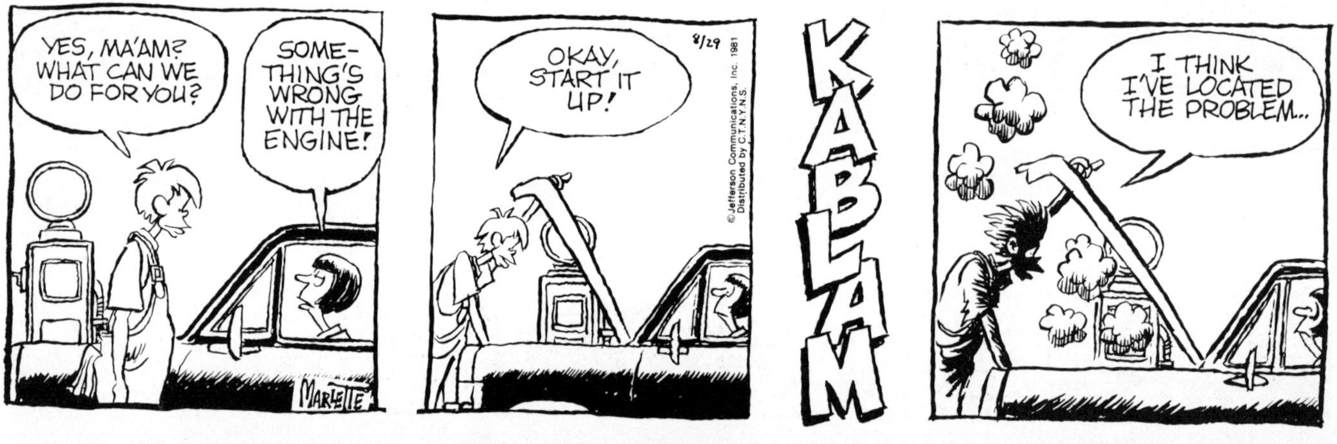
YES, MA'AM? WHAT CAN WE DO FOR YOU?
SOMETHING'S WRONG WITH THE ENGINE!
MARLETTE
8/29
OKAY, START IT UP!
© Jefferson Communications, Inc. 1981
Distributed by C.T.N.Y.N.S.
KABLAM
I THINK I'VE LOCATED THE PROBLEM...

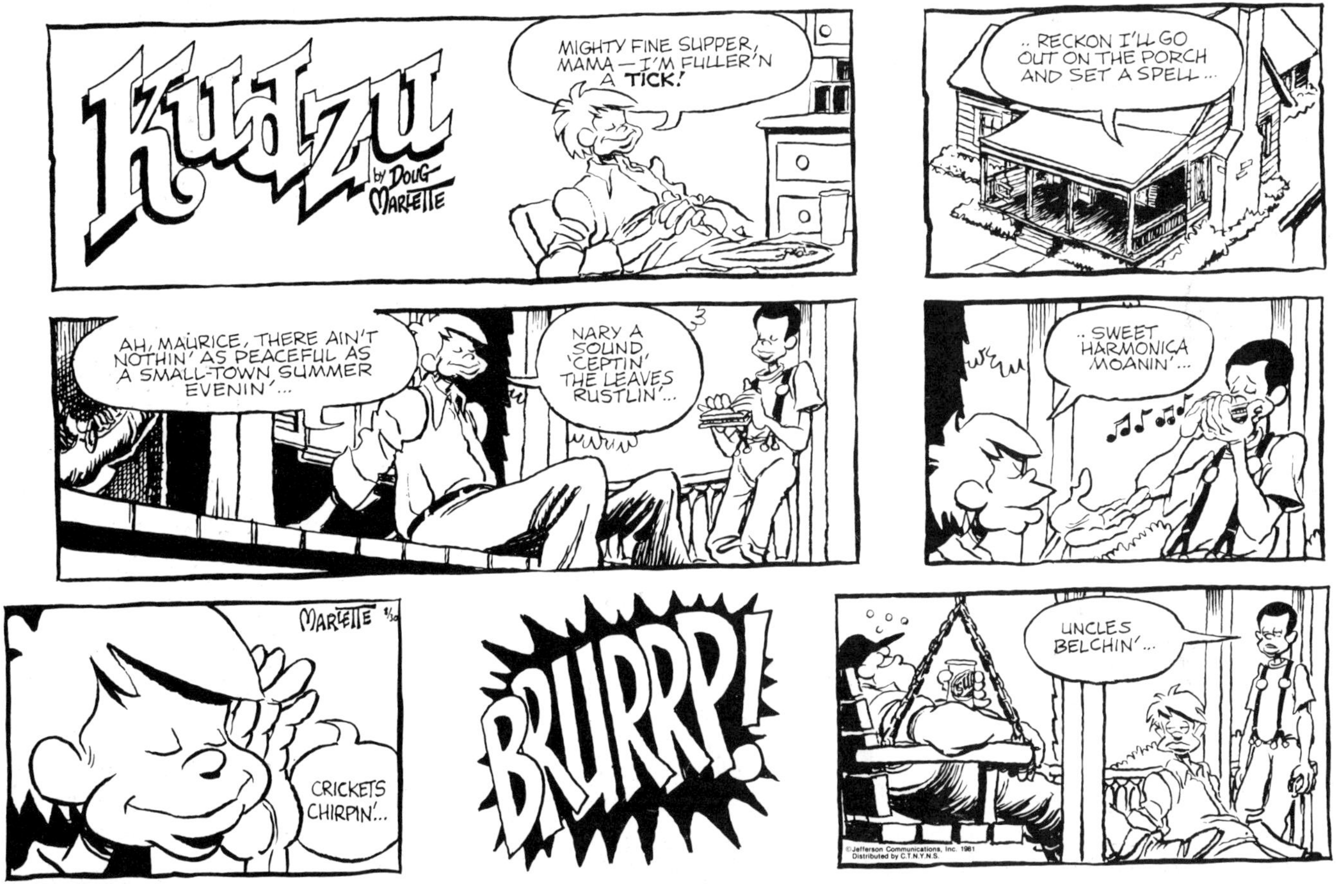
KUDZU
by DOUG MARLETTE
MIGHTY FINE SUPPER, MAMA — I'M FULLER'N A TICK!
.. RECKON I'LL GO OUT ON THE PORCH AND SET A SPELL...
AH, MAURICE, THERE AIN'T NOTHIN' AS PEACEFUL AS A SMALL-TOWN SUMMER EVENIN'...
NARY A SOUND 'CEPTIN' THE LEAVES RUSTLIN'...
.. SWEET HARMONICA MOANIN'...
MARLETTE 8/30
CRICKETS CHIRPIN'...
BRURRP!
UNCLES BELCHIN'...
©Jefferson Communications, Inc. 1981
Distributed by C.T.N.Y.N.S.

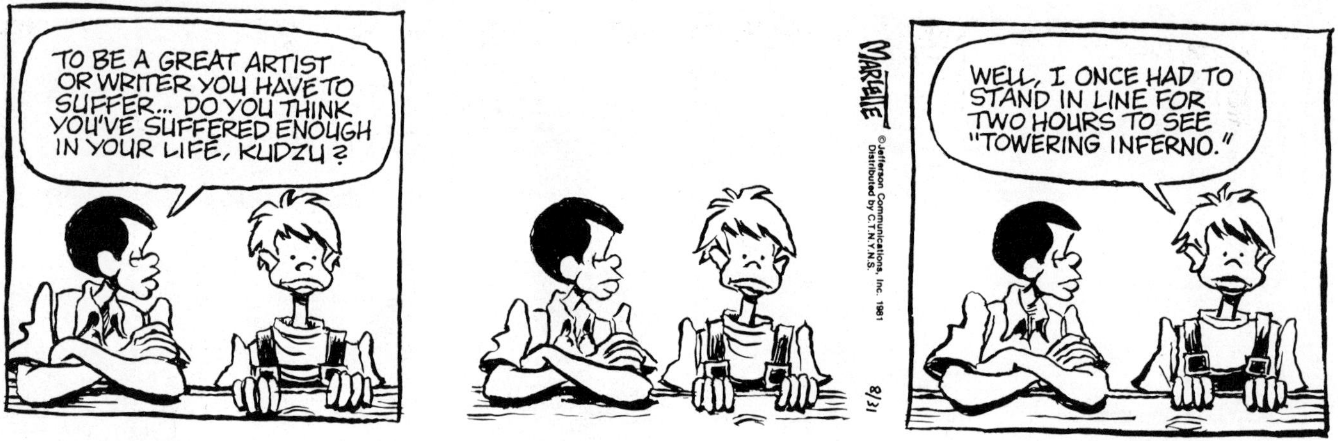
TO BE A GREAT ARTIST OR WRITER YOU HAVE TO SUFFER... DO YOU THINK YOU'VE SUFFERED ENOUGH IN YOUR LIFE, KUDZU?
MARLETTE
© Jefferson Communications, Inc. 1981
Distributed by C.T.N.Y.N.S.
8/31
WELL, I ONCE HAD TO STAND IN LINE FOR TWO HOURS TO SEE "TOWERING INFERNO."

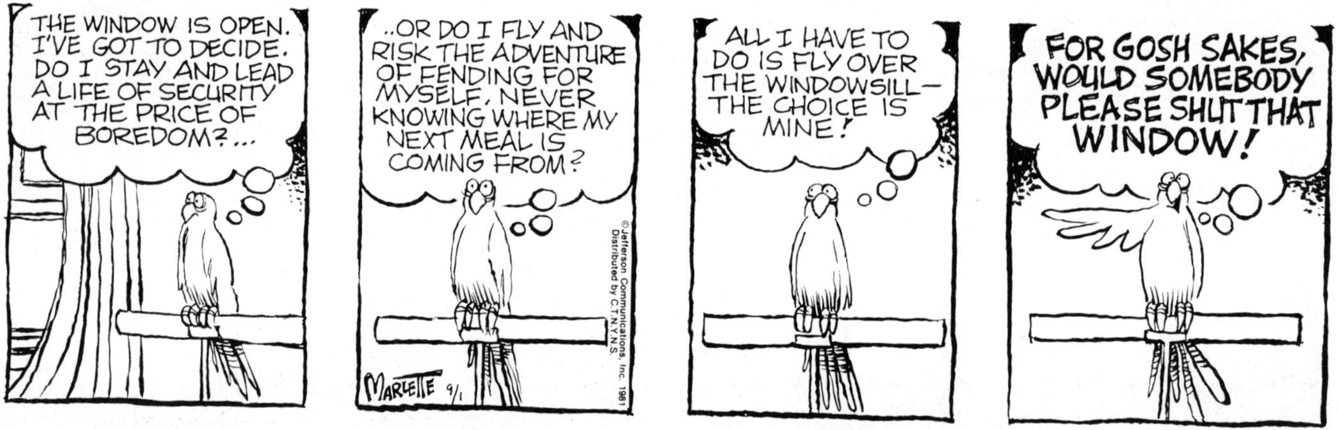
THE WINDOW IS OPEN. I'VE GOT TO DECIDE. DO I STAY AND LEAD A LIFE OF SECURITY AT THE PRICE OF BOREDOM?...
..OR DO I FLY AND RISK THE ADVENTURE OF FENDING FOR MYSELF, NEVER KNOWING WHERE MY NEXT MEAL IS COMING FROM?
© Jefferson Communications, Inc. 1981
Distributed by C.T.N.Y.N.S.
MARLETTE 9/1
ALL I HAVE TO DO IS FLY OVER THE WINDOWSILL— THE CHOICE IS MINE!
FOR GOSH SAKES, WOULD SOMEBODY PLEASE SHUT THAT WINDOW!

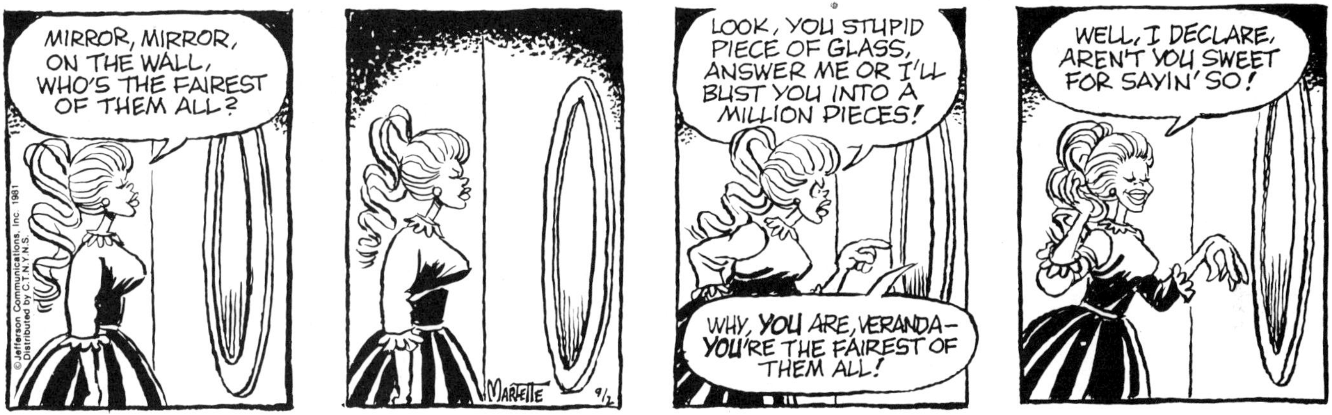
MIRROR, MIRROR, ON THE WALL, WHO'S THE FAIREST OF THEM ALL?
© Jefferson Communications, Inc. 1981 Distributed by C.T.N.Y.N.S.
MARLETTE
9/2
LOOK, YOU STUPID PIECE OF GLASS, ANSWER ME OR I'LL BUST YOU INTO A MILLION PIECES!
WHY, YOU ARE, VERANDA— YOU'RE THE FAIREST OF THEM ALL!
WELL, I DECLARE, AREN'T YOU SWEET FOR SAYIN' SO!

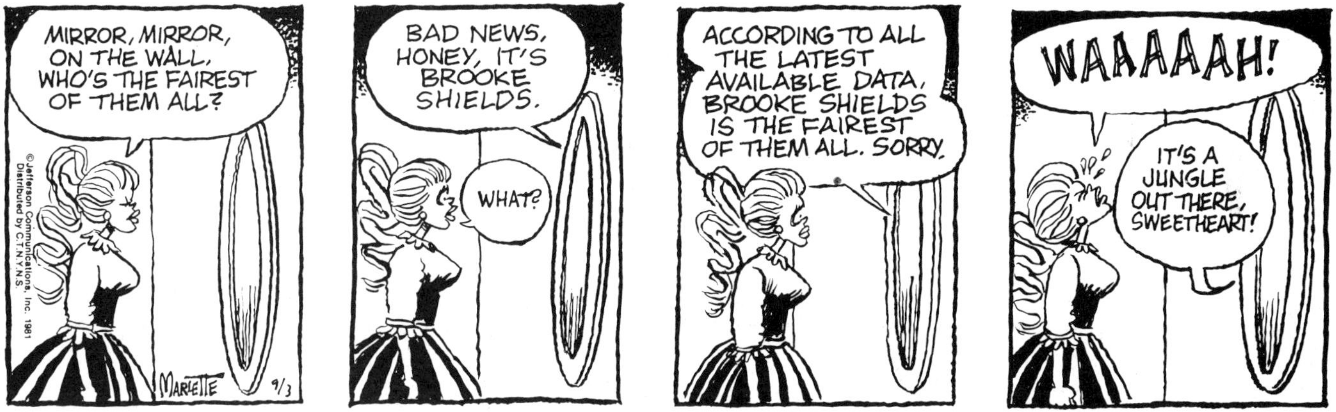
MIRROR, MIRROR, ON THE WALL, WHO'S THE FAIREST OF THEM ALL?
© Jefferson Communications, Inc. 1981 Distributed by C.T.N.Y.N.S.
MARLETTE
9/3
BAD NEWS, HONEY, IT'S BROOKE SHIELDS.
WHAT?
ACCORDING TO ALL THE LATEST AVAILABLE DATA, BROOKE SHIELDS IS THE FAIREST OF THEM ALL. SORRY.
WAAAAAH!
IT'S A JUNGLE OUT THERE, SWEETHEART!

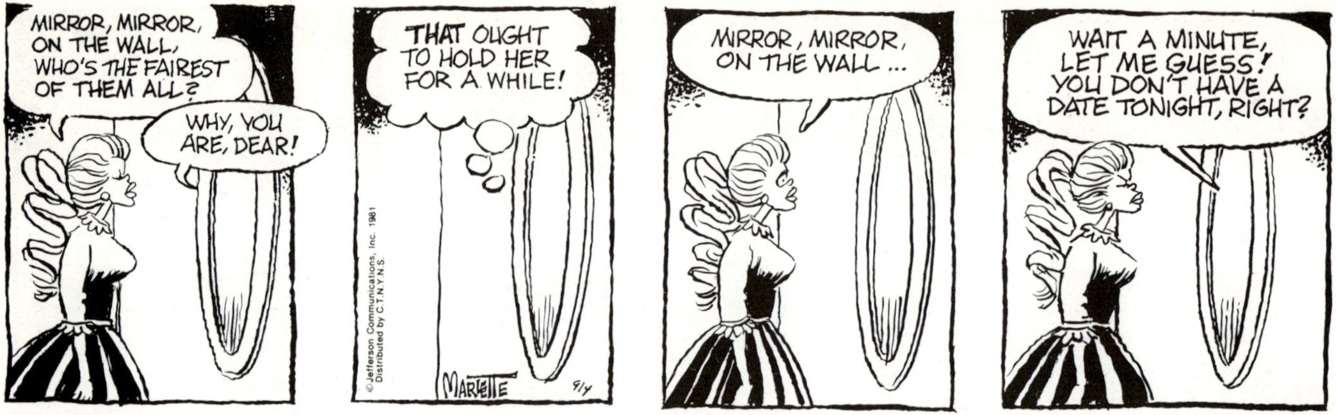
MIRROR, MIRROR, ON THE WALL, WHO'S THE FAIREST OF THEM ALL?
WHY, YOU ARE, DEAR!
THAT OUGHT TO HOLD HER FOR A WHILE!
© Jefferson Communications, Inc. 1981 Distributed by C.T.N.Y.N.S.
MARLETTE
9/4
MIRROR, MIRROR, ON THE WALL ...
WAIT A MINUTE, LET ME GUESS! YOU DON'T HAVE A DATE TONIGHT, RIGHT?

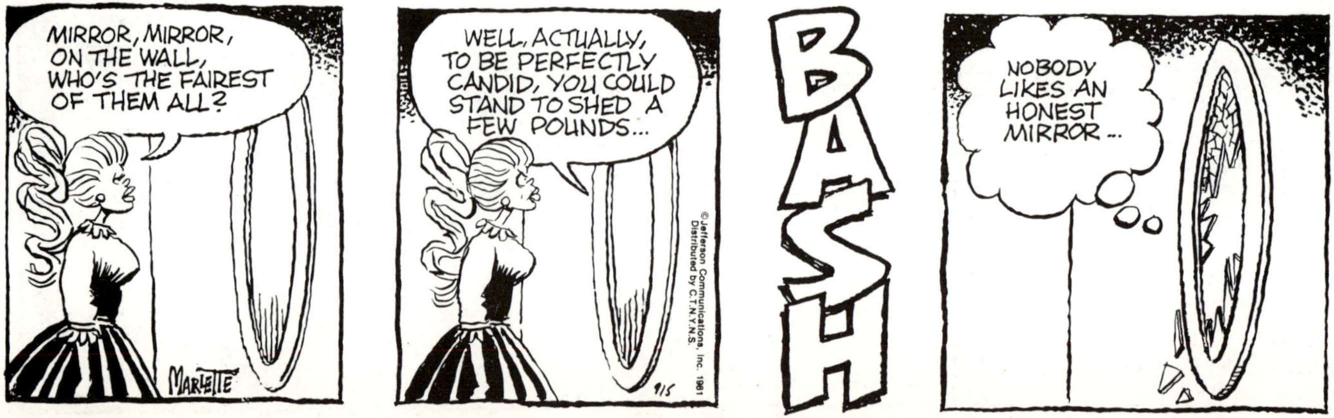
MIRROR, MIRROR, ON THE WALL, WHO'S THE FAIREST OF THEM ALL?
MARLETTE
WELL, ACTUALLY, TO BE PERFECTLY CANDID, YOU COULD STAND TO SHED A FEW POUNDS...
©Jefferson Communications, Inc. 1981 Distributed by C.T.N.Y.N.S.
9/5
BASH
NOBODY LIKES AN HONEST MIRROR...

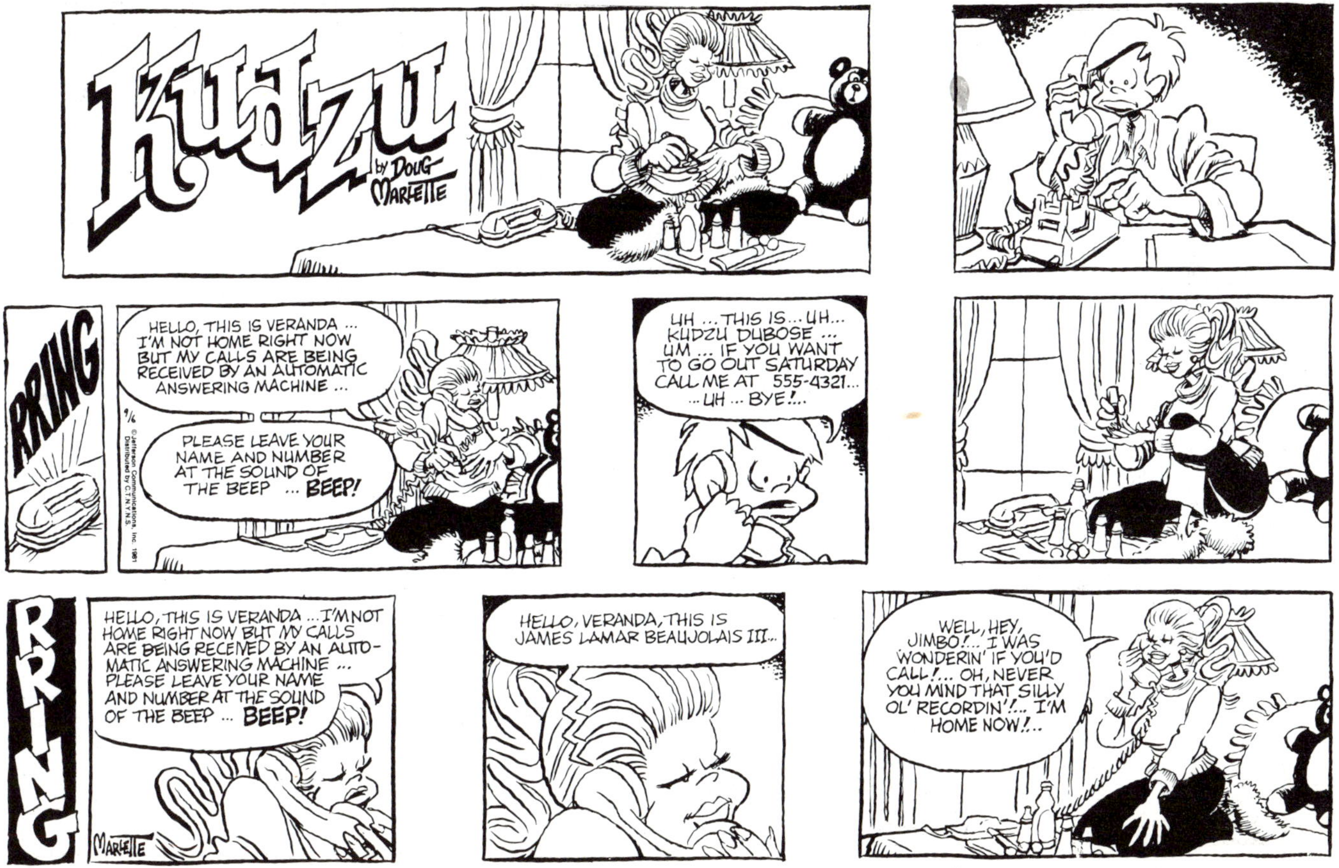
Kudzu
by Doug Marlette
RRING
HELLO, THIS IS VERANDA ... I'M NOT HOME RIGHT NOW BUT MY CALLS ARE BEING RECEIVED BY AN AUTOMATIC ANSWERING MACHINE ...
PLEASE LEAVE YOUR NAME AND NUMBER AT THE SOUND OF THE BEEP ... BEEP!
9/6
©Jefferson Communications, Inc. 1981
Distributed by C.T.N.Y.N.S.
UH ... THIS IS ... UH ... KUDZU DUBOSE ... UM ... IF YOU WANT TO GO OUT SATURDAY CALL ME AT 555-4321 ... ... UH ... BYE!...
RRING
HELLO, THIS IS VERANDA ... I'M NOT HOME RIGHT NOW BUT MY CALLS ARE BEING RECEIVED BY AN AUTOMATIC ANSWERING MACHINE ... PLEASE LEAVE YOUR NAME AND NUMBER AT THE SOUND OF THE BEEP ... BEEP!
MARLETTE
HELLO, VERANDA, THIS IS JAMES LAMAR BEAUJOLAIS III...
WELL, HEY, JIMBO!... I WAS WONDERIN' IF YOU'D CALL!... OH, NEVER YOU MIND THAT SILLY OL' RECORDIN'!... I'M HOME NOW!...

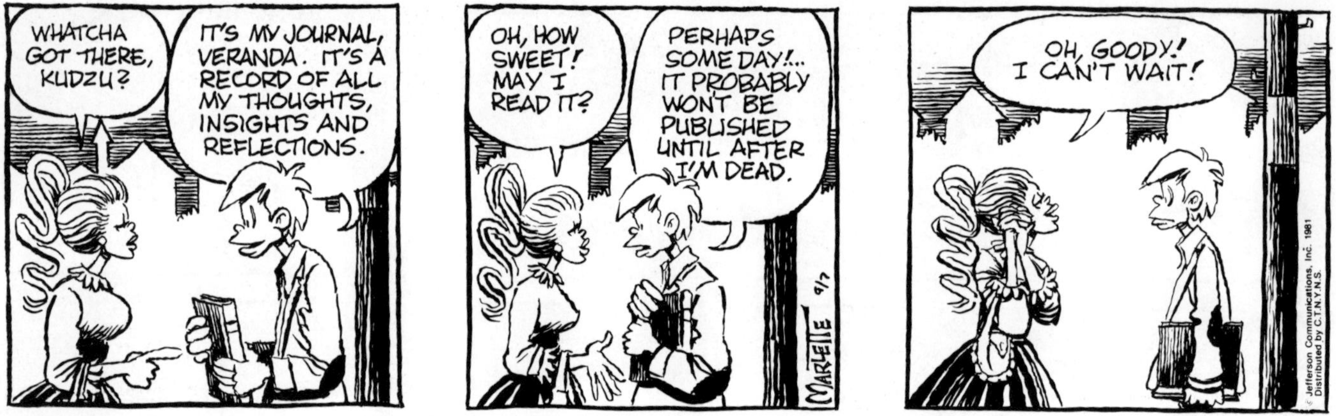
WHATCHA GOT THERE, KUDZU?
IT'S MY JOURNAL, VERANDA. IT'S A RECORD OF ALL MY THOUGHTS, INSIGHTS AND REFLECTIONS.
OH, HOW SWEET! MAY I READ IT?
PERHAPS SOMEDAY!... IT PROBABLY WON'T BE PUBLISHED UNTIL AFTER I'M DEAD.
MARLETTE 9/7
OH, GOODY! I CAN'T WAIT!
© Jefferson Communications, Inc. 1981 Distributed by C.T.N.Y.N.S.

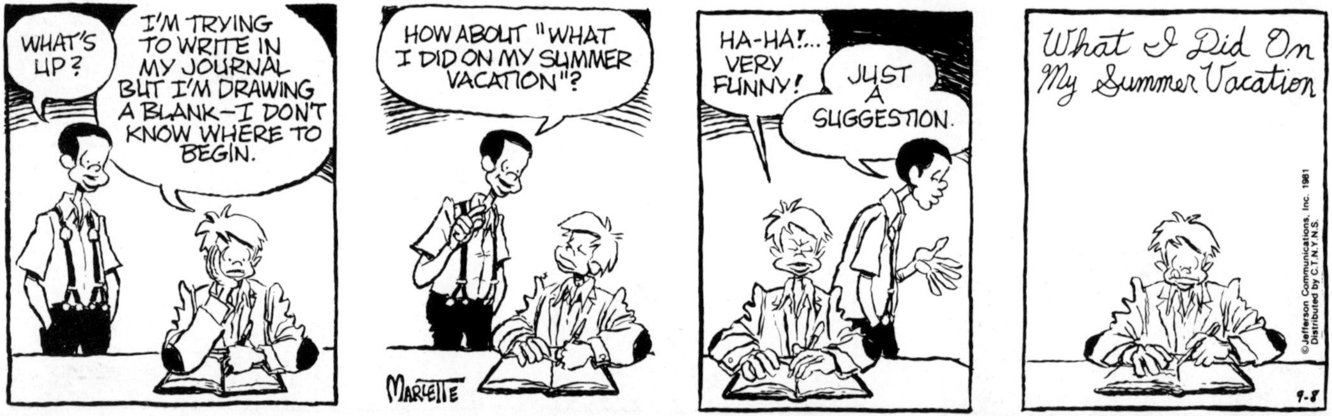
WHAT'S UP?
I'M TRYING TO WRITE IN MY JOURNAL BUT I'M DRAWING A BLANK—I DON'T KNOW WHERE TO BEGIN.
HOW ABOUT "WHAT I DID ON MY SUMMER VACATION"?
MARLETTE
HA-HA!... VERY FUNNY!
JUST A SUGGESTION.
What I Did On My Summer Vacation
© Jefferson Communications, Inc. 1981 Distributed by C.T.N.Y.N.S.
9-8

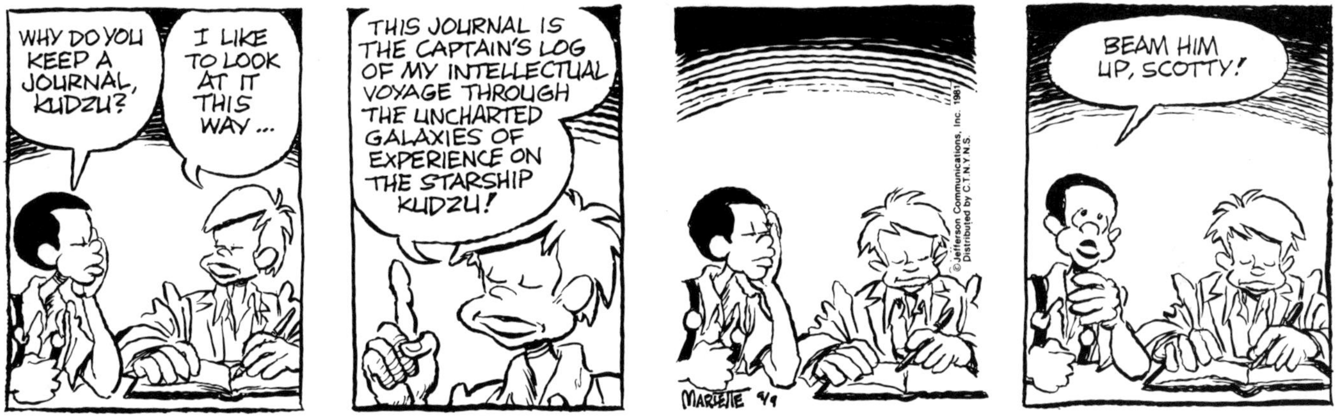
WHY DO YOU KEEP A JOURNAL, KUDZU?
I LIKE TO LOOK AT IT THIS WAY ...
THIS JOURNAL IS THE CAPTAIN'S LOG OF MY INTELLECTUAL VOYAGE THROUGH THE UNCHARTED GALAXIES OF EXPERIENCE ON THE STARSHIP KUDZU!
© Jefferson Communications, Inc. 1981
Distributed by C.T.N.Y.N.S.
MARLETTE 9/9
BEAM HIM UP, SCOTTY!

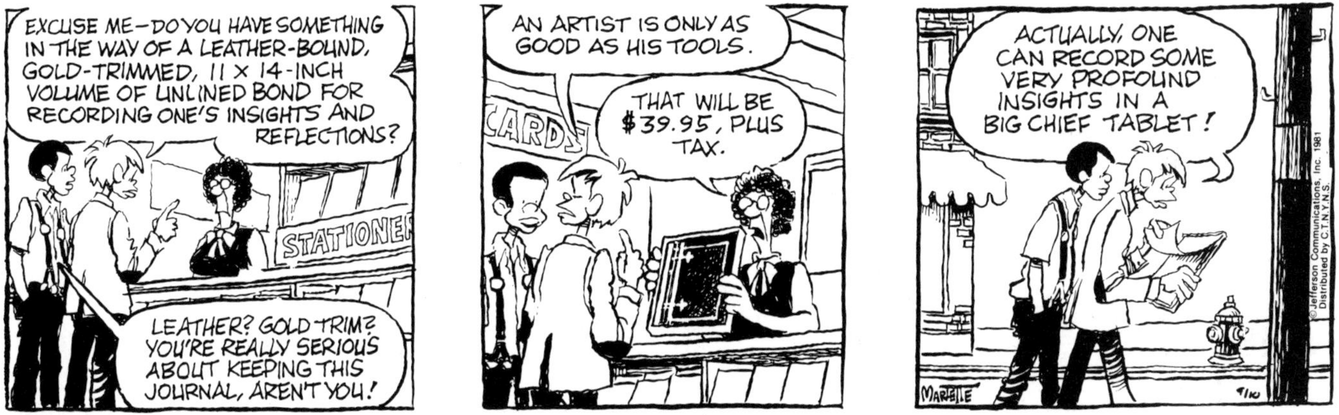
EXCUSE ME—DO YOU HAVE SOMETHING IN THE WAY OF A LEATHER-BOUND, GOLD-TRIMMED, 11 X 14-INCH VOLUME OF UNLINED BOND FOR RECORDING ONE'S INSIGHTS AND REFLECTIONS?
STATIONER
LEATHER? GOLD TRIM? YOU'RE REALLY SERIOUS ABOUT KEEPING THIS JOURNAL, AREN'T YOU!
AN ARTIST IS ONLY AS GOOD AS HIS TOOLS.
CARDS
THAT WILL BE $39.95, PLUS TAX.
ACTUALLY, ONE CAN RECORD SOME VERY PROFOUND INSIGHTS IN A BIG CHIEF TABLET!
© Jefferson Communications, Inc. 1981
Distributed by C.T.N.Y.N.S.
MARLETTE 9/10

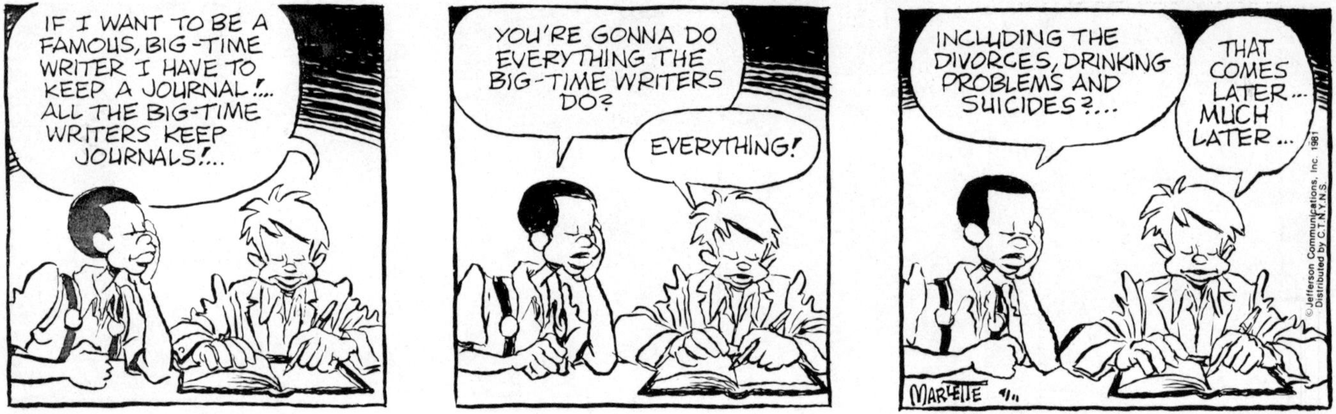
IF I WANT TO BE A FAMOUS, BIG-TIME WRITER I HAVE TO KEEP A JOURNAL!... ALL THE BIG-TIME WRITERS KEEP JOURNALS!...
YOU'RE GONNA DO EVERYTHING THE BIG-TIME WRITERS DO?
EVERYTHING!
INCLUDING THE DIVORCES, DRINKING PROBLEMS AND SUICIDES?...
THAT COMES LATER... MUCH LATER...
© Jefferson Communications, Inc. 1981 Distributed by C.T.N.Y.N.S.
MARLETTE 9/11

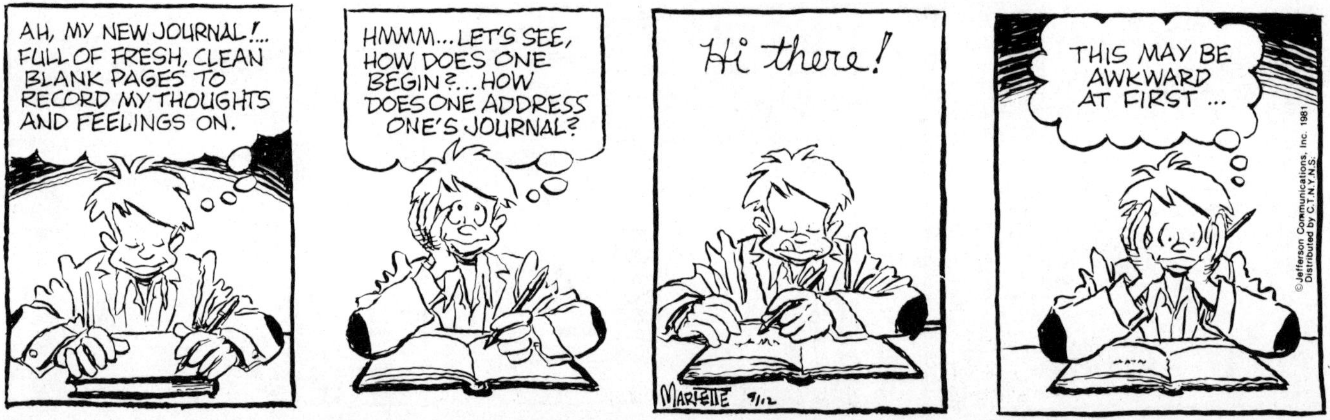
AH, MY NEW JOURNAL!... FULL OF FRESH, CLEAN BLANK PAGES TO RECORD MY THOUGHTS AND FEELINGS ON.
HMMM... LET'S SEE, HOW DOES ONE BEGIN?... HOW DOES ONE ADDRESS ONE'S JOURNAL?
Hi there!
THIS MAY BE AWKWARD AT FIRST...
© Jefferson Communications, Inc. 1981 Distributed by C.T.N.Y.N.S.
MARLETTE 9/12

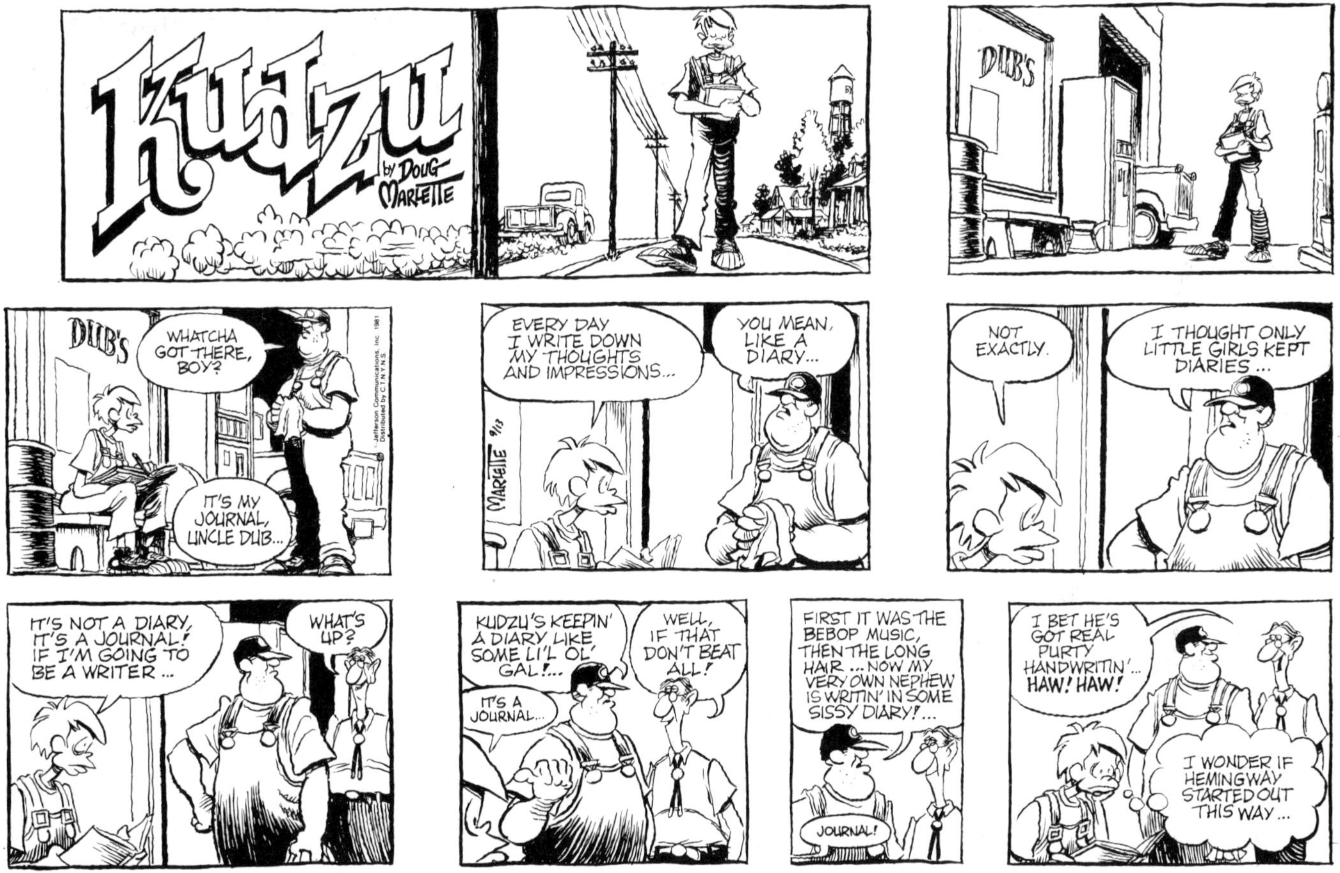
KUDZU
by DOUG MARLETTE
DUB'S
DUB'S
WHATCHA GOT THERE, BOY?
IT'S MY JOURNAL, UNCLE DUB...
©1981 Jefferson Communications, Inc. Distributed by C.T.N.Y.N.S.
MARLETTE 9/13
EVERY DAY I WRITE DOWN MY THOUGHTS AND IMPRESSIONS...
YOU MEAN, LIKE A DIARY...
NOT EXACTLY.
I THOUGHT ONLY LITTLE GIRLS KEPT DIARIES ...
IT'S NOT A DIARY, IT'S A JOURNAL! IF I'M GOING TO BE A WRITER ...
WHAT'S UP?
KUDZU'S KEEPIN' A DIARY LIKE SOME LI'L OL' GAL!...
WELL, IF THAT DON'T BEAT ALL!
IT'S A JOURNAL...
FIRST IT WAS THE BEBOP MUSIC, THEN THE LONG HAIR ... NOW MY VERY OWN NEPHEW IS WRITIN' IN SOME SISSY DIARY!...
JOURNAL!
I BET HE'S GOT REAL PURTY HANDWRITIN'... HAW! HAW!
I WONDER IF HEMINGWAY STARTED OUT THIS WAY...

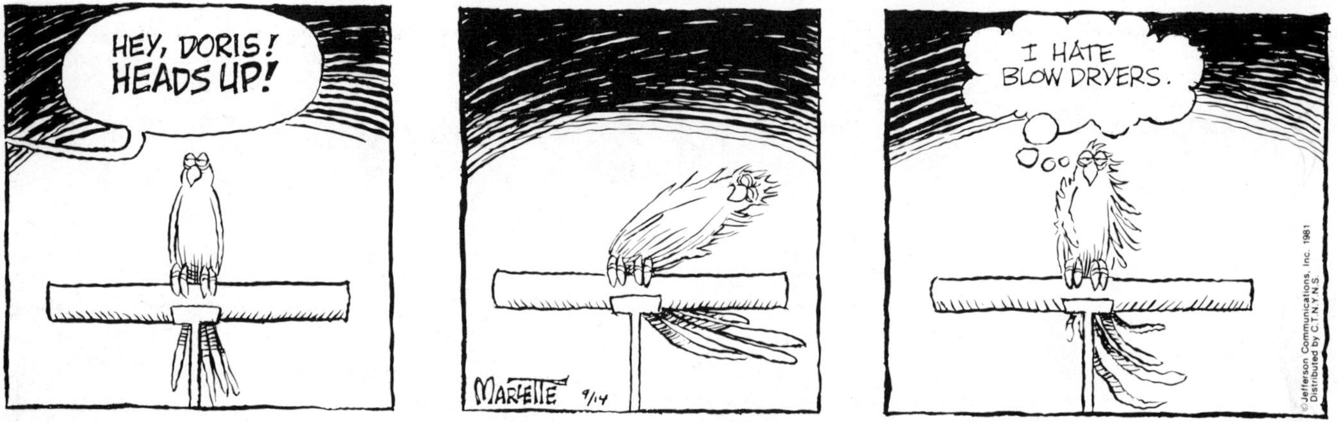
HEY, DORIS! HEADS UP!
MARLETTE 9/14
I HATE BLOW DRYERS.
© Jefferson Communications, Inc. 1981 Distributed by C.T.N.Y.N.S.

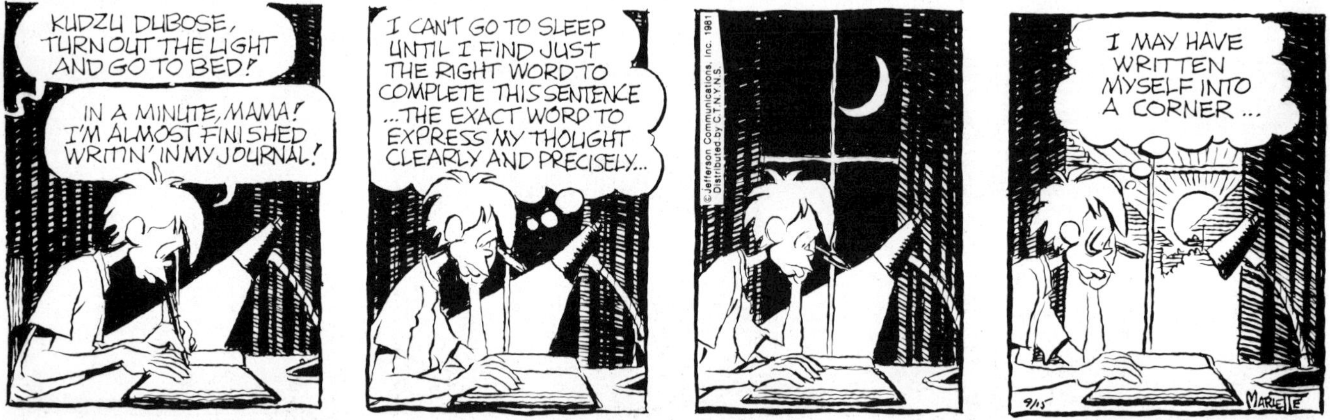
KUDZU DUBOSE, TURN OUT THE LIGHT AND GO TO BED!
IN A MINUTE, MAMA! I'M ALMOST FINISHED WRITIN' IN MY JOURNAL!
I CAN'T GO TO SLEEP UNTIL I FIND JUST THE RIGHT WORD TO COMPLETE THIS SENTENCE ...THE EXACT WORD TO EXPRESS MY THOUGHT CLEARLY AND PRECISELY...
© Jefferson Communications, Inc. 1981 Distributed by C.T.N.Y.N.S.
I MAY HAVE WRITTEN MYSELF INTO A CORNER...
9/15
MARLETTE

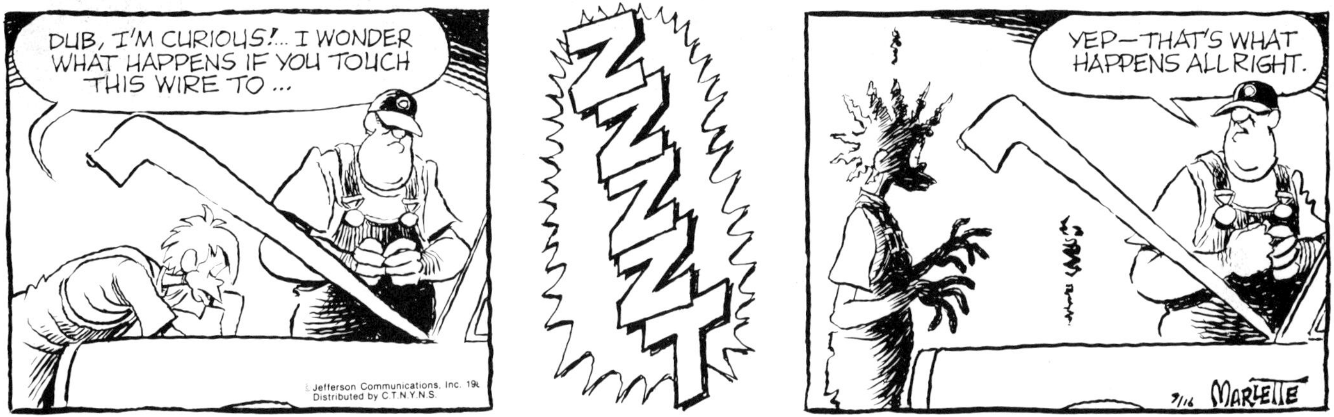
DUB, I'M CURIOUS!... I WONDER WHAT HAPPENS IF YOU TOUCH THIS WIRE TO ...
ZZZZZT
YEP—THAT'S WHAT HAPPENS ALL RIGHT.
© Jefferson Communications, Inc. 19
Distributed by C.T.N.Y.N.S.
9/16
MARLETTE

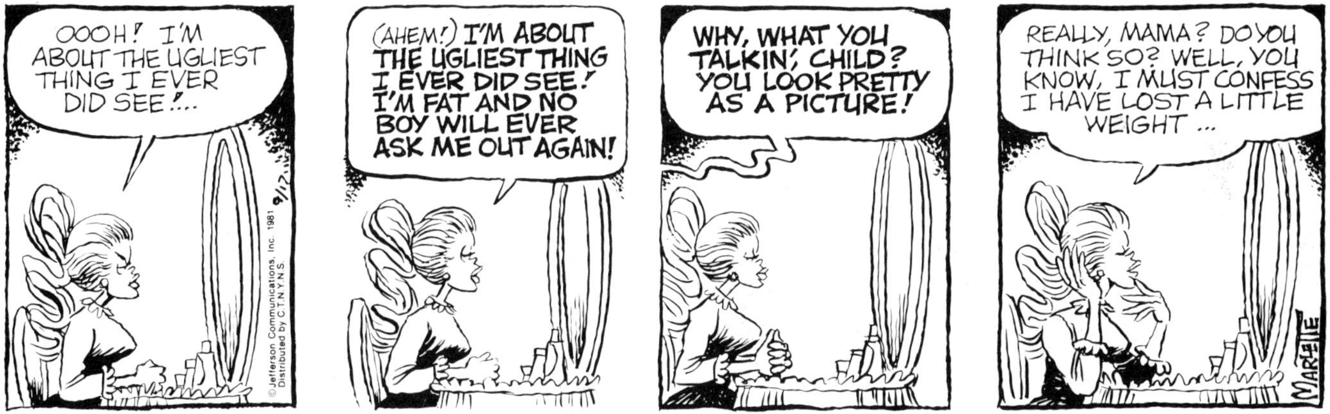
OOOH! I'M ABOUT THE UGLIEST THING I EVER DID SEE!...
(AHEM!) I'M ABOUT THE UGLIEST THING I EVER DID SEE! I'M FAT AND NO BOY WILL EVER ASK ME OUT AGAIN!
WHY, WHAT YOU TALKIN', CHILD? YOU LOOK PRETTY AS A PICTURE!
REALLY, MAMA? DO YOU THINK SO? WELL, YOU KNOW, I MUST CONFESS I HAVE LOST A LITTLE WEIGHT ...
© Jefferson Communications, Inc. 1981
Distributed by C.T.N.Y.N.S.
9/17
MARLETTE

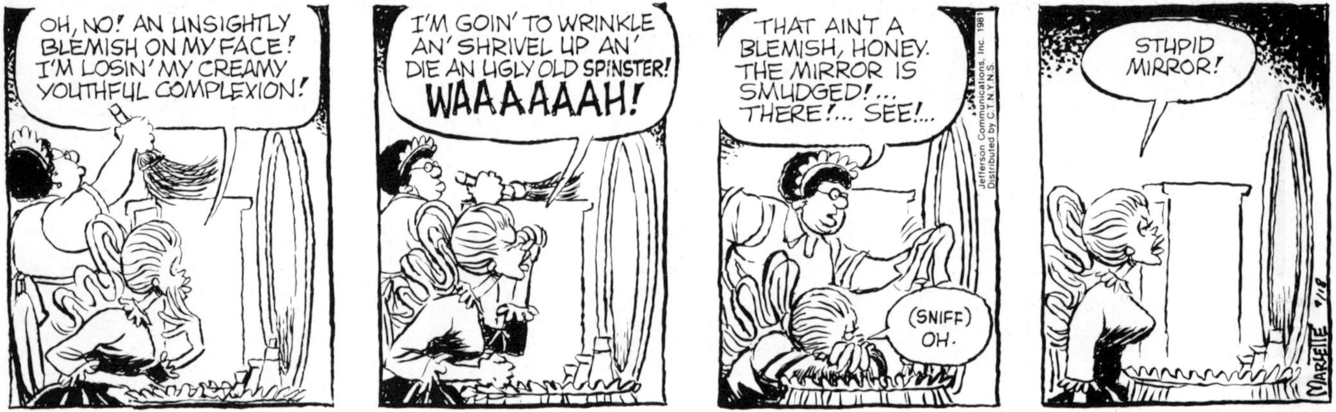
OH, NO! AN UNSIGHTLY BLEMISH ON MY FACE! I'M LOSIN' MY CREAMY YOUTHFUL COMPLEXION!
I'M GOIN' TO WRINKLE AN' SHRIVEL UP AN' DIE AN UGLY OLD SPINSTER! WAAAAAAH!
THAT AIN'T A BLEMISH, HONEY. THE MIRROR IS SMUDGED!... THERE!... SEE!...
(SNIFF) OH.
Jefferson Communications, Inc. 1981 Distributed by C.T.N.Y.N.S.
STUPID MIRROR!
MARLETTE 9/18

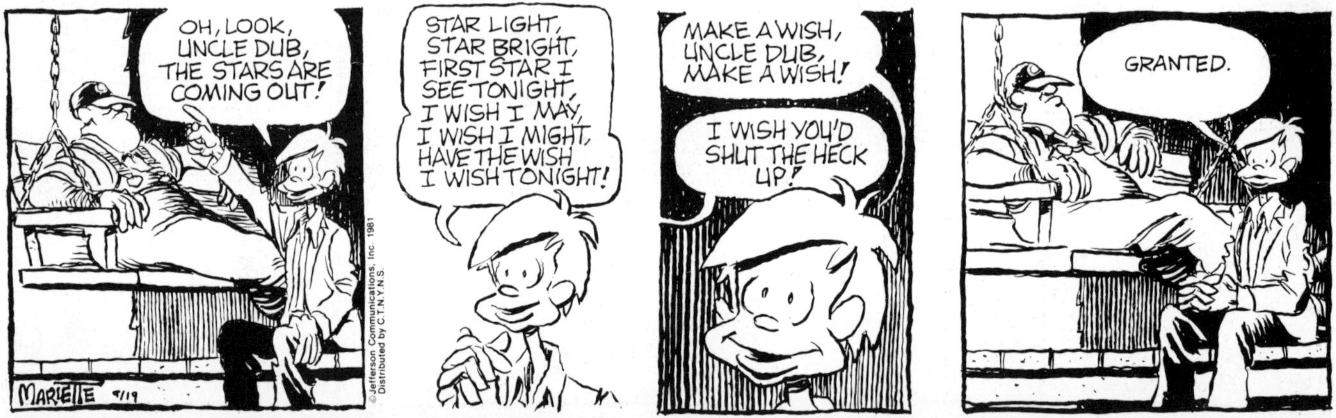
OH, LOOK, UNCLE DUB, THE STARS ARE COMING OUT!
MARLETTE 9/19
©Jefferson Communications, Inc. 1981 Distributed by C.T.N.Y.N.S.
STAR LIGHT, STAR BRIGHT, FIRST STAR I SEE TONIGHT, I WISH I MAY, I WISH I MIGHT, HAVE THE WISH I WISH TONIGHT!
MAKE A WISH, UNCLE DUB, MAKE A WISH!
I WISH YOU'D SHUT THE HECK UP!
GRANTED.

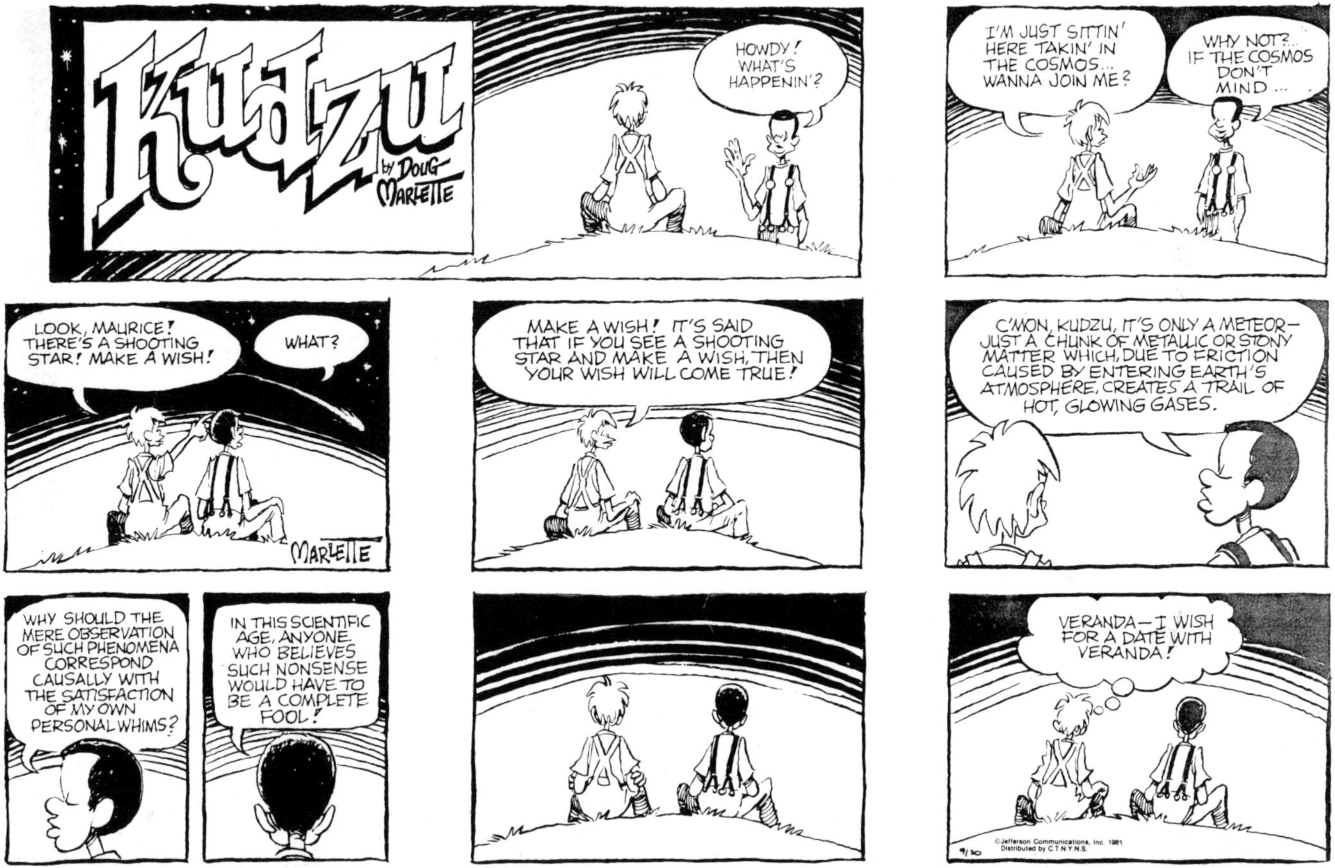
KUDZU
by DOUG MARLETTE
HOWDY! WHAT'S HAPPENIN'?
I'M JUST SITTIN' HERE TAKIN' IN THE COSMOS... WANNA JOIN ME?
WHY NOT?... IF THE COSMOS DON'T MIND...
LOOK, MAURICE! THERE'S A SHOOTING STAR! MAKE A WISH!
WHAT?
MARLETTE
MAKE A WISH! IT'S SAID THAT IF YOU SEE A SHOOTING STAR AND MAKE A WISH, THEN YOUR WISH WILL COME TRUE!
C'MON, KUDZU, IT'S ONLY A METEOR—JUST A CHUNK OF METALLIC OR STONY MATTER WHICH, DUE TO FRICTION CAUSED BY ENTERING EARTH'S ATMOSPHERE, CREATES A TRAIL OF HOT, GLOWING GASES.
WHY SHOULD THE MERE OBSERVATION OF SUCH PHENOMENA CORRESPOND CAUSALLY WITH THE SATISFACTION OF MY OWN PERSONAL WHIMS?
IN THIS SCIENTIFIC AGE, ANYONE WHO BELIEVES SUCH NONSENSE WOULD HAVE TO BE A COMPLETE FOOL!
VERANDA—I WISH FOR A DATE WITH VERANDA!
©Jefferson Communications, Inc. 1981
Distributed by C.T.N.Y.N.S.
9/20

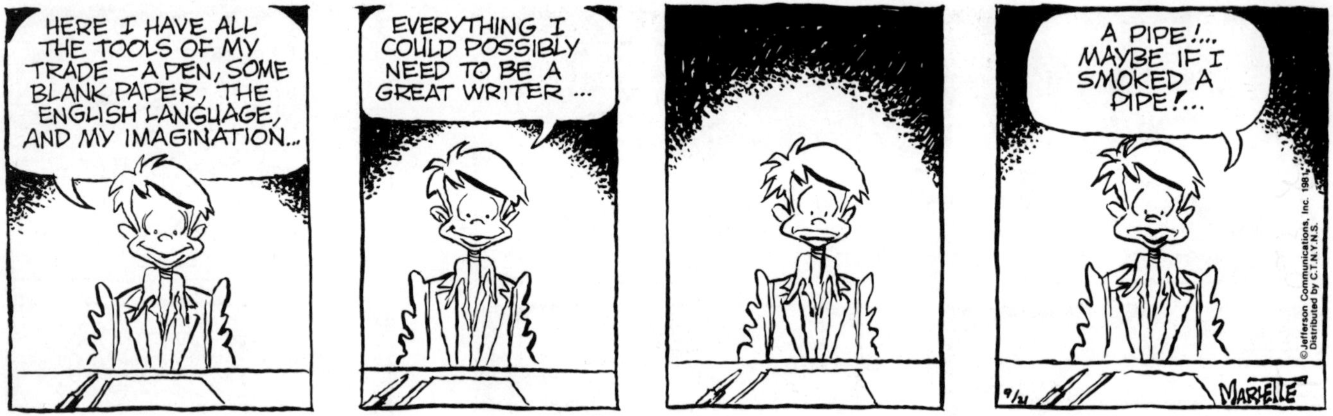
HERE I HAVE ALL THE TOOLS OF MY TRADE — A PEN, SOME BLANK PAPER, THE ENGLISH LANGUAGE, AND MY IMAGINATION...
EVERYTHING I COULD POSSIBLY NEED TO BE A GREAT WRITER ...
A PIPE!... MAYBE IF I SMOKED A PIPE!...
9/21
MARLETTE
© Jefferson Communications, Inc. 1981
Distributed by C.T.N.Y.N.S.

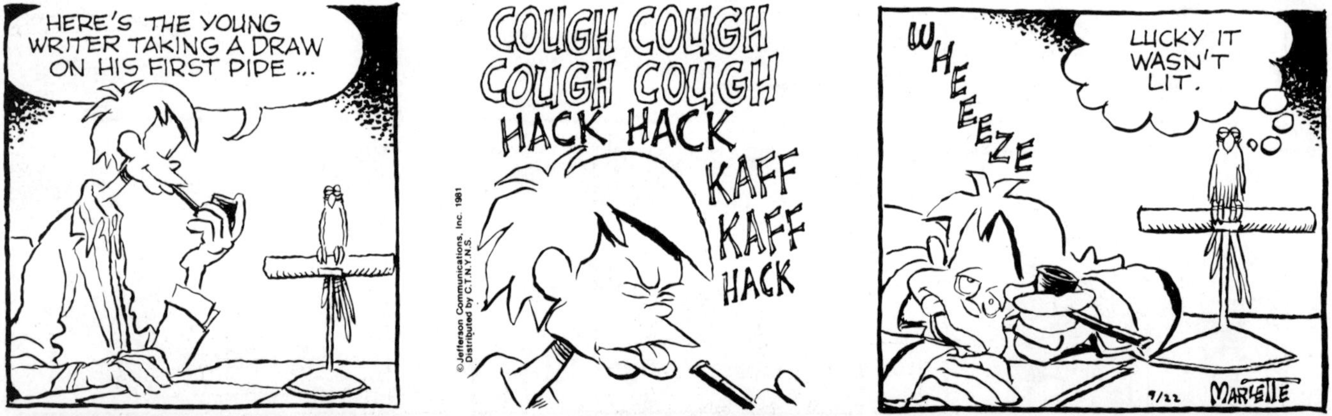
HERE'S THE YOUNG WRITER TAKING A DRAW ON HIS FIRST PIPE ...
COUGH COUGH
COUGH COUGH
HACK HACK
KAFF
KAFF
HACK
© Jefferson Communications, Inc. 1981
Distributed by C.T.N.Y.N.S.
WHEEEEZE
LUCKY IT WASN'T LIT.
9/22
MARLETTE

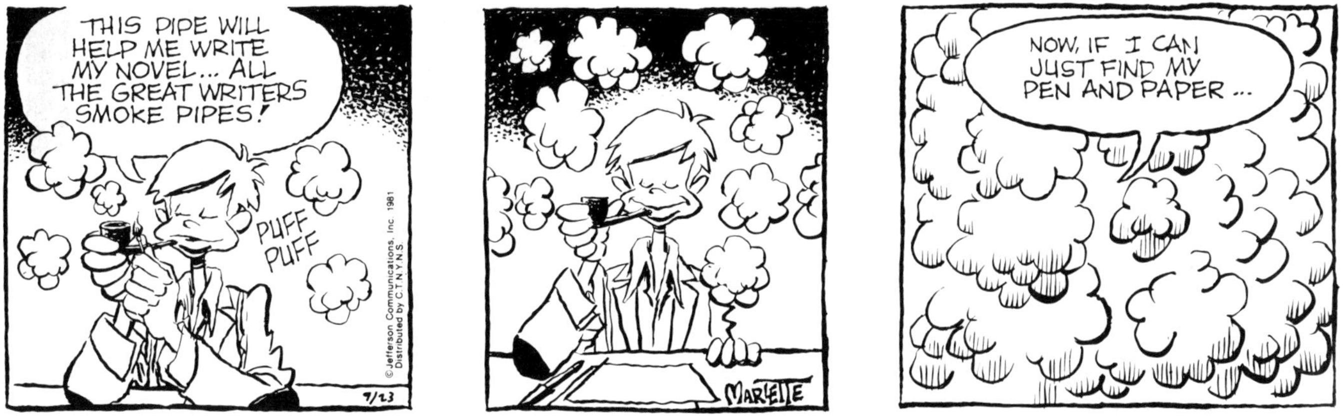
THIS PIPE WILL HELP ME WRITE MY NOVEL... ALL THE GREAT WRITERS SMOKE PIPES!
PUFF PUFF
© Jefferson Communications, Inc. 1981
Distributed by C.T.N.Y.N.S.
9/23
MARLETTE
NOW, IF I CAN JUST FIND MY PEN AND PAPER ...

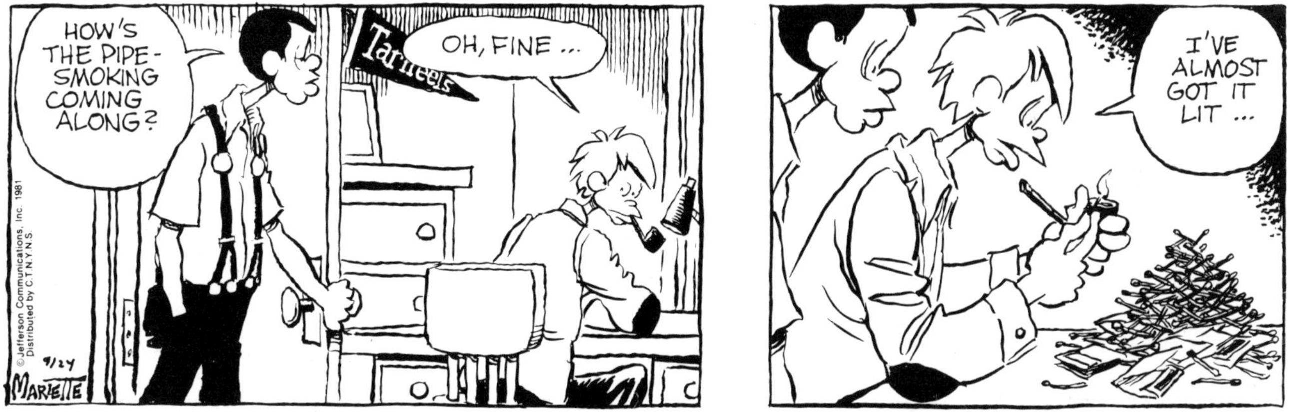
HOW'S THE PIPE-SMOKING COMING ALONG?
Tarheels
OH, FINE ...
© Jefferson Communications, Inc. 1981
Distributed by C.T.N.Y.N.S.
9/24
MARLETTE
I'VE ALMOST GOT IT LIT ...

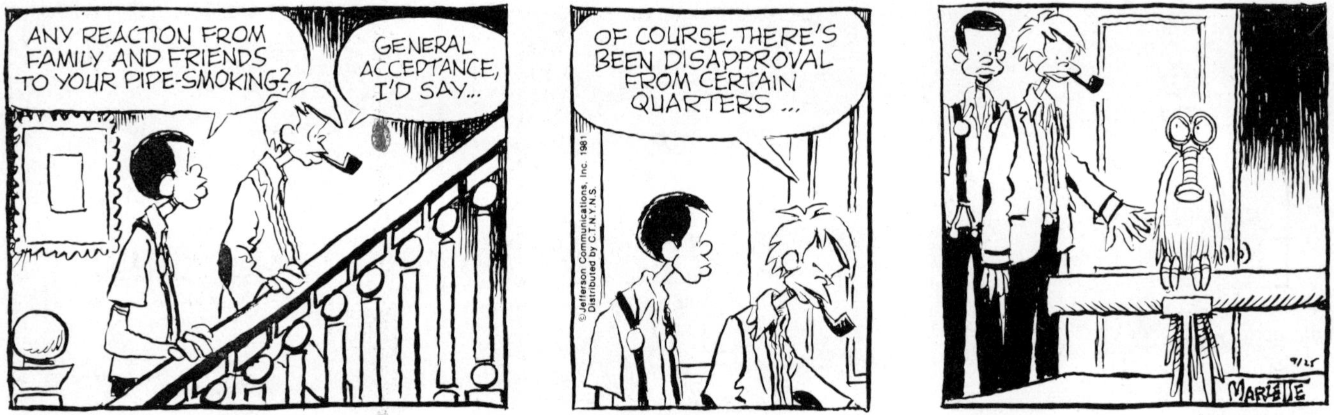
ANY REACTION FROM FAMILY AND FRIENDS TO YOUR PIPE-SMOKING?
GENERAL ACCEPTANCE, I'D SAY...
OF COURSE, THERE'S BEEN DISAPPROVAL FROM CERTAIN QUARTERS ...
© Jefferson Communications, Inc. 1981
Distributed by C.T.N.Y.N.S.
9/25
MARLETTE

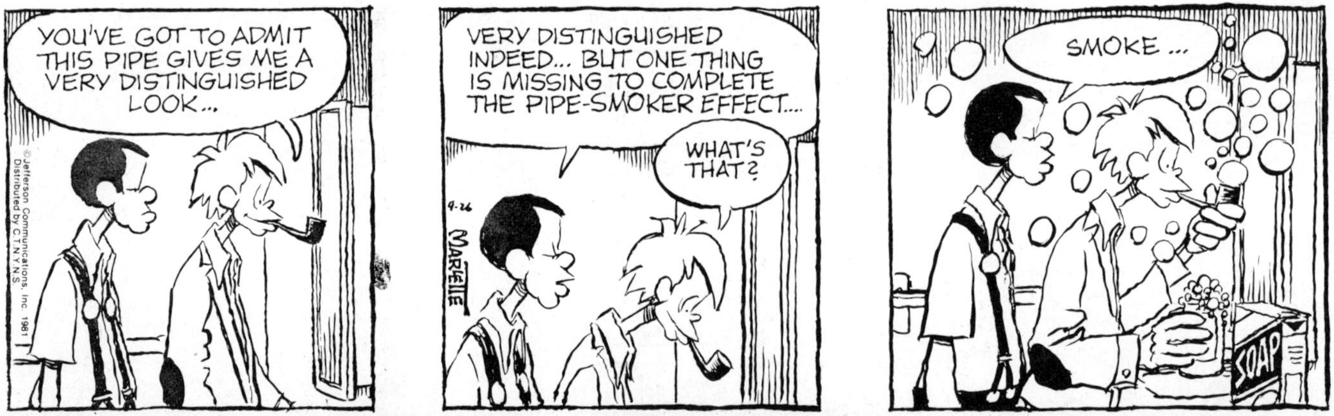
YOU'VE GOT TO ADMIT THIS PIPE GIVES ME A VERY DISTINGUISHED LOOK...
© Jefferson Communications, Inc. 1981
Distributed by C.T.N.Y.N.S.
VERY DISTINGUISHED INDEED... BUT ONE THING IS MISSING TO COMPLETE THE PIPE-SMOKER EFFECT....
WHAT'S THAT?
9-26
MARLETTE
SMOKE ...
SOAP

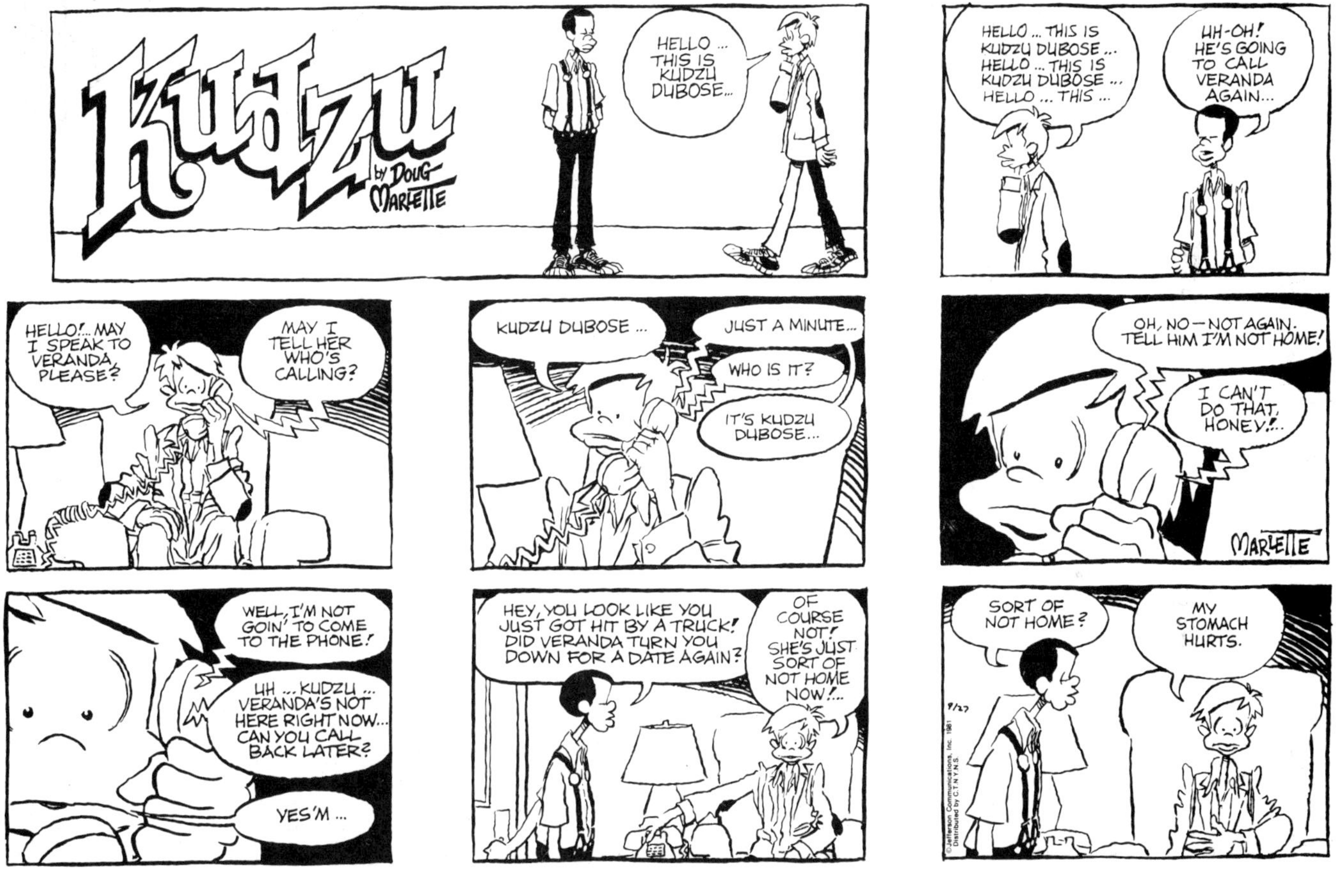
Kudzu
by DOUG MARLETTE
HELLO ... THIS IS KUDZU DUBOSE...
HELLO ... THIS IS KUDZU DUBOSE ... HELLO ... THIS IS KUDZU DUBOSE ... HELLO ... THIS ...
UH-OH! HE'S GOING TO CALL VERANDA AGAIN...
HELLO!... MAY I SPEAK TO VERANDA, PLEASE?
MAY I TELL HER WHO'S CALLING?
KUDZU DUBOSE ...
JUST A MINUTE...
WHO IS IT?
IT'S KUDZU DUBOSE...
OH, NO—NOT AGAIN. TELL HIM I'M NOT HOME!
I CAN'T DO THAT, HONEY!...
MARLETTE
WELL, I'M NOT GOIN' TO COME TO THE PHONE!
UH ... KUDZU ... VERANDA'S NOT HERE RIGHT NOW... CAN YOU CALL BACK LATER?
YES'M ...
HEY, YOU LOOK LIKE YOU JUST GOT HIT BY A TRUCK! DID VERANDA TURN YOU DOWN FOR A DATE AGAIN?
OF COURSE NOT! SHE'S JUST SORT OF NOT HOME NOW!...
SORT OF NOT HOME?
MY STOMACH HURTS.
9/27
©Jefferson Communications, Inc. 1981 Distributed by C.T.N.Y.N.S.

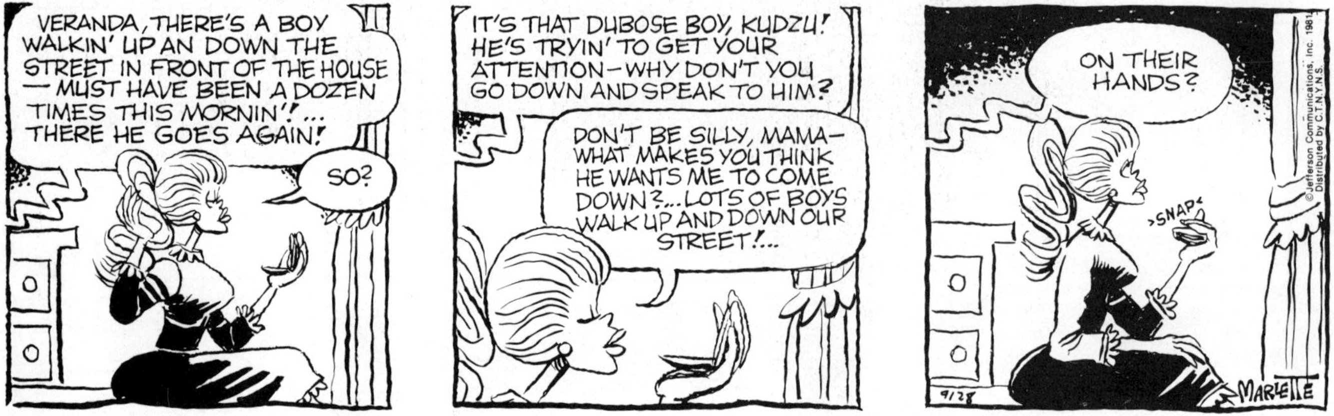
VERANDA, THERE'S A BOY WALKIN' UP AN DOWN THE STREET IN FRONT OF THE HOUSE — MUST HAVE BEEN A DOZEN TIMES THIS MORNIN'!... THERE HE GOES AGAIN!
SO?
IT'S THAT DUBOSE BOY, KUDZU! HE'S TRYIN' TO GET YOUR ATTENTION—WHY DON'T YOU GO DOWN AND SPEAK TO HIM?
DON'T BE SILLY, MAMA—WHAT MAKES YOU THINK HE WANTS ME TO COME DOWN?... LOTS OF BOYS WALK UP AND DOWN OUR STREET!...
ON THEIR HANDS?
>SNAP<
©Jefferson Communications, Inc. 1981 Distributed by C.T.N.Y.N.S.
9/28
MARLETTE

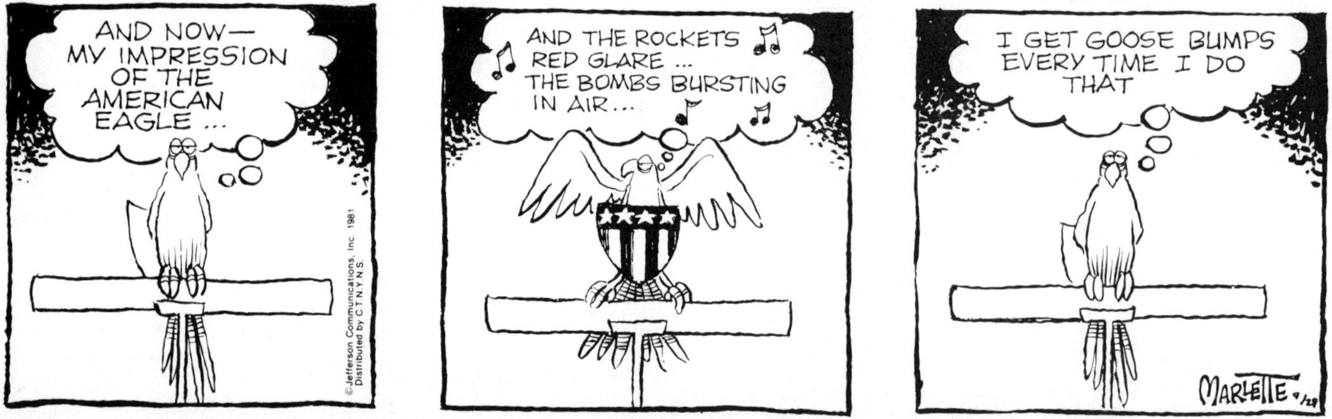
AND NOW— MY IMPRESSION OF THE AMERICAN EAGLE...
© Jefferson Communications, Inc. 1981 Distributed by C.T.N.Y.N.S.
AND THE ROCKETS RED GLARE ... THE BOMBS BURSTING IN AIR...
I GET GOOSE BUMPS EVERY TIME I DO THAT
MARLETTE 9/29

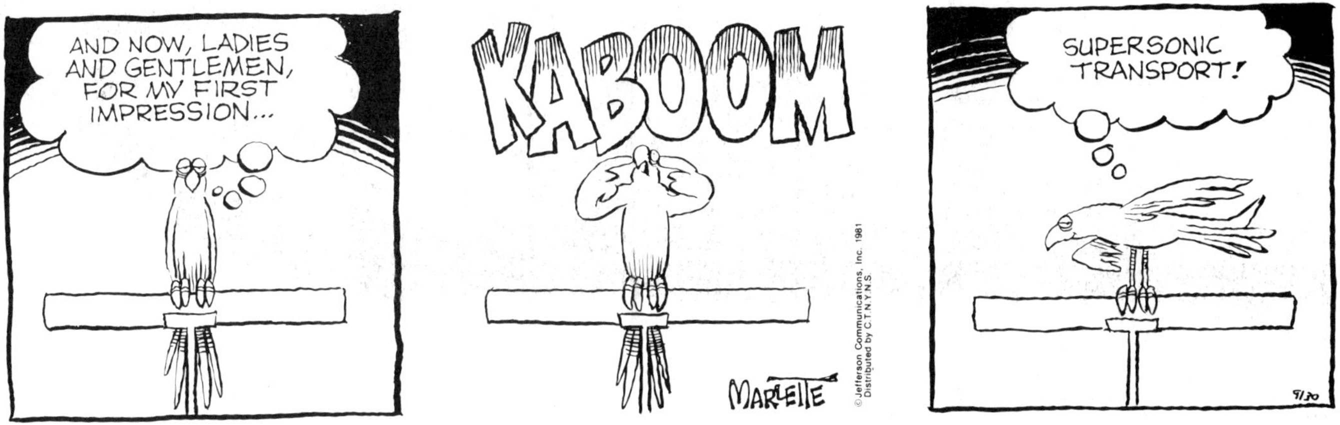
AND NOW, LADIES AND GENTLEMEN, FOR MY FIRST IMPRESSION...
KABOOM
SUPERSONIC TRANSPORT!
MARLETTE
9/30
© Jefferson Communications, Inc. 1981
Distributed by C.T.N.Y.N.S.

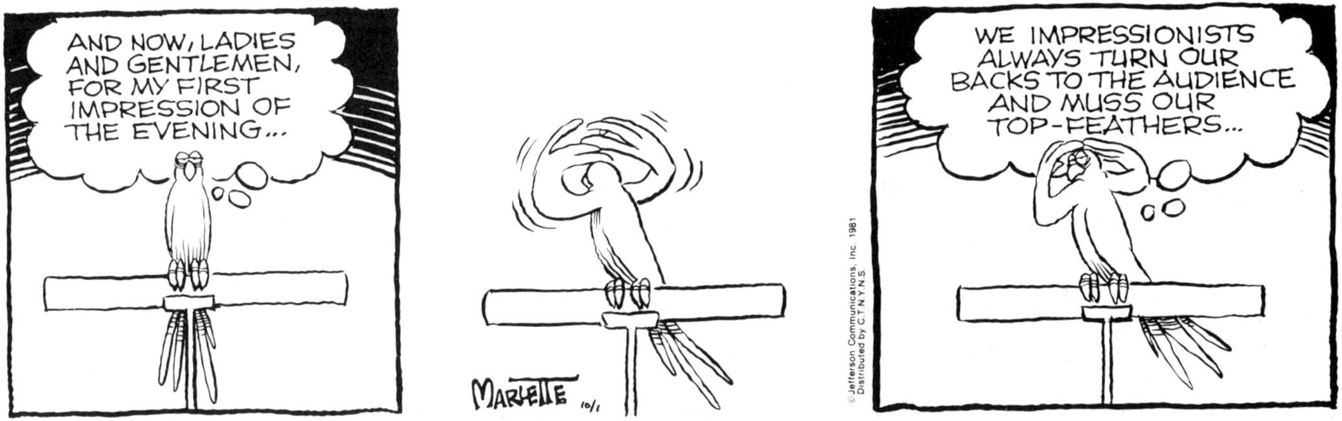
AND NOW, LADIES AND GENTLEMEN, FOR MY FIRST IMPRESSION OF THE EVENING...
WE IMPRESSIONISTS ALWAYS TURN OUR BACKS TO THE AUDIENCE AND MUSS OUR TOP-FEATHERS...
MARLETTE
10/1
© Jefferson Communications, Inc. 1981
Distributed by C.T.N.Y.N.S.

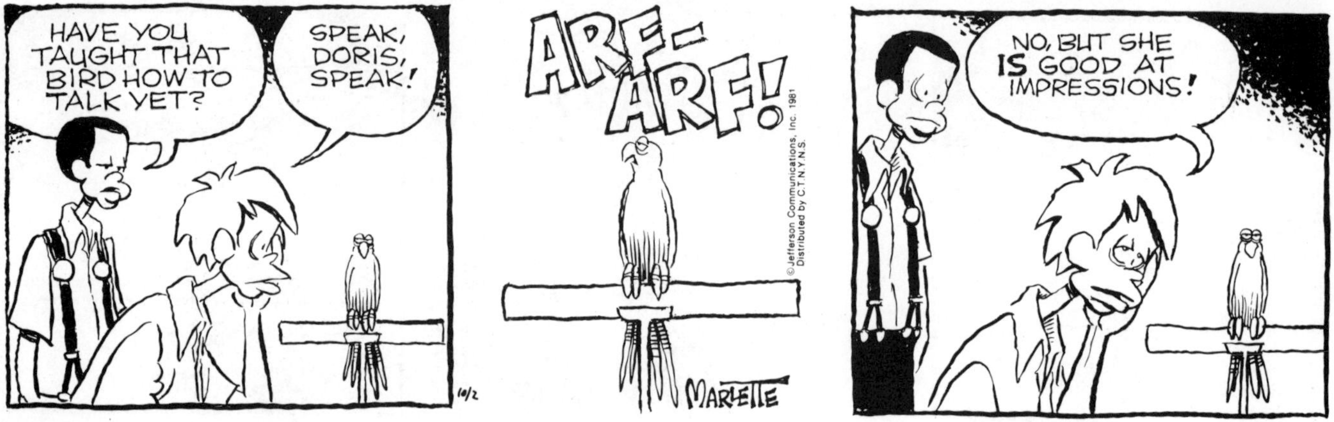
HAVE YOU TAUGHT THAT BIRD HOW TO TALK YET?
SPEAK, DORIS, SPEAK!
ARF-ARF!
© Jefferson Communications, Inc. 1981 Distributed by C.T.N.Y.N.S.
MARLETTE
NO, BUT SHE IS GOOD AT IMPRESSIONS!

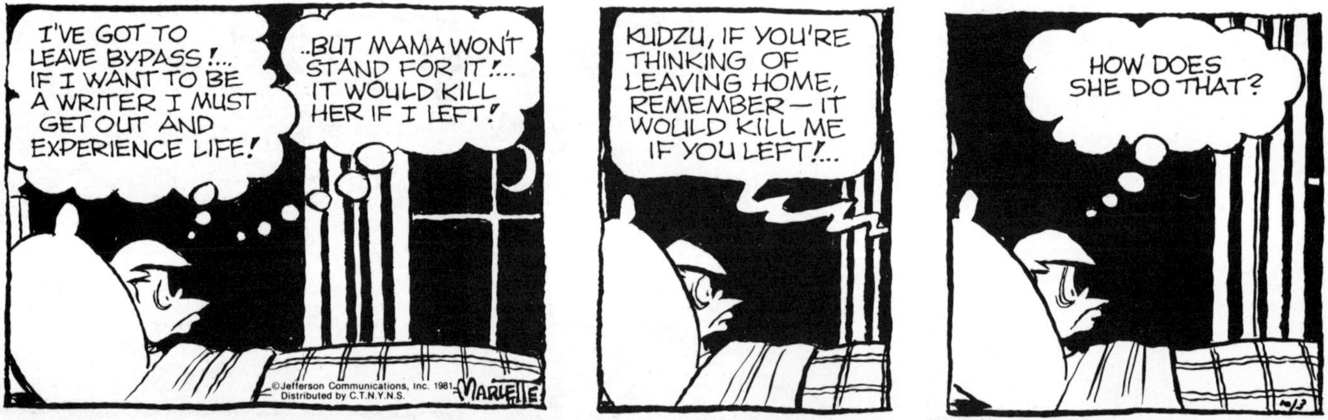
I'VE GOT TO LEAVE BYPASS!... IF I WANT TO BE A WRITER I MUST GET OUT AND EXPERIENCE LIFE!
..BUT MAMA WON'T STAND FOR IT!... IT WOULD KILL HER IF I LEFT!
©Jefferson Communications, Inc. 1981 Distributed by C.T.N.Y.N.S.
MARLETTE
KUDZU, IF YOU'RE THINKING OF LEAVING HOME, REMEMBER — IT WOULD KILL ME IF YOU LEFT!...
HOW DOES SHE DO THAT?

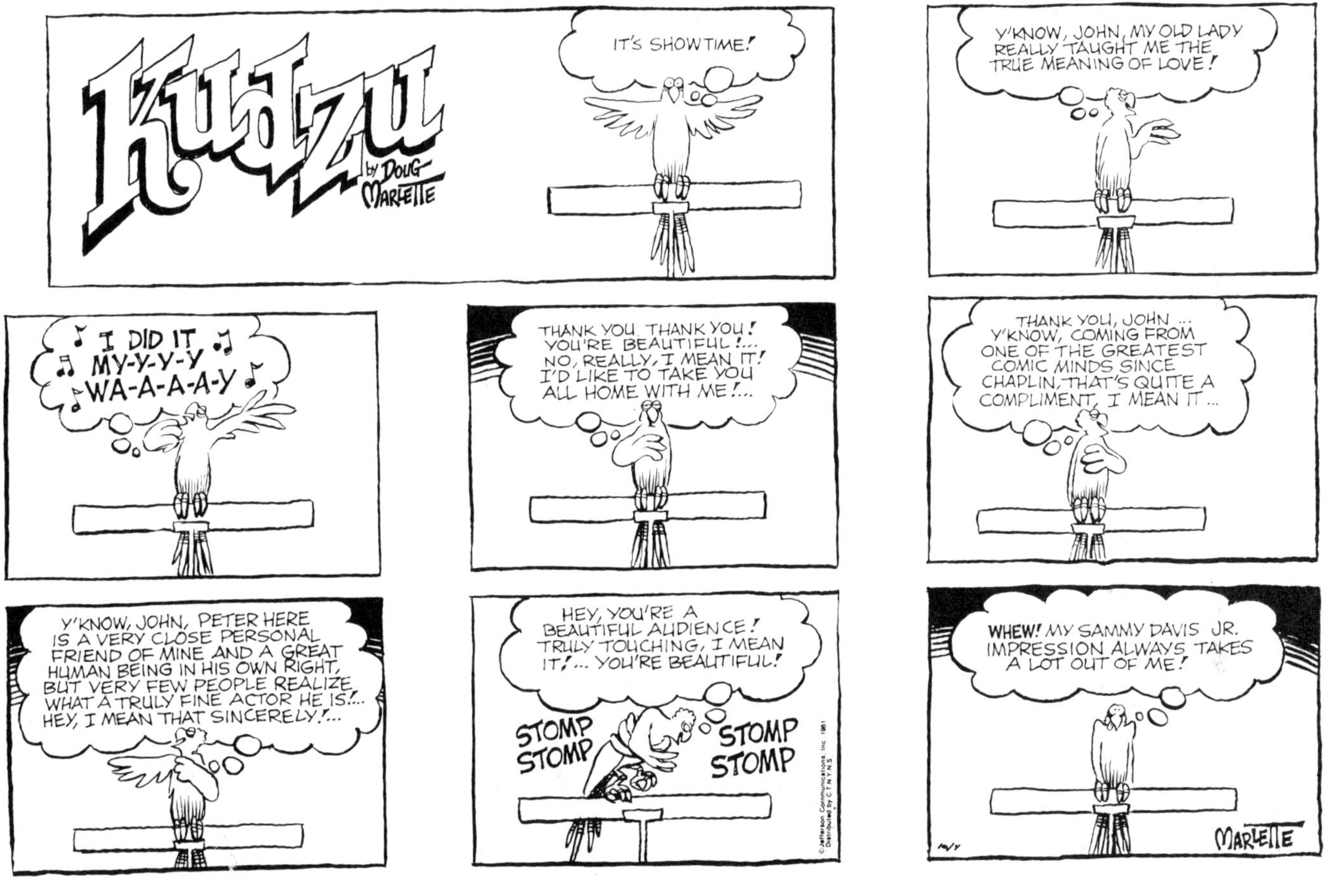
Kudzu
by Doug Marlette
IT'S SHOWTIME!
Y'KNOW, JOHN, MY OLD LADY REALLY TAUGHT ME THE TRUE MEANING OF LOVE!
♪ I DID IT ♫ MY-Y-Y-Y WA-A-A-A-Y ♪
THANK YOU. THANK YOU! YOU'RE BEAUTIFUL!... NO, REALLY, I MEAN IT! I'D LIKE TO TAKE YOU ALL HOME WITH ME!...
THANK YOU, JOHN ... Y'KNOW, COMING FROM ONE OF THE GREATEST COMIC MINDS SINCE CHAPLIN, THAT'S QUITE A COMPLIMENT, I MEAN IT ...
Y'KNOW, JOHN, PETER HERE IS A VERY CLOSE PERSONAL FRIEND OF MINE AND A GREAT HUMAN BEING IN HIS OWN RIGHT, BUT VERY FEW PEOPLE REALIZE WHAT A TRULY FINE ACTOR HE IS!... HEY, I MEAN THAT SINCERELY!...
HEY, YOU'RE A BEAUTIFUL AUDIENCE! TRULY TOUCHING, I MEAN IT!... YOU'RE BEAUTIFUL!
STOMP STOMP
STOMP STOMP
© Jefferson Communications, Inc. 1981
Distributed by C.T.N.Y.N.S.
WHEW! MY SAMMY DAVIS JR. IMPRESSION ALWAYS TAKES A LOT OUT OF ME!
MARLETTE

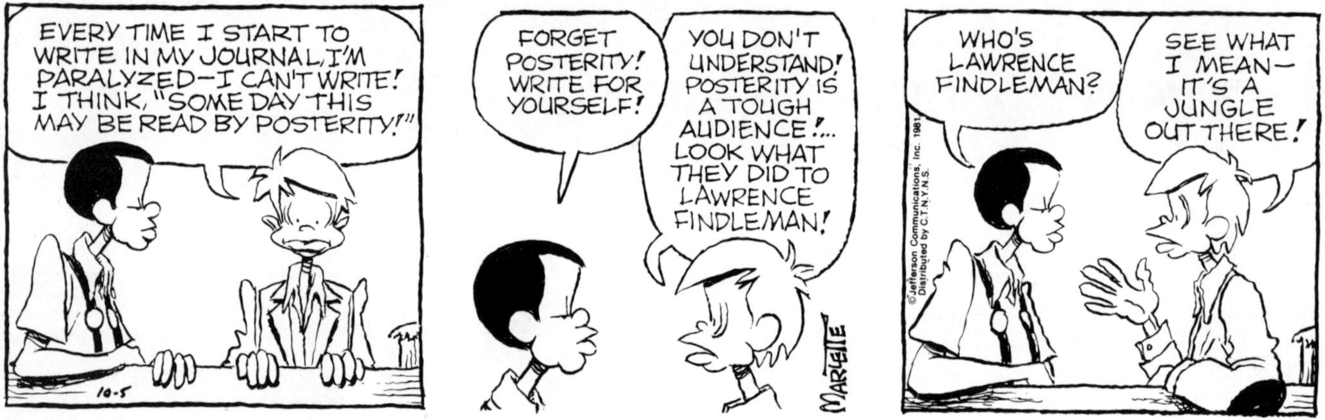
EVERY TIME I START TO WRITE IN MY JOURNAL, I'M PARALYZED—I CAN'T WRITE! I THINK, "SOME DAY THIS MAY BE READ BY POSTERITY!"
10-5
FORGET POSTERITY! WRITE FOR YOURSELF!
YOU DON'T UNDERSTAND! POSTERITY IS A TOUGH AUDIENCE!... LOOK WHAT THEY DID TO LAWRENCE FINDLEMAN!
MARLETTE
WHO'S LAWRENCE FINDLEMAN?
SEE WHAT I MEAN— IT'S A JUNGLE OUT THERE!
©Jefferson Communications, Inc. 1981 Distributed by C.T.N.Y.N.S.

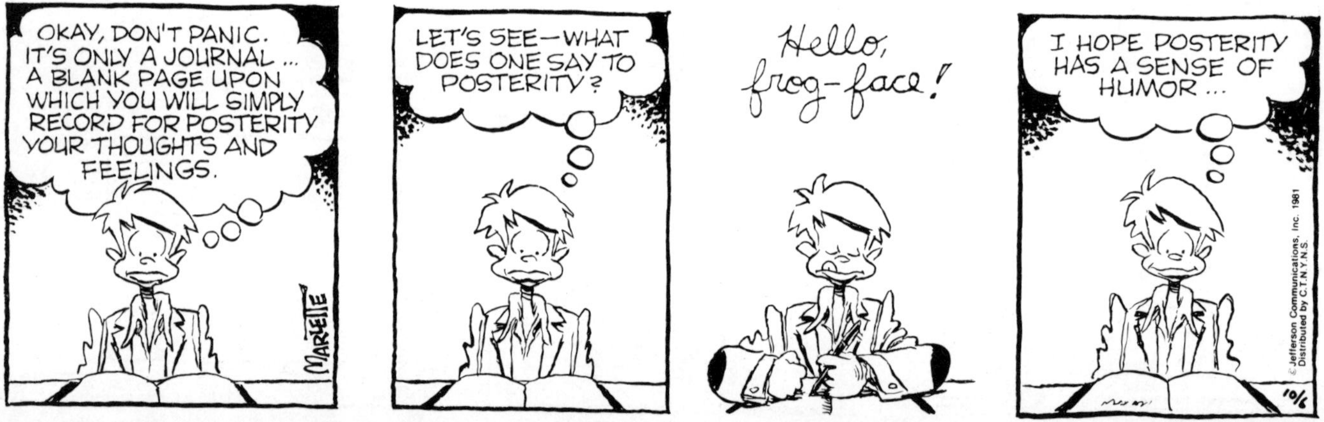
OKAY, DON'T PANIC. IT'S ONLY A JOURNAL ... A BLANK PAGE UPON WHICH YOU WILL SIMPLY RECORD FOR POSTERITY YOUR THOUGHTS AND FEELINGS.
MARLETTE
LET'S SEE—WHAT DOES ONE SAY TO POSTERITY?
Hello, frog-face!
I HOPE POSTERITY HAS A SENSE OF HUMOR ...
©Jefferson Communications, Inc. 1981 Distributed by C.T.N.Y.N.S.
10/6

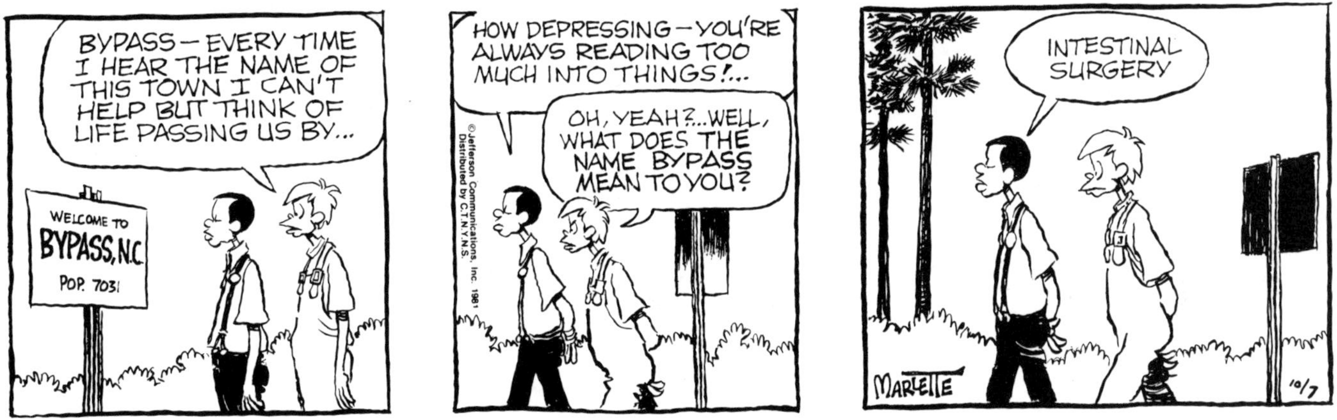
BYPASS—EVERY TIME I HEAR THE NAME OF THIS TOWN I CAN'T HELP BUT THINK OF LIFE PASSING US BY...
WELCOME TO BYPASS, N.C. POP. 7031
HOW DEPRESSING—YOU'RE ALWAYS READING TOO MUCH INTO THINGS!...
OH, YEAH?...WELL, WHAT DOES THE NAME BYPASS MEAN TO YOU?
©Jefferson Communications, Inc. 1981 Distributed by C.T.N.Y.N.S.
INTESTINAL SURGERY
MARLETTE
10/7

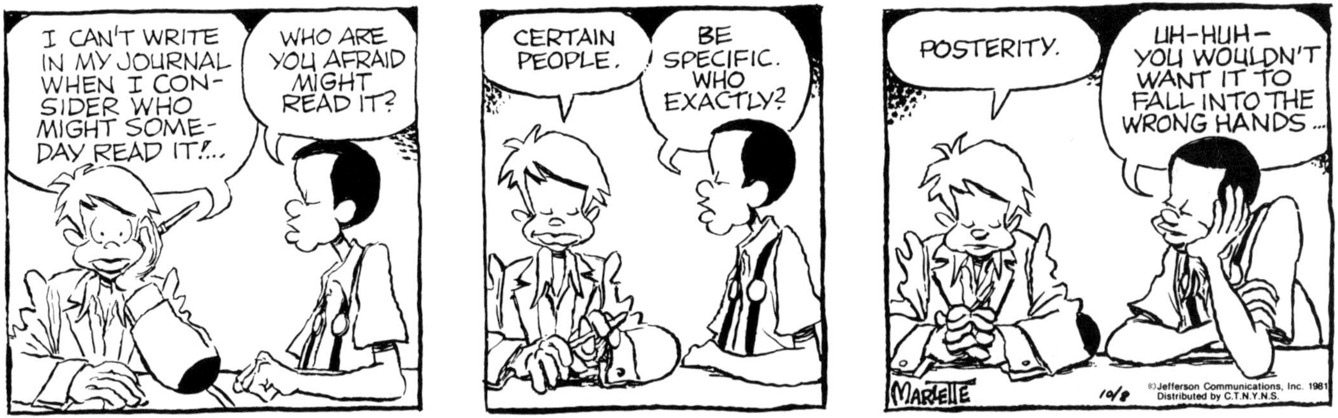
I CAN'T WRITE IN MY JOURNAL WHEN I CONSIDER WHO MIGHT SOMEDAY READ IT!...
WHO ARE YOU AFRAID MIGHT READ IT?
CERTAIN PEOPLE.
BE SPECIFIC. WHO EXACTLY?
POSTERITY.
UH-HUH—YOU WOULDN'T WANT IT TO FALL INTO THE WRONG HANDS...
MARLETTE
10/8
©Jefferson Communications, Inc. 1981 Distributed by C.T.N.Y.N.S.

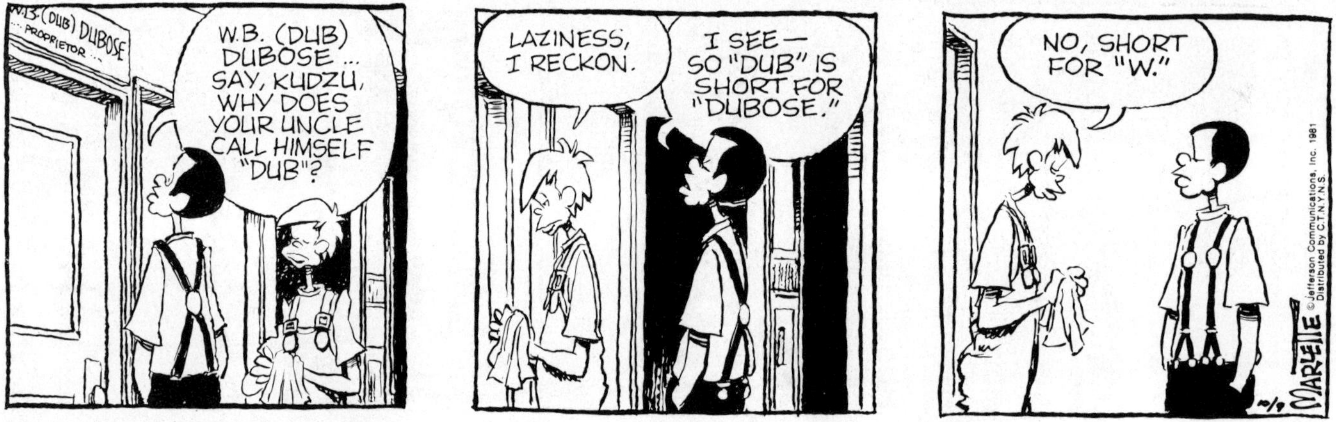
W.B. (DUB) DUBOSE
... PROPRIETOR ...
W.B. (DUB) DUBOSE ... SAY, KUDZU, WHY DOES YOUR UNCLE CALL HIMSELF "DUB"?
LAZINESS, I RECKON.
I SEE— SO "DUB" IS SHORT FOR "DUBOSE."
NO, SHORT FOR "W."
© Jefferson Communications, Inc. 1981
Distributed by C.T.N.Y.N.S.
MARLETTE
10/9

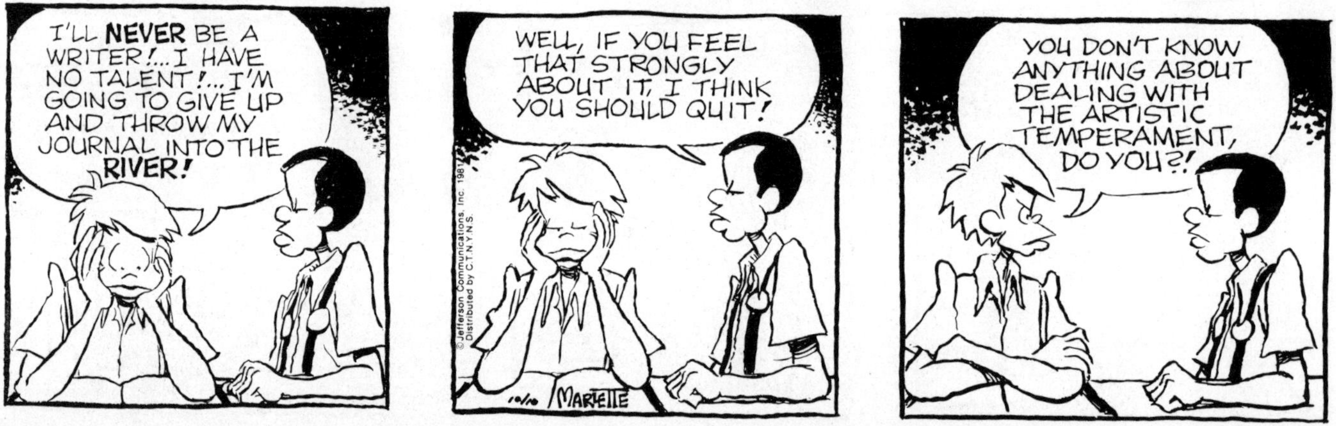
I'LL **NEVER** BE A WRITER!... I HAVE NO TALENT!... I'M GOING TO GIVE UP AND THROW MY JOURNAL INTO THE **RIVER**!
© Jefferson Communications, Inc. 1981
Distributed by C.T.N.Y.N.S.
WELL, IF YOU FEEL THAT STRONGLY ABOUT IT, I THINK YOU SHOULD QUIT!
10/10
MARLETTE
YOU DON'T KNOW ANYTHING ABOUT DEALING WITH THE ARTISTIC TEMPERAMENT, DO YOU?!

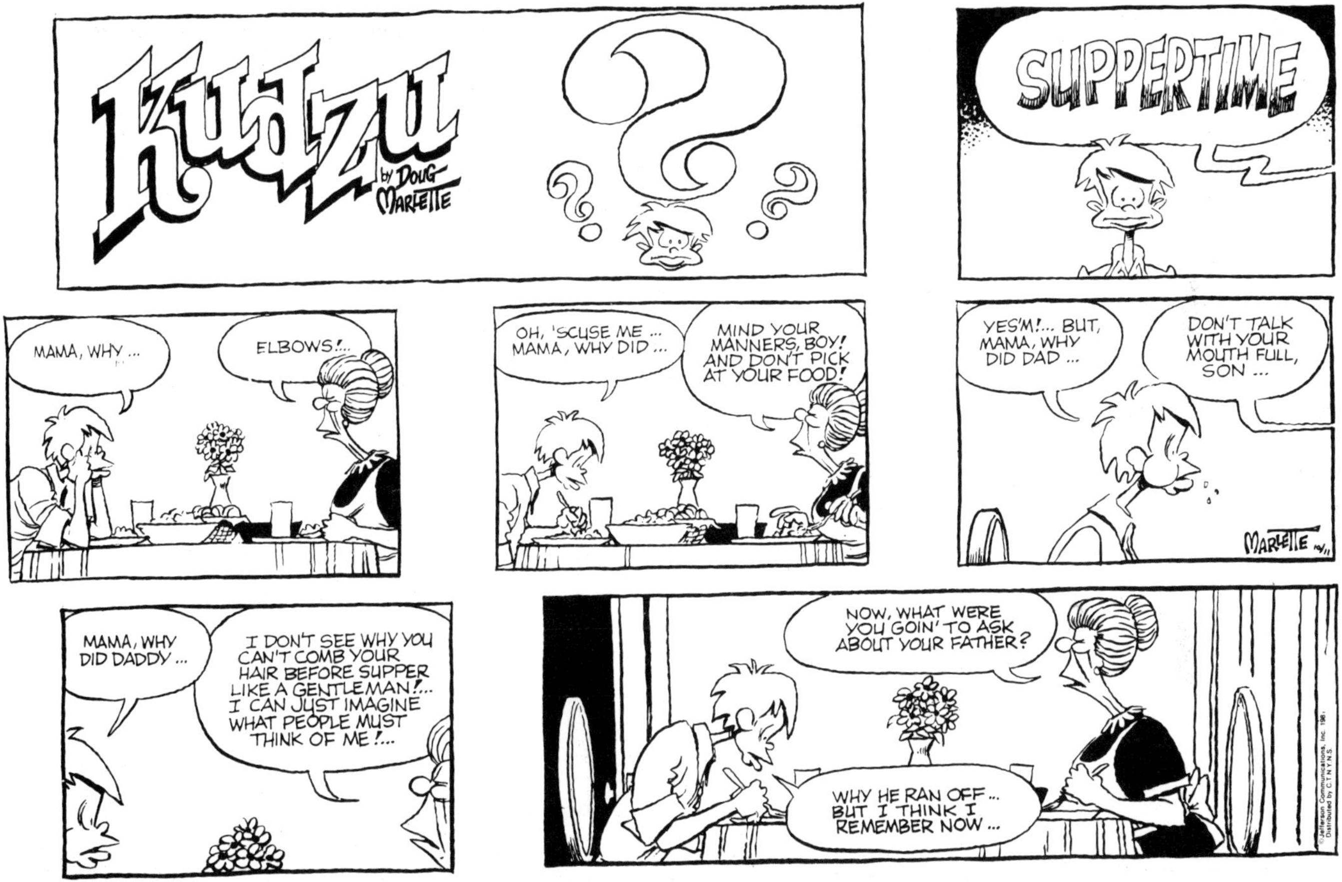

KUDZU
by DOUG MARLETTE
SUPPERTIME
MAMA, WHY ...
ELBOWS!...
OH, 'SCUSE ME ... MAMA, WHY DID ...
MIND YOUR MANNERS, BOY! AND DON'T PICK AT YOUR FOOD!
YES'M!... BUT, MAMA, WHY DID DAD ...
DON'T TALK WITH YOUR MOUTH FULL, SON ...
MARLETTE
MAMA, WHY DID DADDY ...
I DON'T SEE WHY YOU CAN'T COMB YOUR HAIR BEFORE SUPPER LIKE A GENTLEMAN!... I CAN JUST IMAGINE WHAT PEOPLE MUST THINK OF ME!...
NOW, WHAT WERE YOU GOIN' TO ASK ABOUT YOUR FATHER?
WHY HE RAN OFF... BUT I THINK I REMEMBER NOW ...
© Jefferson Communications, Inc. 1981. Distributed by C.T.N.Y.N.S.

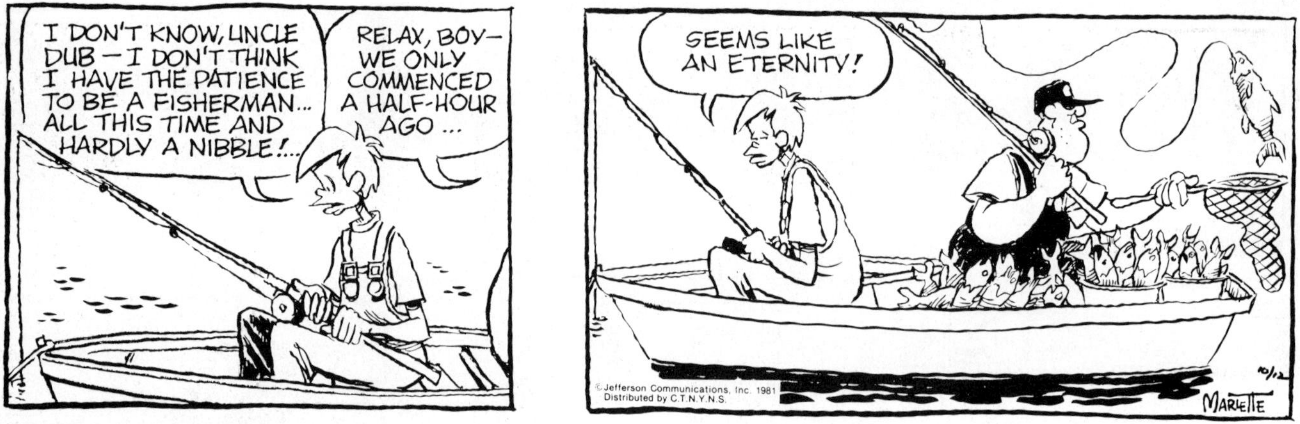
I DON'T KNOW, UNCLE DUB — I DON'T THINK I HAVE THE PATIENCE TO BE A FISHERMAN... ALL THIS TIME AND HARDLY A NIBBLE!...
RELAX, BOY— WE ONLY COMMENCED A HALF-HOUR AGO ...
SEEMS LIKE AN ETERNITY!
© Jefferson Communications, Inc. 1981 Distributed by C.T.N.Y.N.S.
10/12
MARLETTE

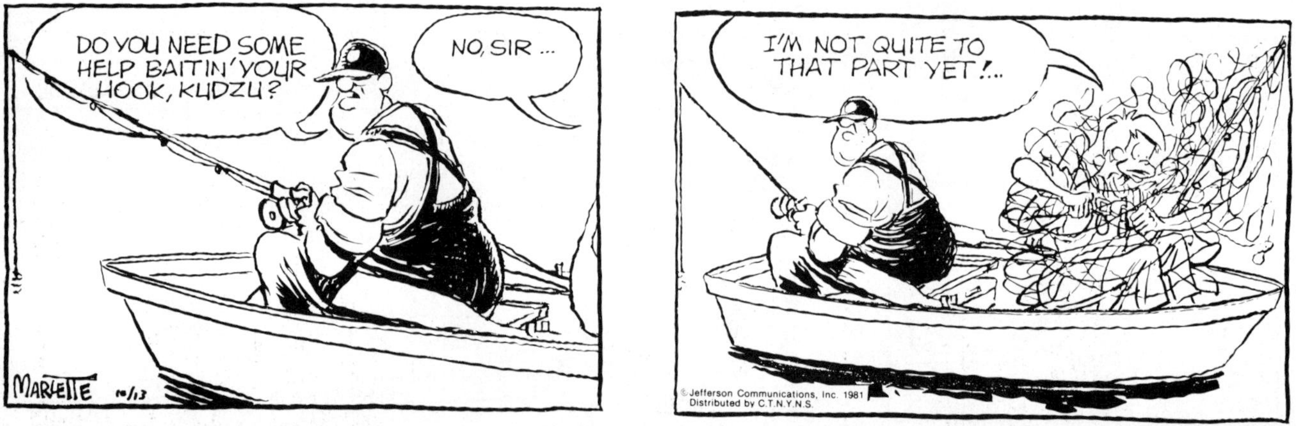
DO YOU NEED SOME HELP BAITIN' YOUR HOOK, KUDZU?
NO, SIR ...
MARLETTE 10/13
I'M NOT QUITE TO THAT PART YET!...
© Jefferson Communications, Inc. 1981 Distributed by C.T.N.Y.N.S.

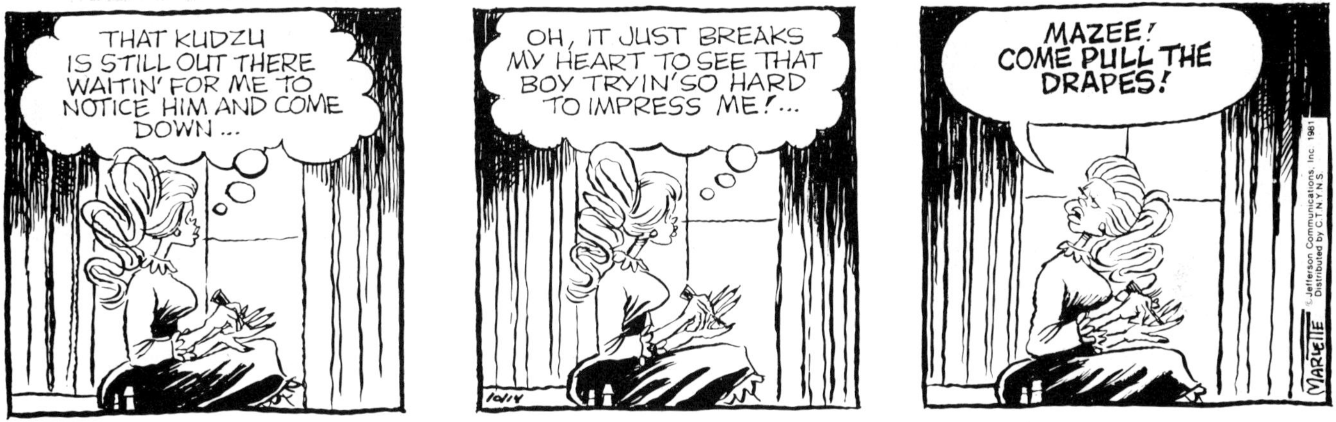
THAT KUDZU IS STILL OUT THERE WAITIN' FOR ME TO NOTICE HIM AND COME DOWN ...
OH, IT JUST BREAKS MY HEART TO SEE THAT BOY TRYIN' SO HARD TO IMPRESS ME! ...
10/14
MAZEE! COME PULL THE DRAPES!
© Jefferson Communications, Inc. 1981
Distributed by C.T.N.Y.N.S.
MARLETTE

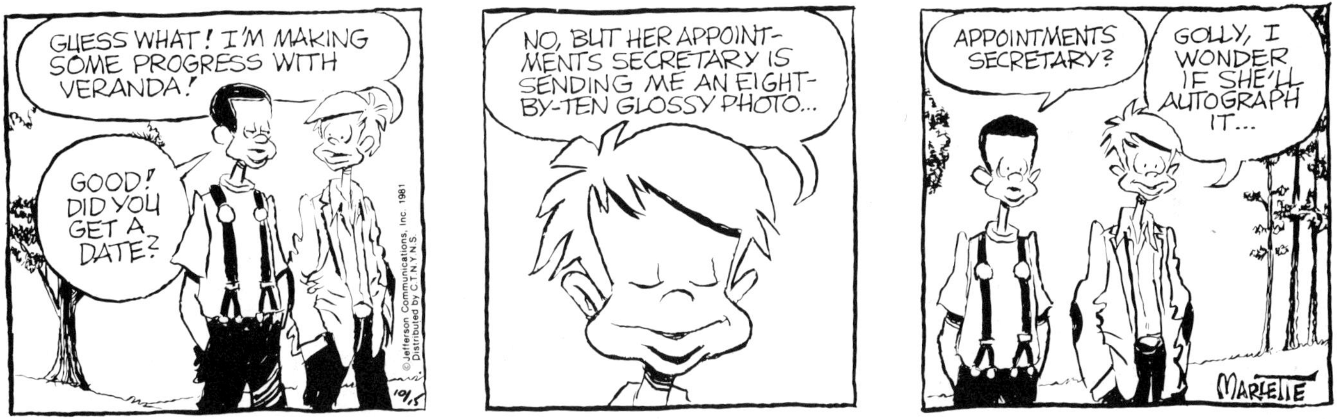
GUESS WHAT! I'M MAKING SOME PROGRESS WITH VERANDA!
GOOD! DID YOU GET A DATE?
© Jefferson Communications, Inc. 1981
Distributed by C.T.N.Y.N.S.
10/15
NO, BUT HER APPOINT-MENTS SECRETARY IS SENDING ME AN EIGHT-BY-TEN GLOSSY PHOTO...
APPOINTMENTS SECRETARY?
GOLLY, I WONDER IF SHE'LL AUTOGRAPH IT...
MARLETTE

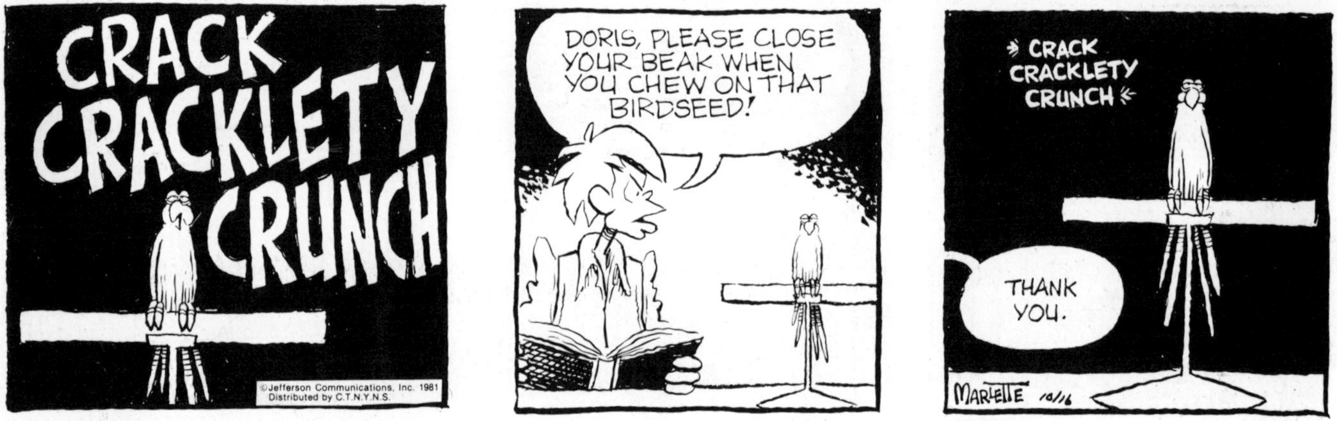
CRACK CRACKLETY CRUNCH
©Jefferson Communications, Inc. 1981 Distributed by C.T.N.Y.N.S.
DORIS, PLEASE CLOSE YOUR BEAK WHEN YOU CHEW ON THAT BIRDSEED!
CRACK CRACKLETY CRUNCH
THANK YOU.
MARLETTE 10/16

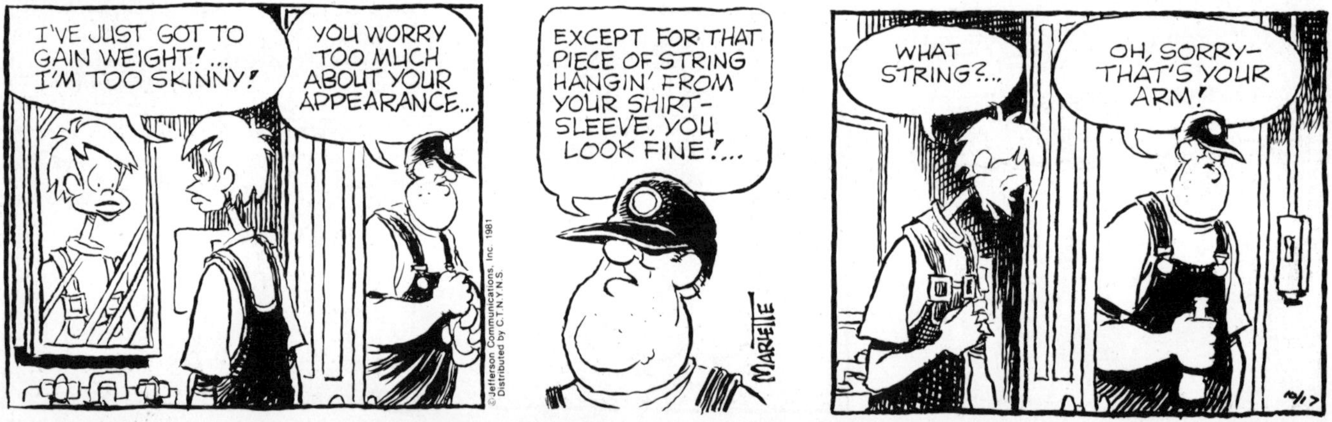
I'VE JUST GOT TO GAIN WEIGHT!... I'M TOO SKINNY!
YOU WORRY TOO MUCH ABOUT YOUR APPEARANCE...
©Jefferson Communications, Inc. 1981 Distributed by C.T.N.Y.N.S.
EXCEPT FOR THAT PIECE OF STRING HANGIN' FROM YOUR SHIRT-SLEEVE, YOU LOOK FINE!...
MARLETTE
WHAT STRING?...
OH, SORRY-THAT'S YOUR ARM!
10/17

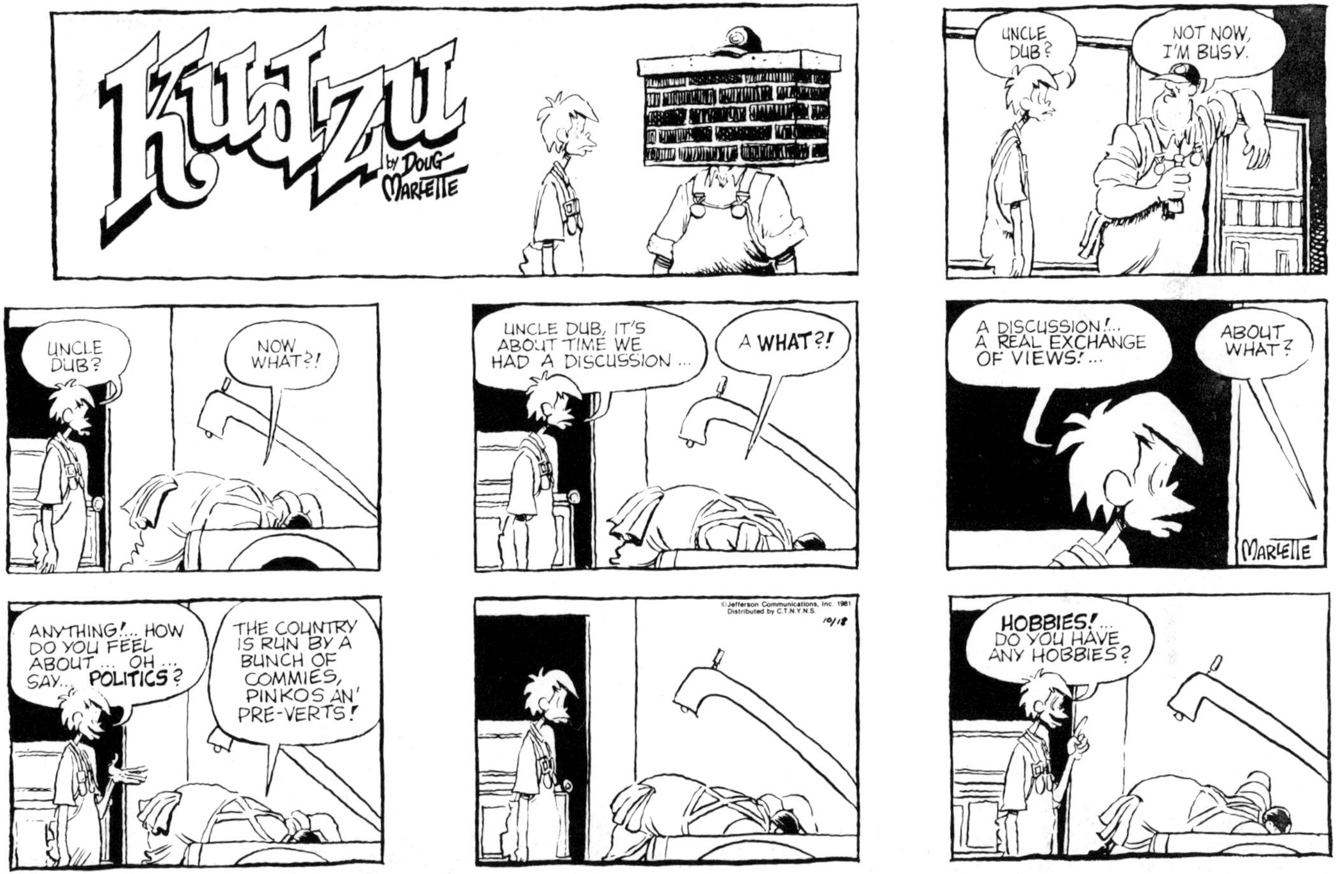

Kudzu
by Doug Marlette
UNCLE DUB?
NOT NOW, I'M BUSY.
UNCLE DUB?
NOW WHAT?!
UNCLE DUB, IT'S ABOUT TIME WE HAD A DISCUSSION ...
A **WHAT**?!
A DISCUSSION!... A REAL EXCHANGE OF VIEWS!...
ABOUT WHAT?
MARLETTE
ANYTHING!... HOW DO YOU FEEL ABOUT... OH ... SAY... **POLITICS**?
THE COUNTRY IS RUN BY A BUNCH OF COMMIES, PINKOS AN' PRE-VERTS!
©Jefferson Communications, Inc. 1981
Distributed by C.T.N.Y.N.S.
10/18
HOBBIES!... DO YOU HAVE ANY HOBBIES?

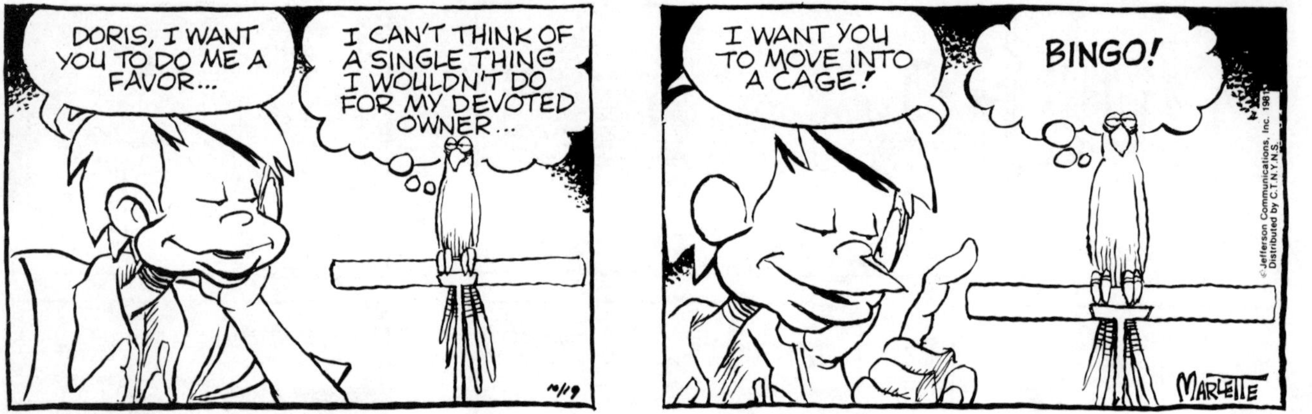
DORIS, I WANT YOU TO DO ME A FAVOR...
I CAN'T THINK OF A SINGLE THING I WOULDN'T DO FOR MY DEVOTED OWNER...
10/19
I WANT YOU TO MOVE INTO A CAGE!
BINGO!
© Jefferson Communications, Inc. 1981 Distributed by C.T.N.Y.N.S.
MARLETTE

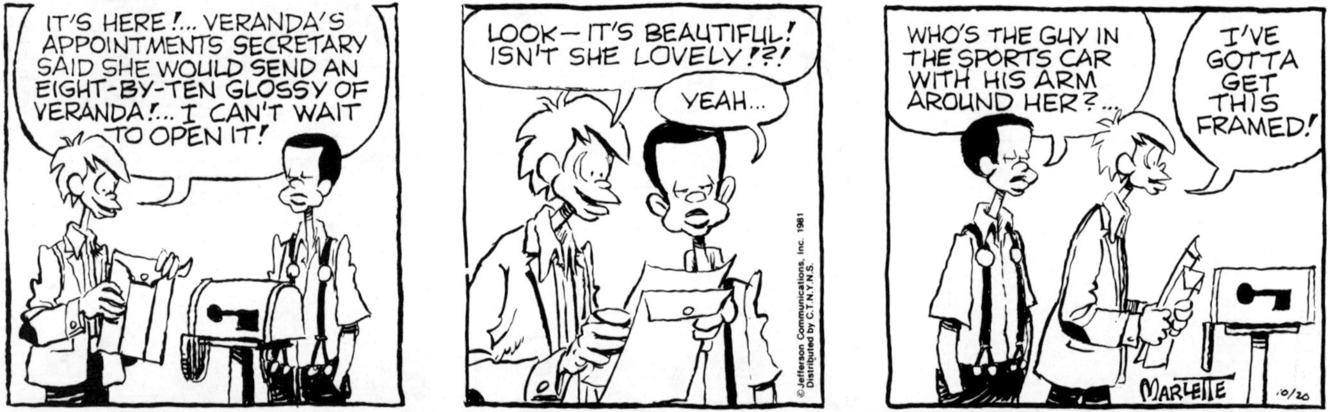
IT'S HERE!... VERANDA'S APPOINTMENTS SECRETARY SAID SHE WOULD SEND AN EIGHT-BY-TEN GLOSSY OF VERANDA!... I CAN'T WAIT TO OPEN IT!
LOOK—IT'S BEAUTIFUL! ISN'T SHE LOVELY!?!
YEAH...
© Jefferson Communications, Inc. 1981 Distributed by C.T.N.Y.N.S.
WHO'S THE GUY IN THE SPORTS CAR WITH HIS ARM AROUND HER?...
I'VE GOTTA GET THIS FRAMED!
MARLETTE
10/20

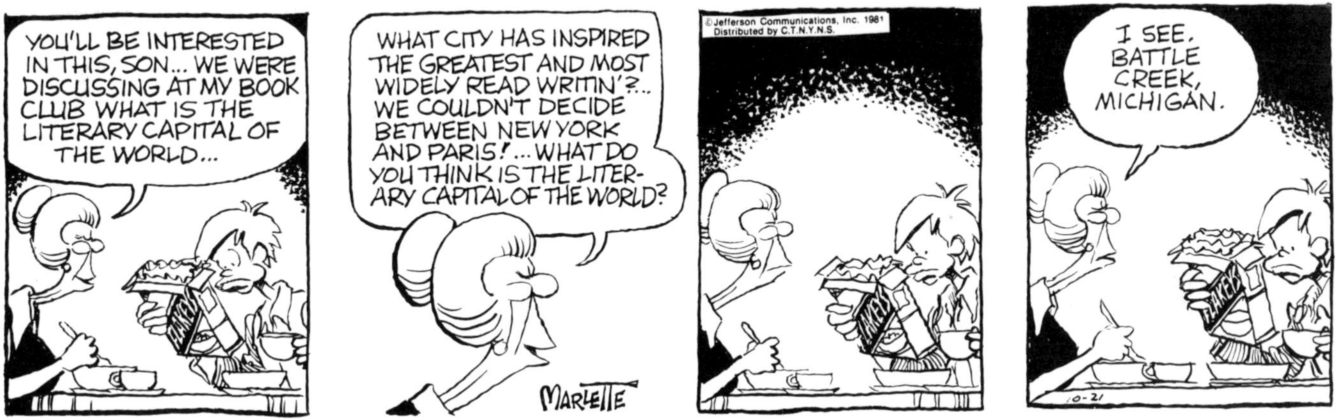
YOU'LL BE INTERESTED IN THIS, SON... WE WERE DISCUSSING AT MY BOOK CLUB WHAT IS THE LITERARY CAPITAL OF THE WORLD...
WHAT CITY HAS INSPIRED THE GREATEST AND MOST WIDELY READ WRITIN'?... WE COULDN'T DECIDE BETWEEN NEW YORK AND PARIS!... WHAT DO YOU THINK IS THE LITERARY CAPITAL OF THE WORLD?
MARLETTE
© Jefferson Communications, Inc. 1981 Distributed by C.T.N.Y.N.S.
I SEE, BATTLE CREEK, MICHIGAN.
10-21

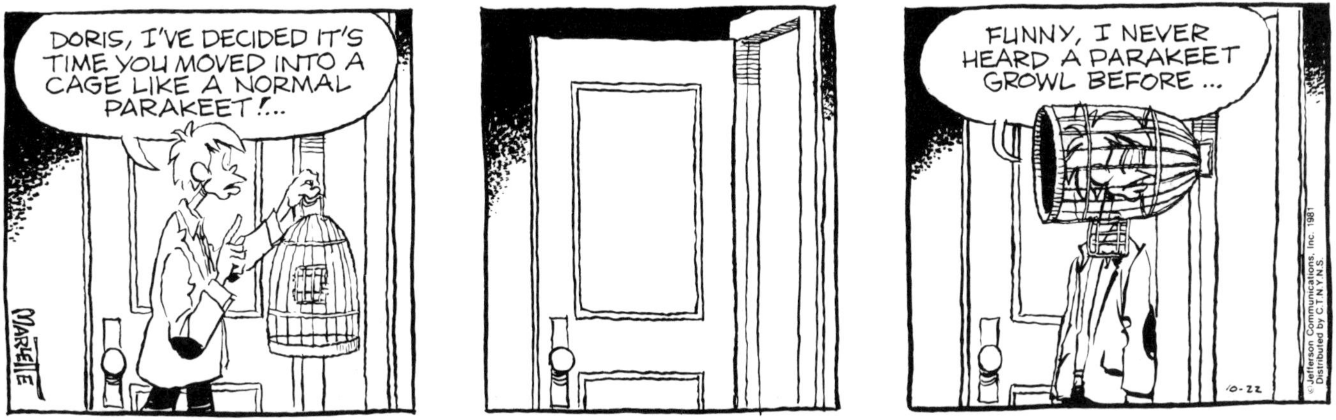
DORIS, I'VE DECIDED IT'S TIME YOU MOVED INTO A CAGE LIKE A NORMAL PARAKEET!...
MARLETTE
FUNNY, I NEVER HEARD A PARAKEET GROWL BEFORE...
10-22
© Jefferson Communications, Inc. 1981 Distributed by C.T.N.Y.N.S.

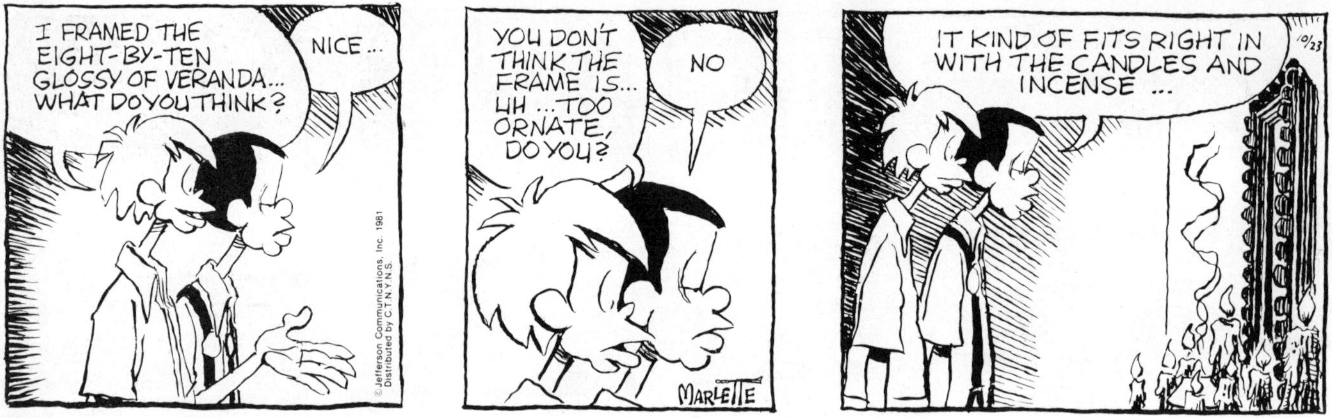
I FRAMED THE EIGHT-BY-TEN GLOSSY OF VERANDA... WHAT DO YOU THINK?
NICE...
© Jefferson Communications, Inc. 1981 Distributed by C.T.N.Y.N.S.
YOU DON'T THINK THE FRAME IS... UH ...TOO ORNATE, DO YOU?
NO
MARLETTE
IT KIND OF FITS RIGHT IN WITH THE CANDLES AND INCENSE...
10/23

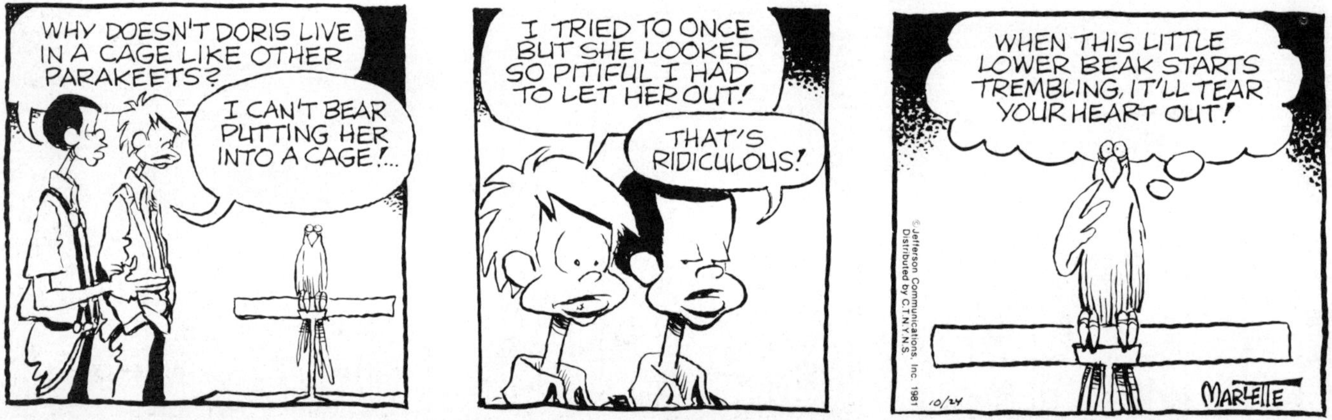
WHY DOESN'T DORIS LIVE IN A CAGE LIKE OTHER PARAKEETS?
I CAN'T BEAR PUTTING HER INTO A CAGE!...
I TRIED TO ONCE BUT SHE LOOKED SO PITIFUL I HAD TO LET HER OUT!
THAT'S RIDICULOUS!
WHEN THIS LITTLE LOWER BEAK STARTS TREMBLING, IT'LL TEAR YOUR HEART OUT!
© Jefferson Communications, Inc. 1981 Distributed by C.T.N.Y.N.S.
10/24
MARLETTE

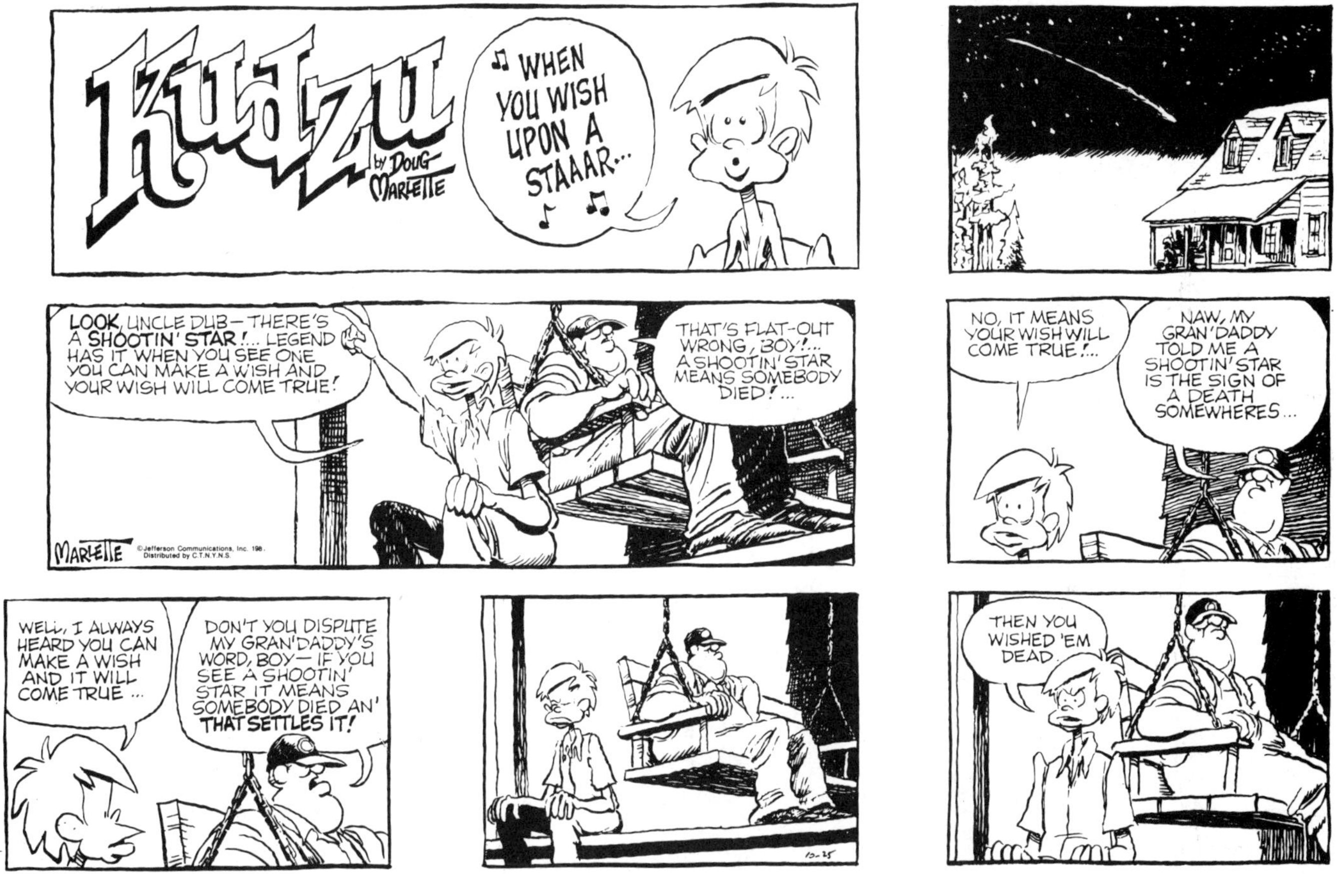

KUDZU
by DOUG MARLETTE
WHEN YOU WISH UPON A STAAAR...
LOOK, UNCLE DUB — THERE'S A SHOOTIN' STAR!... LEGEND HAS IT WHEN YOU SEE ONE YOU CAN MAKE A WISH AND YOUR WISH WILL COME TRUE!
THAT'S FLAT-OUT WRONG, BOY!... A SHOOTIN' STAR MEANS SOMEBODY DIED!...
MARLETTE
©Jefferson Communications, Inc. 198. Distributed by C.T.N.Y.N.S.
NO, IT MEANS YOUR WISH WILL COME TRUE!...
NAW, MY GRAN'DADDY TOLD ME A SHOOTIN' STAR IS THE SIGN OF A DEATH SOMEWHERES...
WELL, I ALWAYS HEARD YOU CAN MAKE A WISH AND IT WILL COME TRUE...
DON'T YOU DISPUTE MY GRAN'DADDY'S WORD, BOY — IF YOU SEE A SHOOTIN' STAR IT MEANS SOMEBODY DIED AN' THAT SETTLES IT!
THEN YOU WISHED 'EM DEAD.

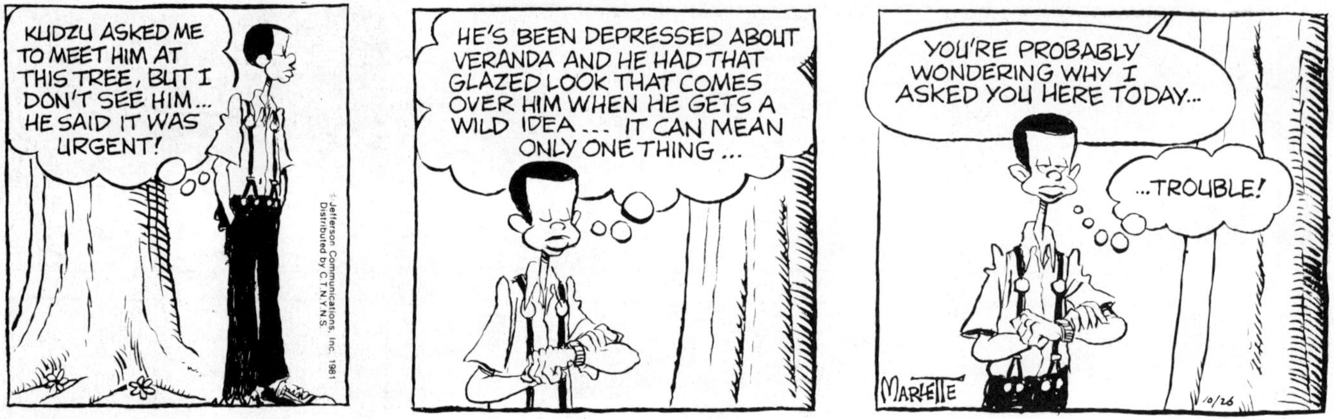
KUDZU ASKED ME TO MEET HIM AT THIS TREE, BUT I DON'T SEE HIM... HE SAID IT WAS URGENT!
© Jefferson Communications, Inc. 1981 Distributed by C.T.N.Y.N.S.
HE'S BEEN DEPRESSED ABOUT VERANDA AND HE HAD THAT GLAZED LOOK THAT COMES OVER HIM WHEN HE GETS A WILD IDEA ... IT CAN MEAN ONLY ONE THING ...
YOU'RE PROBABLY WONDERING WHY I ASKED YOU HERE TODAY...
...TROUBLE!
MARLETTE
10/26

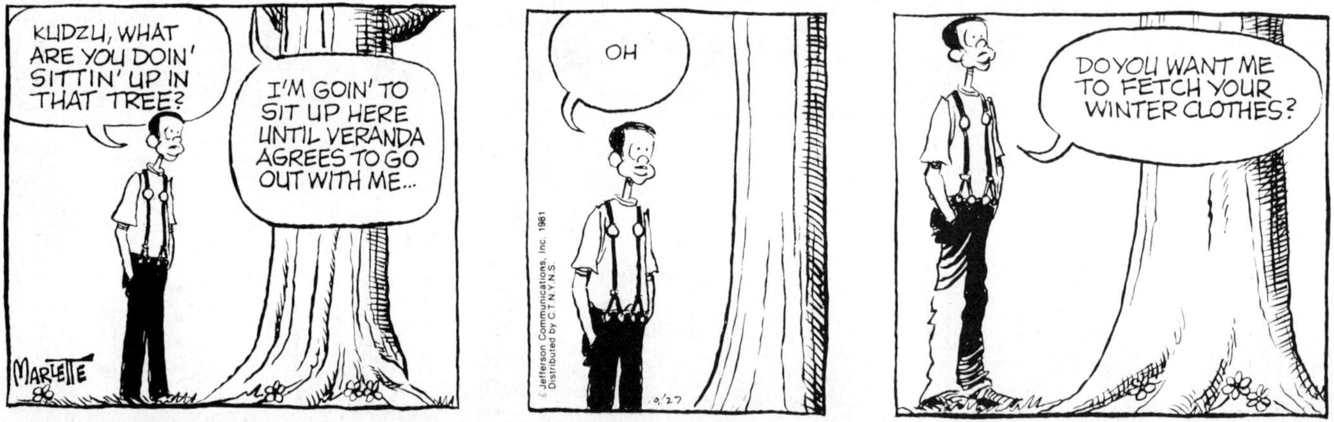
KUDZU, WHAT ARE YOU DOIN' SITTIN' UP IN THAT TREE?
I'M GOIN' TO SIT UP HERE UNTIL VERANDA AGREES TO GO OUT WITH ME...
MARLETTE
OH
© Jefferson Communications, Inc. 1981 Distributed by C.T.N.Y.N.S.
10/27
DO YOU WANT ME TO FETCH YOUR WINTER CLOTHES?

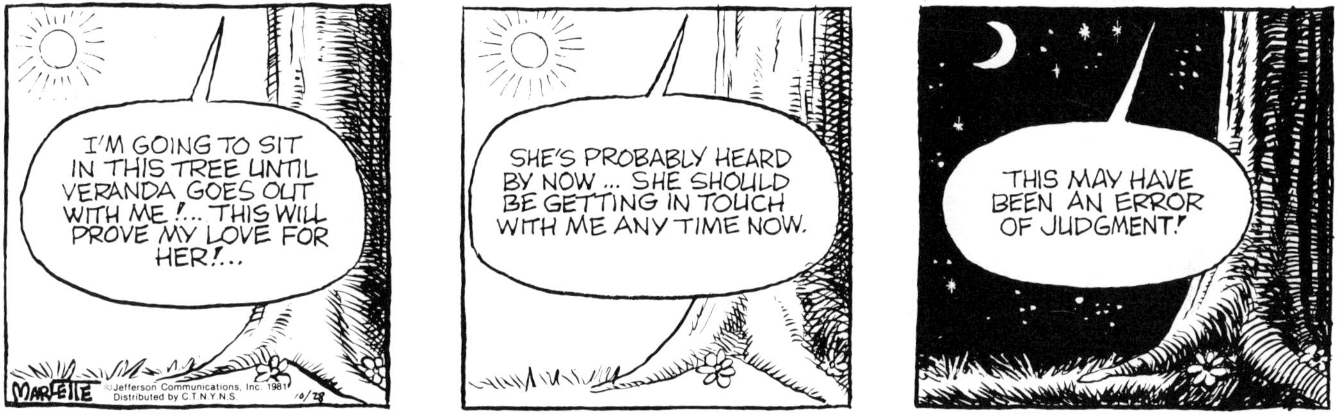
I'M GOING TO SIT IN THIS TREE UNTIL VERANDA GOES OUT WITH ME!... THIS WILL PROVE MY LOVE FOR HER!...
MARLETTE
©Jefferson Communications, Inc. 1981 Distributed by C.T.N.Y.N.S.
10/28
SHE'S PROBABLY HEARD BY NOW ... SHE SHOULD BE GETTING IN TOUCH WITH ME ANY TIME NOW.
THIS MAY HAVE BEEN AN ERROR OF JUDGMENT!

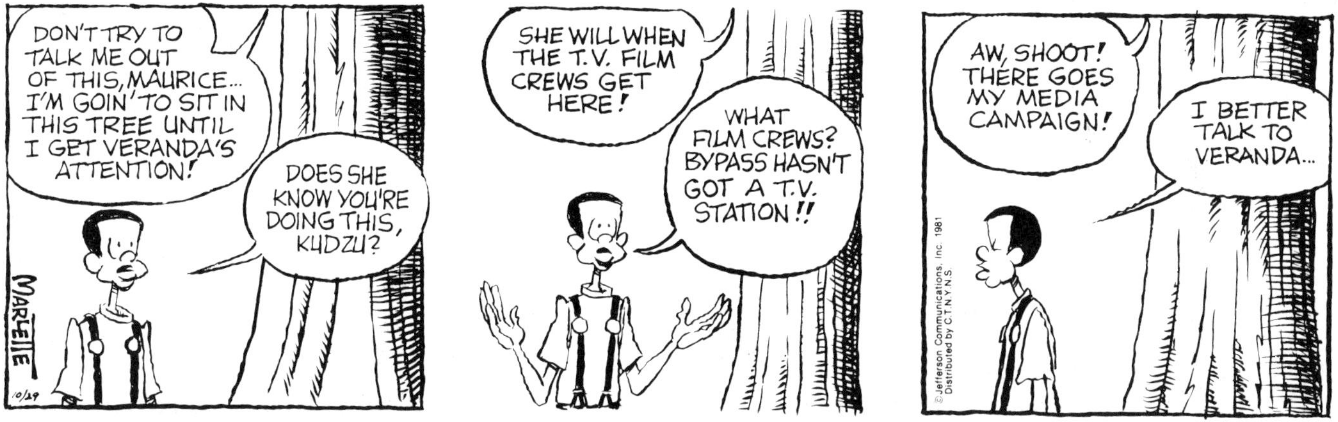
DON'T TRY TO TALK ME OUT OF THIS, MAURICE... I'M GOIN' TO SIT IN THIS TREE UNTIL I GET VERANDA'S ATTENTION!
DOES SHE KNOW YOU'RE DOING THIS, KUDZU?
MARLETTE
10/29
SHE WILL WHEN THE T.V. FILM CREWS GET HERE!
WHAT FILM CREWS? BYPASS HASN'T GOT A T.V. STATION!!
AW, SHOOT! THERE GOES MY MEDIA CAMPAIGN!
I BETTER TALK TO VERANDA...
© Jefferson Communications, Inc. 1981
Distributed by C.T.N.Y.N.S.

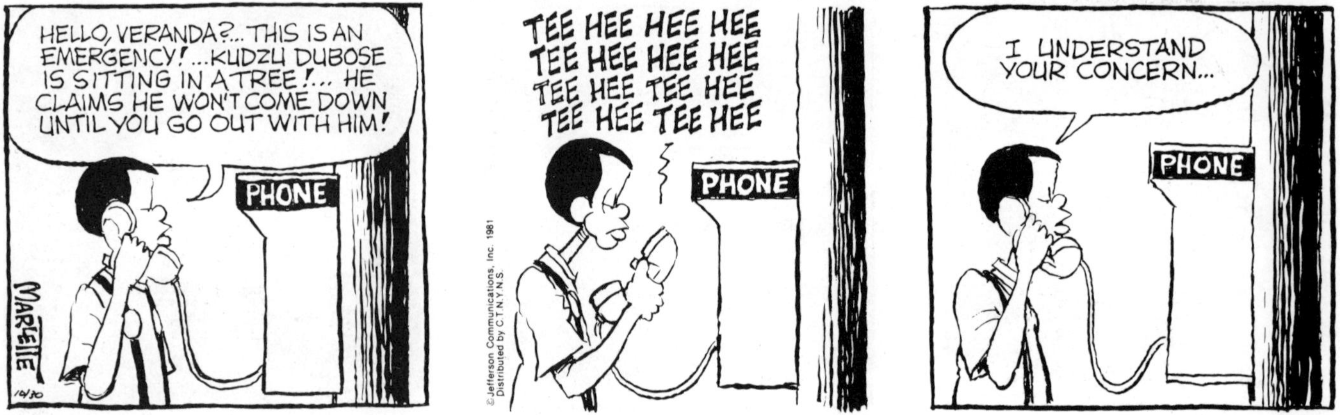
HELLO, VERANDA?... THIS IS AN EMERGENCY!...KUDZU DUBOSE IS SITTING IN A TREE!... HE CLAIMS HE WON'T COME DOWN UNTIL YOU GO OUT WITH HIM!
PHONE
MARLETTE
10/30
TEE HEE HEE HEE TEE HEE HEE HEE TEE HEE TEE HEE TEE HEE TEE HEE
PHONE
© Jefferson Communications, Inc. 1981
Distributed by C.T.N.Y.N.S.
I UNDERSTAND YOUR CONCERN...
PHONE

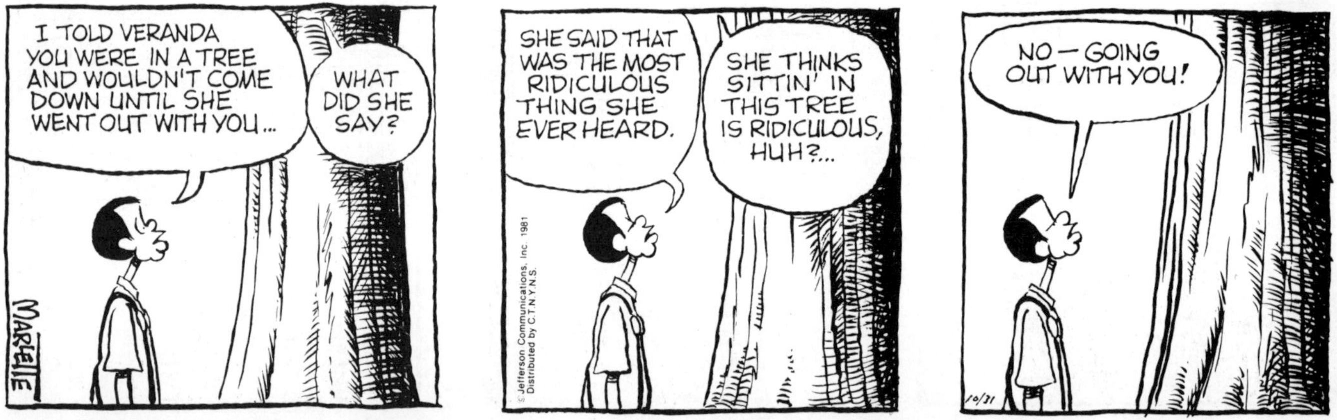
I TOLD VERANDA YOU WERE IN A TREE AND WOULDN'T COME DOWN UNTIL SHE WENT OUT WITH YOU...
WHAT DID SHE SAY?
MARLETTE
SHE SAID THAT WAS THE MOST RIDICULOUS THING SHE EVER HEARD.
SHE THINKS SITTIN' IN THIS TREE IS RIDICULOUS, HUH?...
© Jefferson Communications, Inc. 1981
Distributed by C.T.N.Y.N.S.
NO — GOING OUT WITH YOU!
10/31

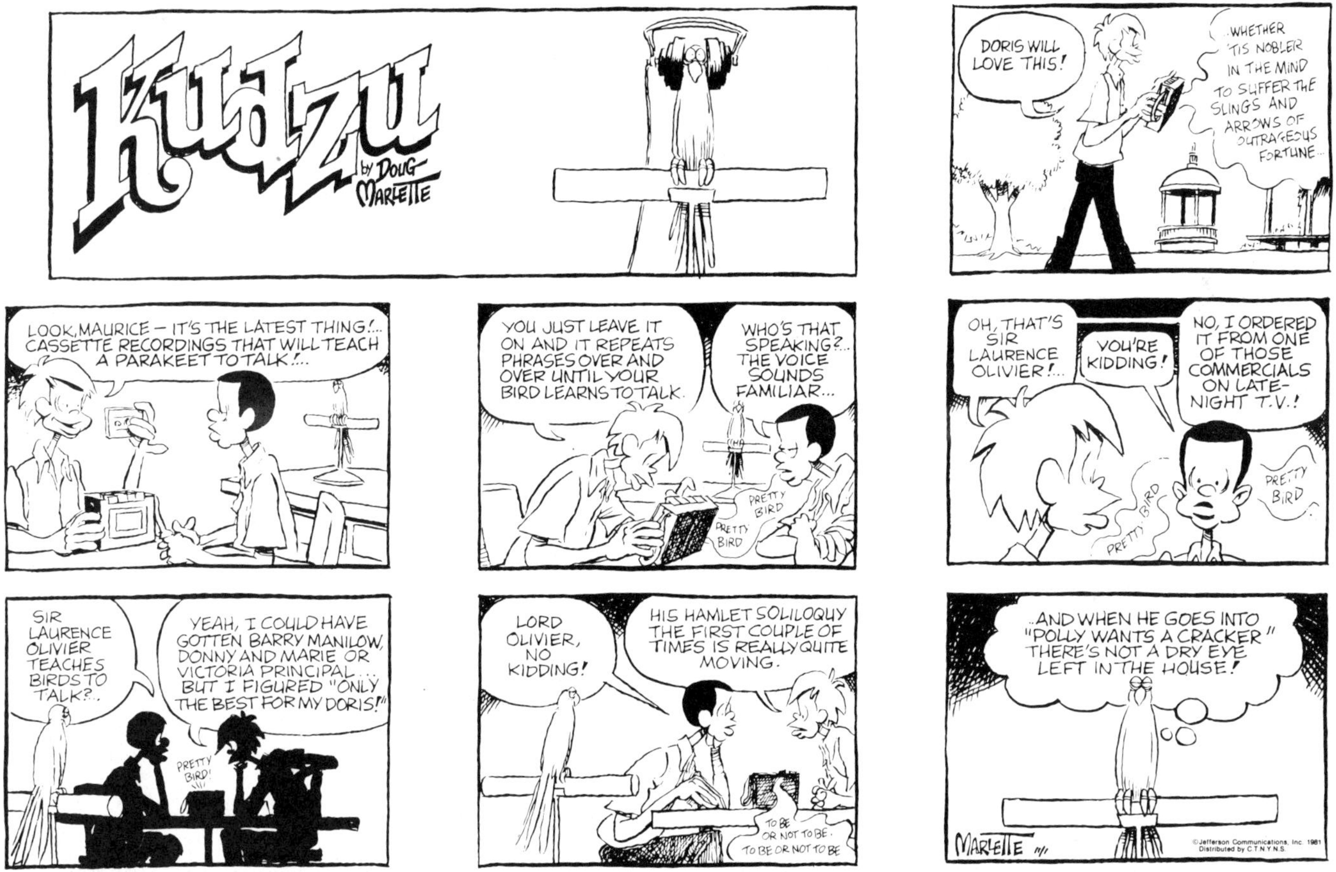
Kudzu
by Doug Marlette
DORIS WILL LOVE THIS!
..WHETHER 'TIS NOBLER IN THE MIND TO SUFFER THE SLINGS AND ARROWS OF OUTRAGEOUS FORTUNE...
LOOK, MAURICE — IT'S THE LATEST THING!... CASSETTE RECORDINGS THAT WILL TEACH A PARAKEET TO TALK!...
YOU JUST LEAVE IT ON AND IT REPEATS PHRASES OVER AND OVER UNTIL YOUR BIRD LEARNS TO TALK.
WHO'S THAT SPEAKING?... THE VOICE SOUNDS FAMILIAR...
PRETTY BIRD
PRETTY BIRD
OH, THAT'S SIR LAURENCE OLIVIER!...
YOU'RE KIDDING!
NO, I ORDERED IT FROM ONE OF THOSE COMMERCIALS ON LATE-NIGHT T.V.!
PRETTY BIRD
PRETTY BIRD
SIR LAURENCE OLIVIER TEACHES BIRDS TO TALK?...
YEAH, I COULD HAVE GOTTEN BARRY MANILOW, DONNY AND MARIE OR VICTORIA PRINCIPAL... BUT I FIGURED "ONLY THE BEST FOR MY DORIS!"
PRETTY BIRD!
LORD OLIVIER, NO KIDDING!
HIS HAMLET SOLILOQUY THE FIRST COUPLE OF TIMES IS REALLY QUITE MOVING.
TO BE OR NOT TO BE. TO BE OR NOT TO BE
..AND WHEN HE GOES INTO "POLLY WANTS A CRACKER" THERE'S NOT A DRY EYE LEFT IN THE HOUSE!
MARLETTE 11/1
©Jefferson Communications, Inc. 1981
Distributed by C.T.N.Y.N.S.

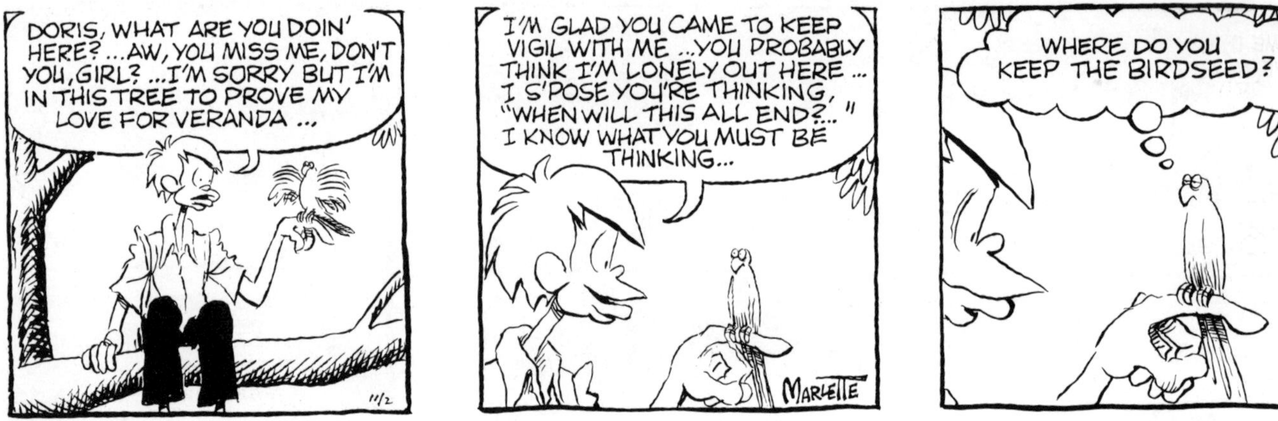
DORIS, WHAT ARE YOU DOIN' HERE? ...AW, YOU MISS ME, DON'T YOU, GIRL? ...I'M SORRY BUT I'M IN THIS TREE TO PROVE MY LOVE FOR VERANDA ...
11/2
I'M GLAD YOU CAME TO KEEP VIGIL WITH ME ...YOU PROBABLY THINK I'M LONELY OUT HERE ... I S'POSE YOU'RE THINKING, "WHEN WILL THIS ALL END?..." I KNOW WHAT YOU MUST BE THINKING...
MARLETTE
WHERE DO YOU KEEP THE BIRDSEED?

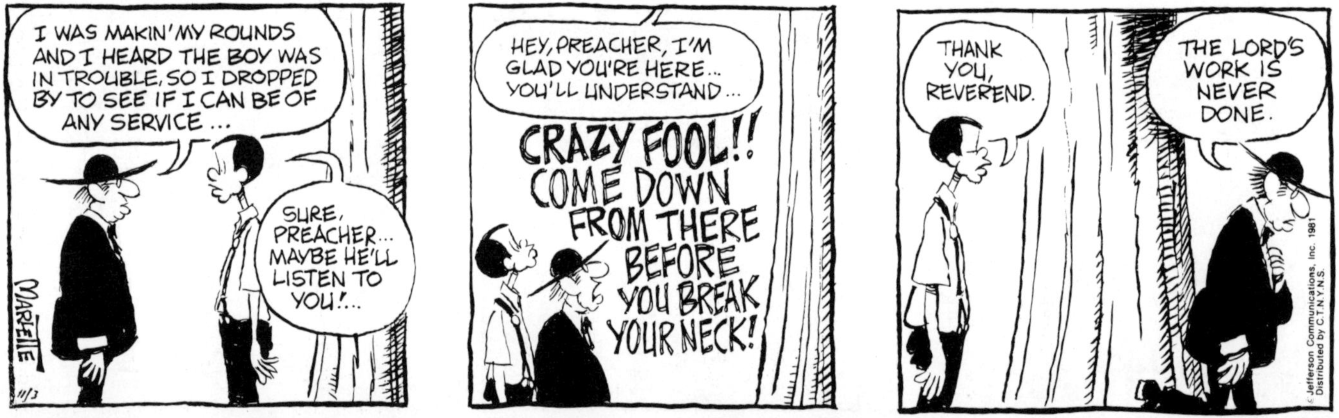
I WAS MAKIN' MY ROUNDS AND I HEARD THE BOY WAS IN TROUBLE, SO I DROPPED BY TO SEE IF I CAN BE OF ANY SERVICE ...
SURE, PREACHER... MAYBE HE'LL LISTEN TO YOU!...
MARLETTE
11/3
HEY, PREACHER, I'M GLAD YOU'RE HERE... YOU'LL UNDERSTAND...
CRAZY FOOL!! COME DOWN FROM THERE BEFORE YOU BREAK YOUR NECK!
THANK YOU, REVEREND.
THE LORD'S WORK IS NEVER DONE.
© Jefferson Communications, Inc. 1981
Distributed by C.T.N.Y.N.S.

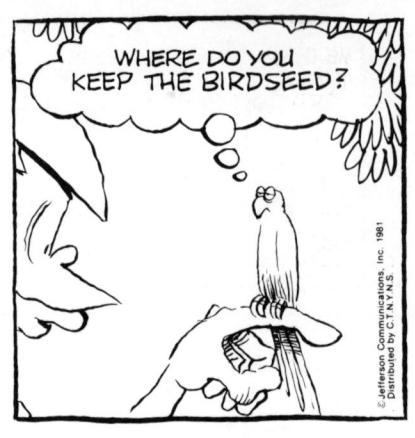

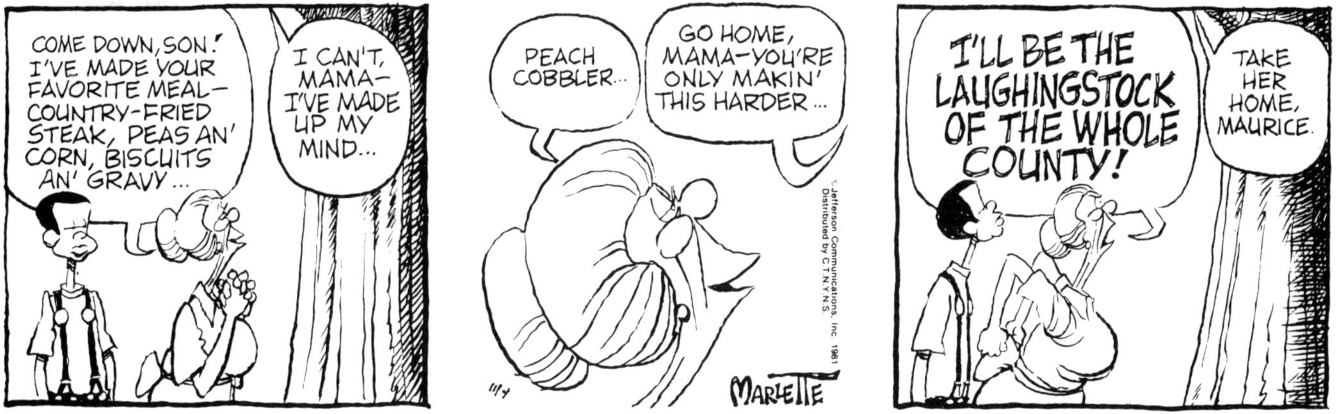
COME DOWN, SON! I'VE MADE YOUR FAVORITE MEAL— COUNTRY-FRIED STEAK, PEAS AN' CORN, BISCUITS AN' GRAVY ...
I CAN'T, MAMA— I'VE MADE UP MY MIND...
PEACH COBBLER...
GO HOME, MAMA—YOU'RE ONLY MAKIN' THIS HARDER ...
I'LL BE THE LAUGHINGSTOCK OF THE WHOLE COUNTY!
TAKE HER HOME, MAURICE.
MARLETTE
11/4

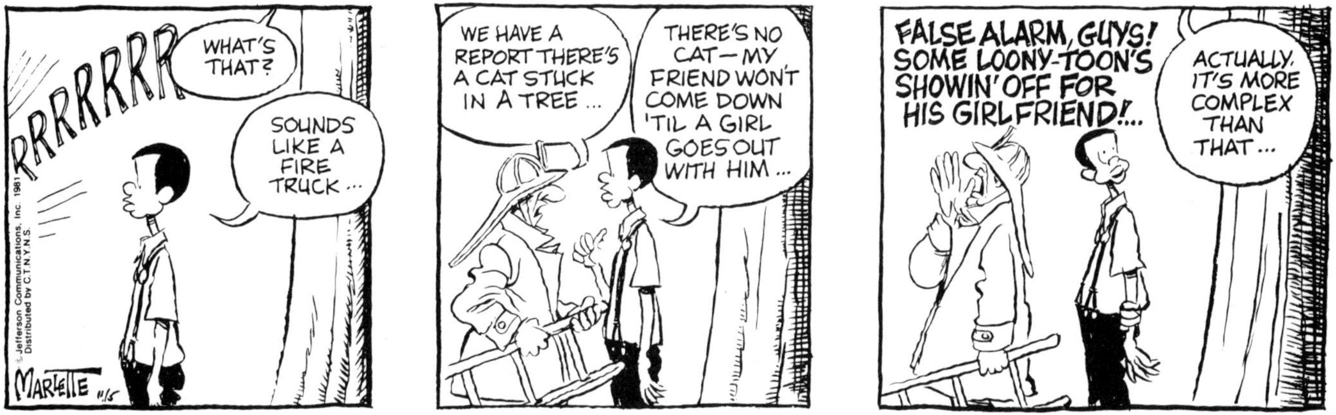
RRRRRRRR
WHAT'S THAT?
SOUNDS LIKE A FIRE TRUCK ...
WE HAVE A REPORT THERE'S A CAT STUCK IN A TREE ...
THERE'S NO CAT—MY FRIEND WON'T COME DOWN 'TIL A GIRL GOES OUT WITH HIM ...
FALSE ALARM, GUYS! SOME LOONY-TOON'S SHOWIN' OFF FOR HIS GIRLFRIEND!...
ACTUALLY, IT'S MORE COMPLEX THAN THAT ...
MARLETTE
11/5

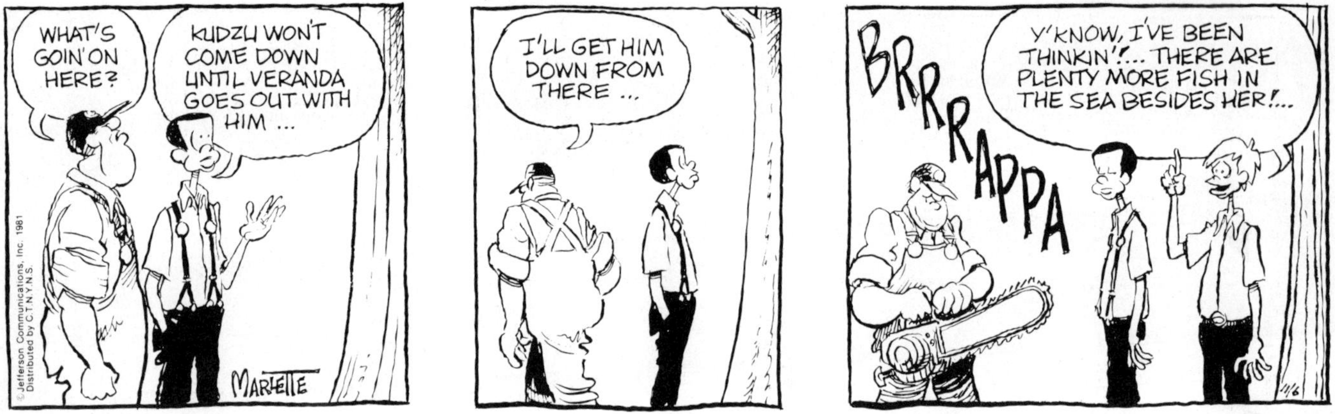
WHAT'S GOIN' ON HERE?
KUDZU WON'T COME DOWN UNTIL VERANDA GOES OUT WITH HIM ...
© Jefferson Communications, Inc. 1981
Distributed by C.T.N.Y.N.S.
MARLETTE
I'LL GET HIM DOWN FROM THERE ...
BRRRAPPA
Y'KNOW, I'VE BEEN THINKIN'!... THERE ARE PLENTY MORE FISH IN THE SEA BESIDES HER!...
11/6

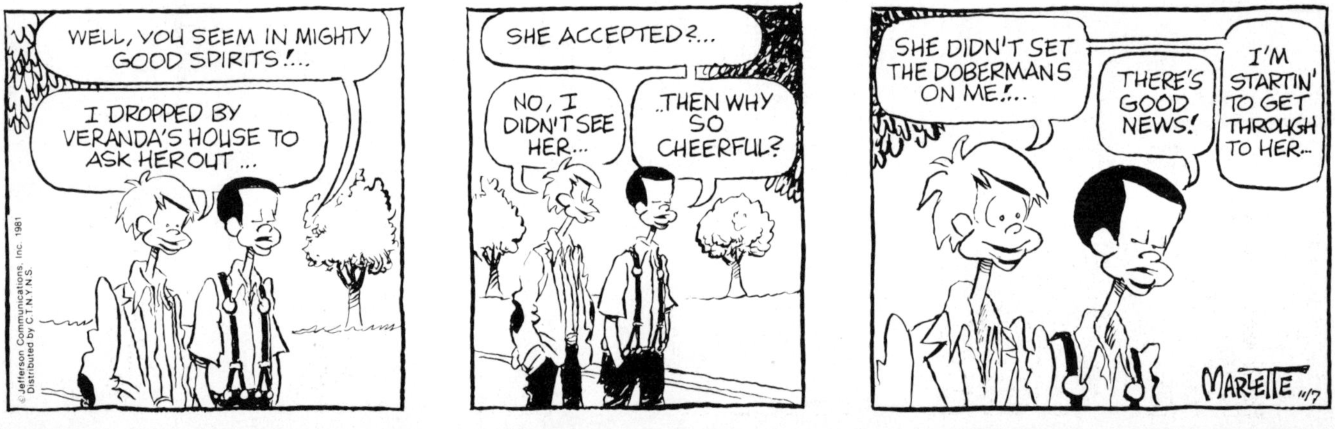
© Jefferson Communications, Inc. 1981
Distributed by C.T.N.Y.N.S.
WELL, YOU SEEM IN MIGHTY GOOD SPIRITS!...
I DROPPED BY VERANDA'S HOUSE TO ASK HER OUT ...
SHE ACCEPTED?...
NO, I DIDN'T SEE HER...
..THEN WHY SO CHEERFUL?
SHE DIDN'T SET THE DOBERMANS ON ME!...
THERE'S GOOD NEWS!
I'M STARTIN' TO GET THROUGH TO HER...
MARLETTE 11/7

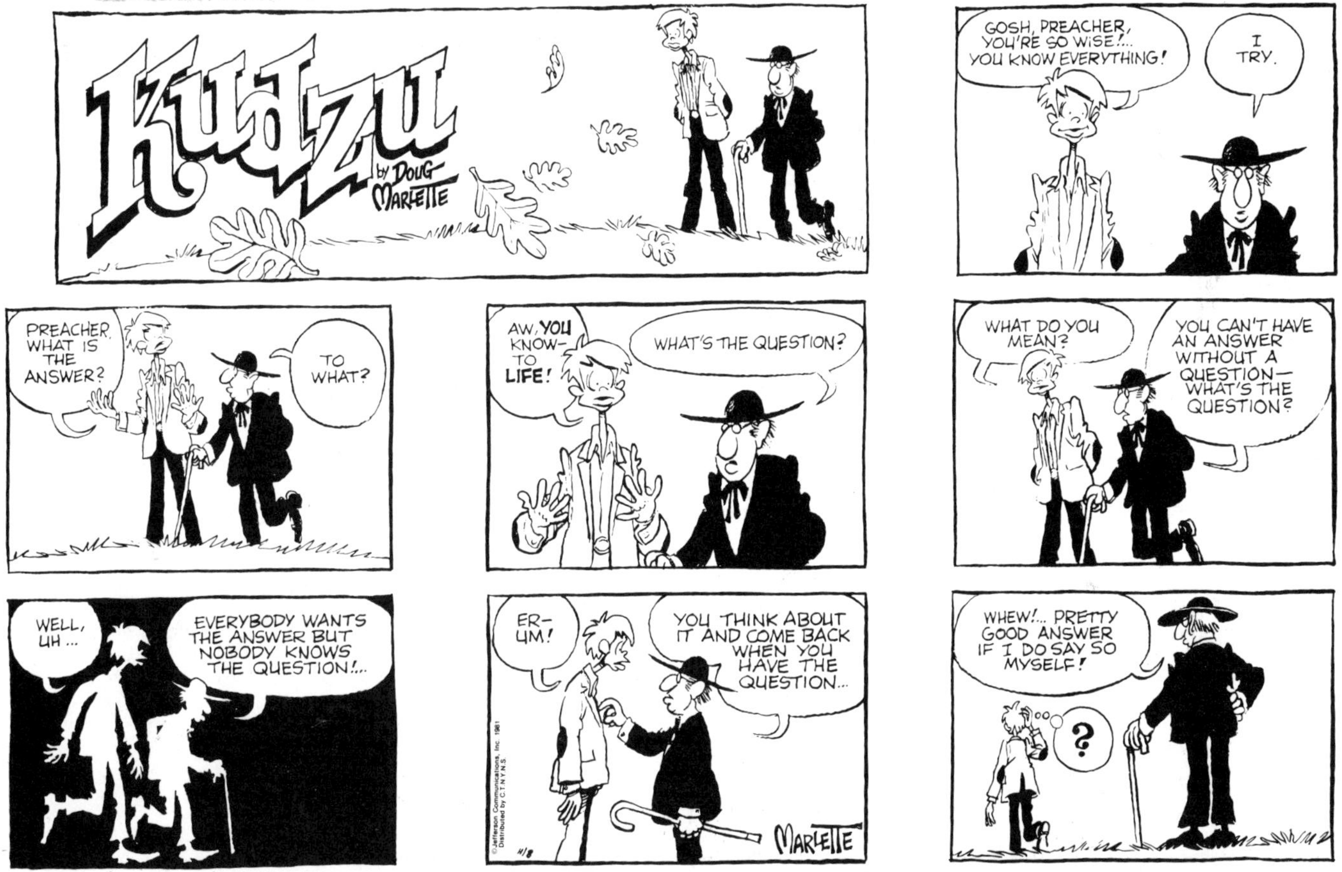
Kudzu
by DOUG MARLETTE
GOSH, PREACHER, YOU'RE SO WISE!... YOU KNOW EVERYTHING!
I TRY.
PREACHER, WHAT IS THE ANSWER?
TO WHAT?
AW, YOU KNOW— TO LIFE!
WHAT'S THE QUESTION?
WHAT DO YOU MEAN?
YOU CAN'T HAVE AN ANSWER WITHOUT A QUESTION— WHAT'S THE QUESTION?
WELL, UH ...
EVERYBODY WANTS THE ANSWER BUT NOBODY KNOWS THE QUESTION!...
ER— UM!
YOU THINK ABOUT IT AND COME BACK WHEN YOU HAVE THE QUESTION...
©Jefferson Communications, Inc. 1981
Distributed by C.T.N.Y.N.S.
MARLETTE
WHEW!... PRETTY GOOD ANSWER IF I DO SAY SO MYSELF!
?

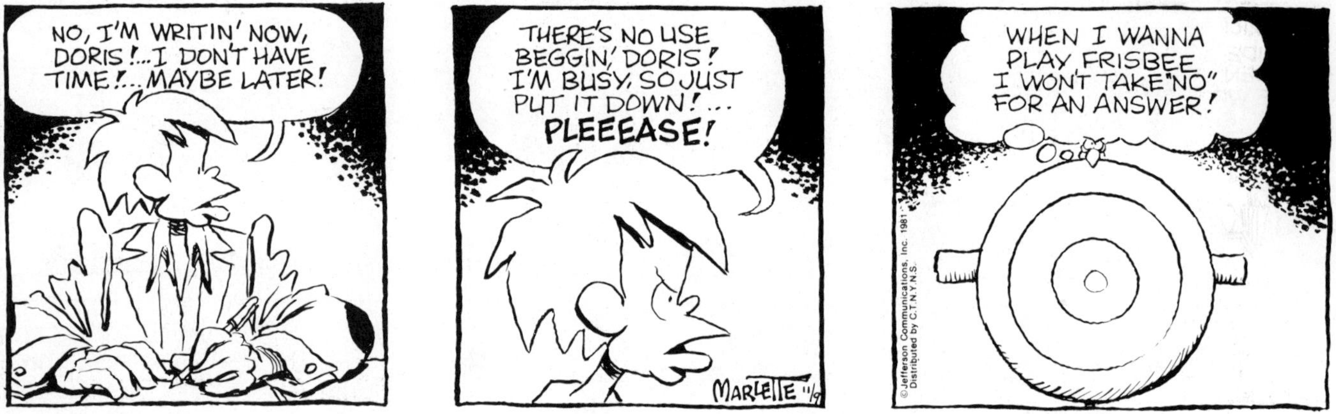
NO, I'M WRITIN' NOW, DORIS!...I DON'T HAVE TIME!...MAYBE LATER!
THERE'S NO USE BEGGIN' DORIS! I'M BUSY, SO JUST PUT IT DOWN!... PLEEEASE!
MARLETTE 11/9
© Jefferson Communications, Inc. 1981 Distributed by C.T.N.Y.N.S.
WHEN I WANNA PLAY FRISBEE I WON'T TAKE "NO" FOR AN ANSWER!

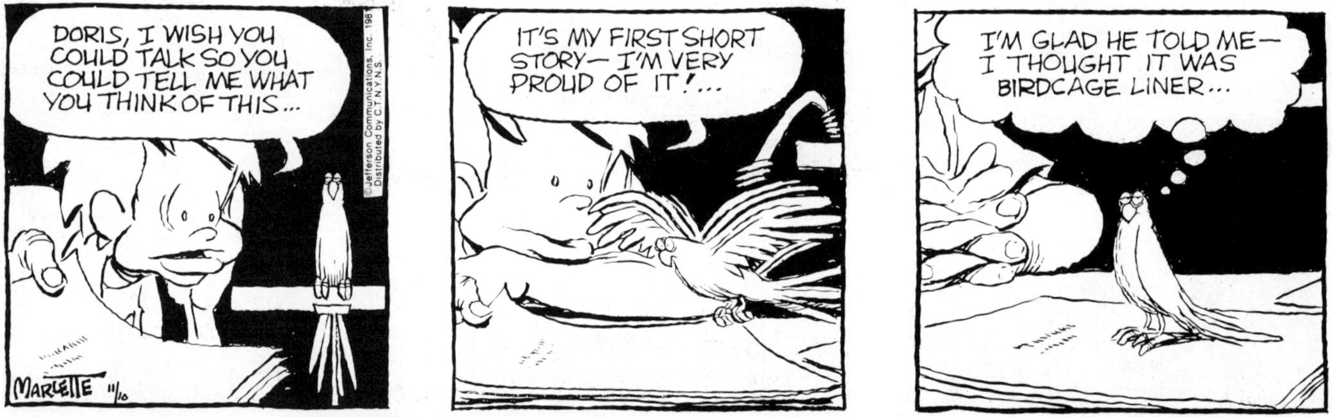
DORIS, I WISH YOU COULD TALK SO YOU COULD TELL ME WHAT YOU THINK OF THIS...
© Jefferson Communications, Inc. 1981 Distributed by C.T.N.Y.N.S.
MARLETTE 11/10
IT'S MY FIRST SHORT STORY— I'M VERY PROUD OF IT!...
I'M GLAD HE TOLD ME— I THOUGHT IT WAS BIRDCAGE LINER...

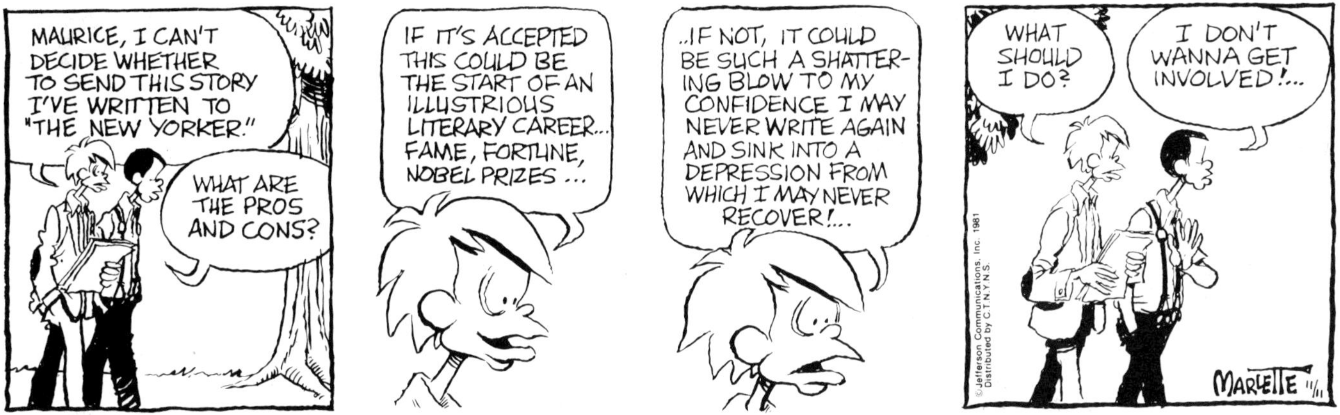

MAURICE, I CAN'T DECIDE WHETHER TO SEND THIS STORY I'VE WRITTEN TO "THE NEW YORKER."
WHAT ARE THE PROS AND CONS?
IF IT'S ACCEPTED THIS COULD BE THE START OF AN ILLUSTRIOUS LITERARY CAREER... FAME, FORTUNE, NOBEL PRIZES ...
..IF NOT, IT COULD BE SUCH A SHATTERING BLOW TO MY CONFIDENCE I MAY NEVER WRITE AGAIN AND SINK INTO A DEPRESSION FROM WHICH I MAY NEVER RECOVER!...
WHAT SHOULD I DO?
I DON'T WANNA GET INVOLVED!...
© Jefferson Communications, Inc. 1981
Distributed by C.T.N.Y.N.S.
MARLETTE 11/11

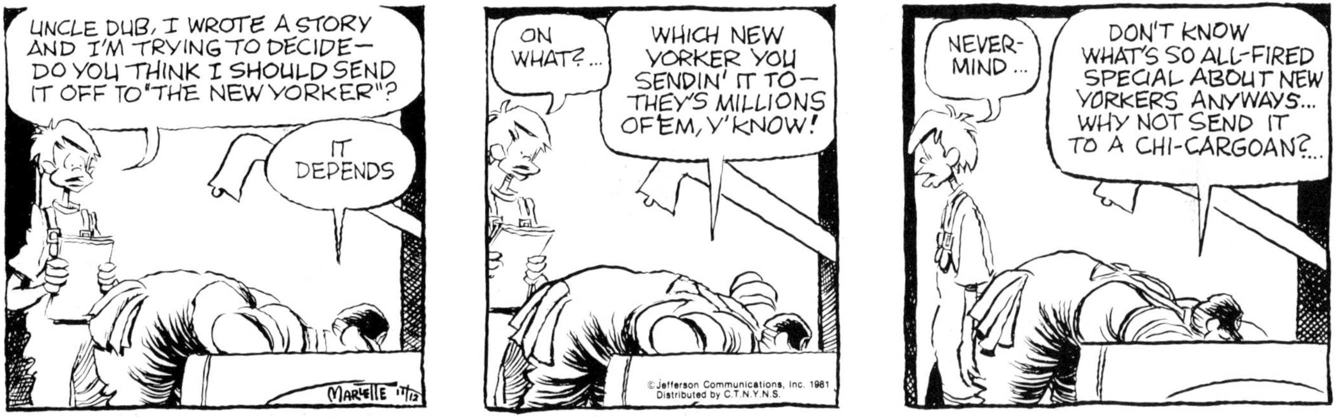

UNCLE DUB, I WROTE A STORY AND I'M TRYING TO DECIDE— DO YOU THINK I SHOULD SEND IT OFF TO "THE NEW YORKER"?
IT DEPENDS
MARLETTE 11/12
ON WHAT?...
WHICH NEW YORKER YOU SENDIN' IT TO— THEY'S MILLIONS OF 'EM, Y'KNOW!
© Jefferson Communications, Inc. 1981
Distributed by C.T.N.Y.N.S.
NEVER-MIND ...
DON'T KNOW WHAT'S SO ALL-FIRED SPECIAL ABOUT NEW YORKERS ANYWAYS... WHY NOT SEND IT TO A CHI-CARGOAN?...

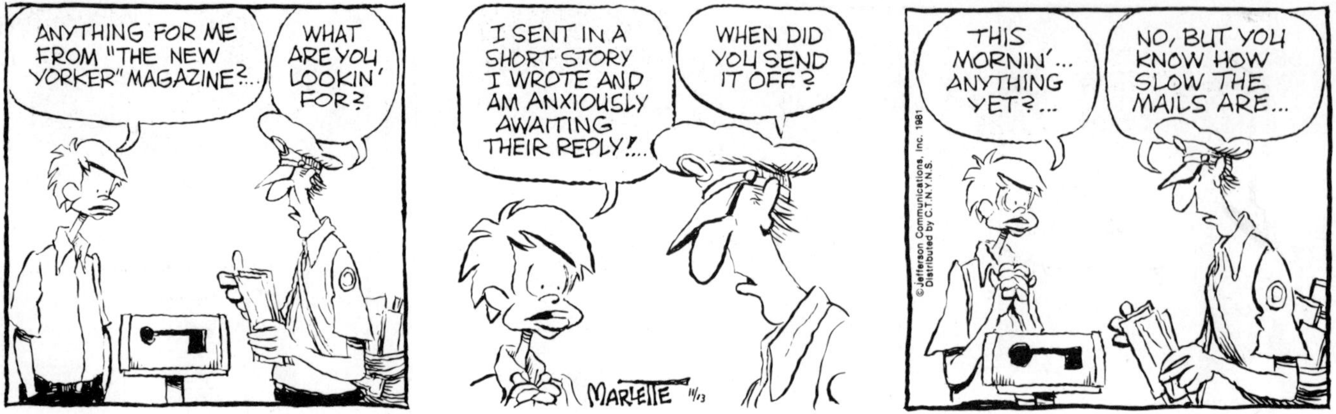
ANYTHING FOR ME FROM "THE NEW YORKER" MAGAZINE?...
WHAT ARE YOU LOOKIN' FOR?
I SENT IN A SHORT STORY I WROTE AND AM ANXIOUSLY AWAITING THEIR REPLY!...
WHEN DID YOU SEND IT OFF?
MARLETTE 11/13
THIS MORNIN'... ANYTHING YET?...
NO, BUT YOU KNOW HOW SLOW THE MAILS ARE...
© Jefferson Communications, Inc. 1981
Distributed by C.T.N.Y.N.S.

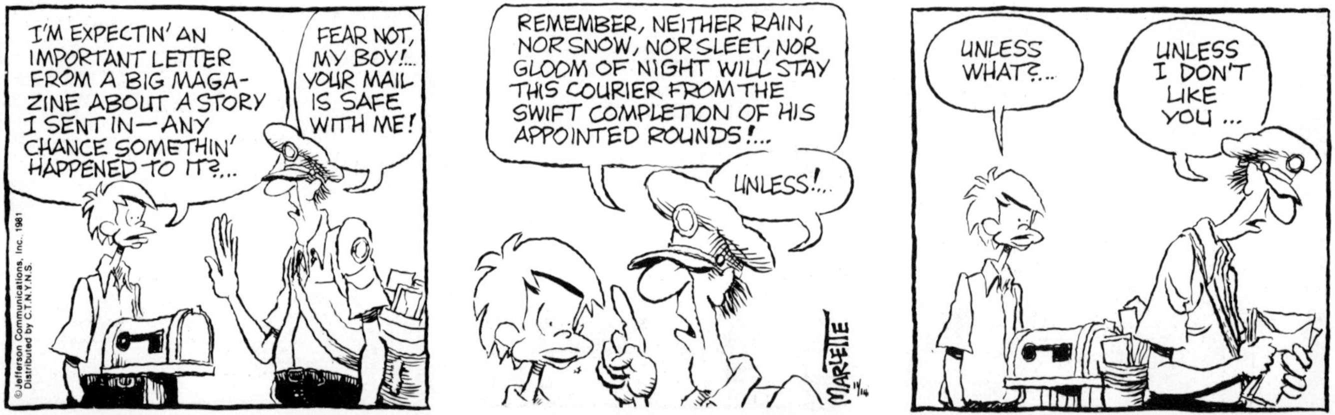
I'M EXPECTIN' AN IMPORTANT LETTER FROM A BIG MAGAZINE ABOUT A STORY I SENT IN—ANY CHANCE SOMETHIN' HAPPENED TO IT?...
FEAR NOT, MY BOY!... YOUR MAIL IS SAFE WITH ME!
© Jefferson Communications, Inc. 1981
Distributed by C.T.N.Y.N.S.
REMEMBER, NEITHER RAIN, NOR SNOW, NOR SLEET, NOR GLOOM OF NIGHT WILL STAY THIS COURIER FROM THE SWIFT COMPLETION OF HIS APPOINTED ROUNDS!...
UNLESS!...
MARLETTE 11/14
UNLESS WHAT?...
UNLESS I DON'T LIKE YOU...

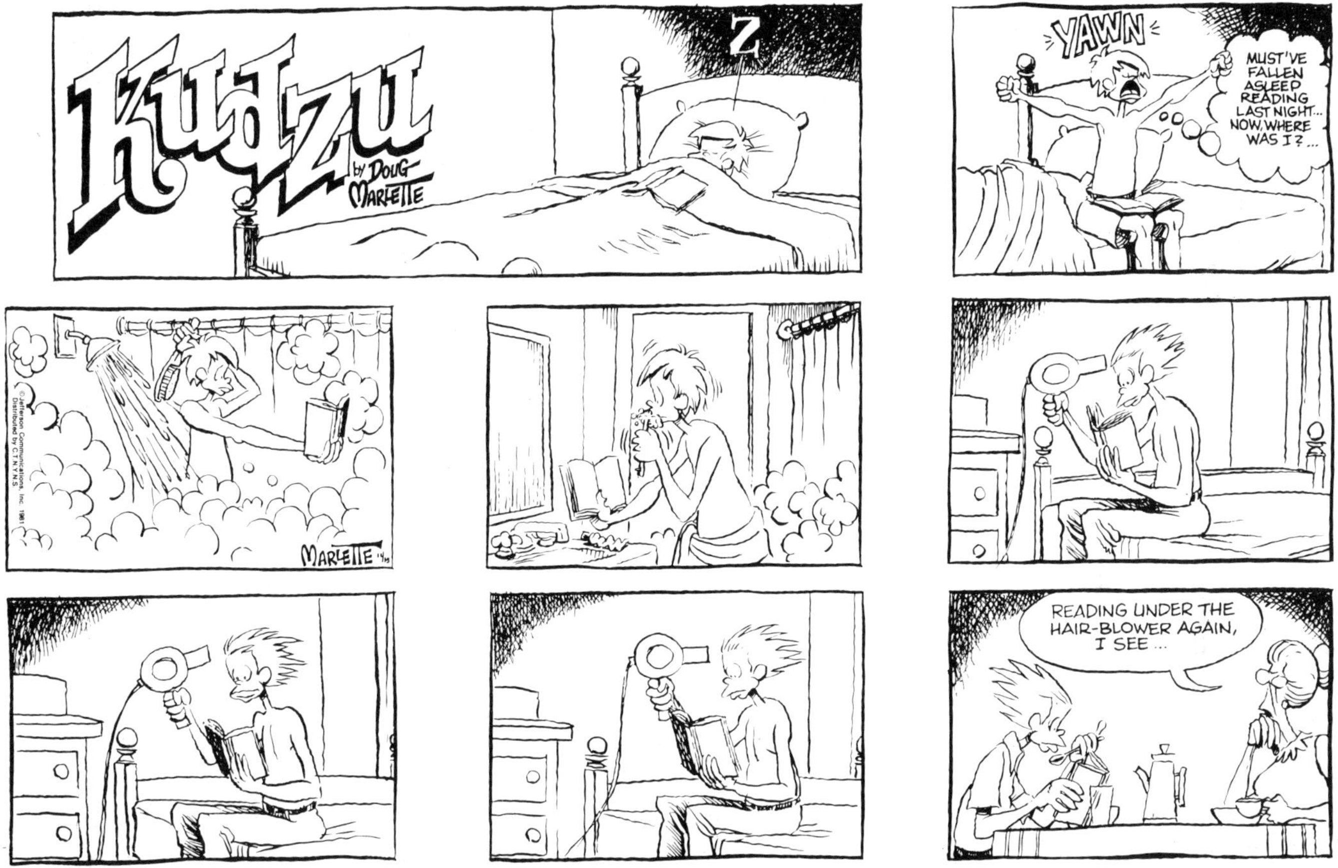
Kudzu
by DOUG MARLETTE
Z
YAWN
MUST'VE FALLEN ASLEEP READING LAST NIGHT... NOW, WHERE WAS I?...
© Jefferson Communications, Inc. 1981
Distributed by C.T.N.Y.N.S.
MARLETTE
READING UNDER THE HAIR-BLOWER AGAIN, I SEE ...

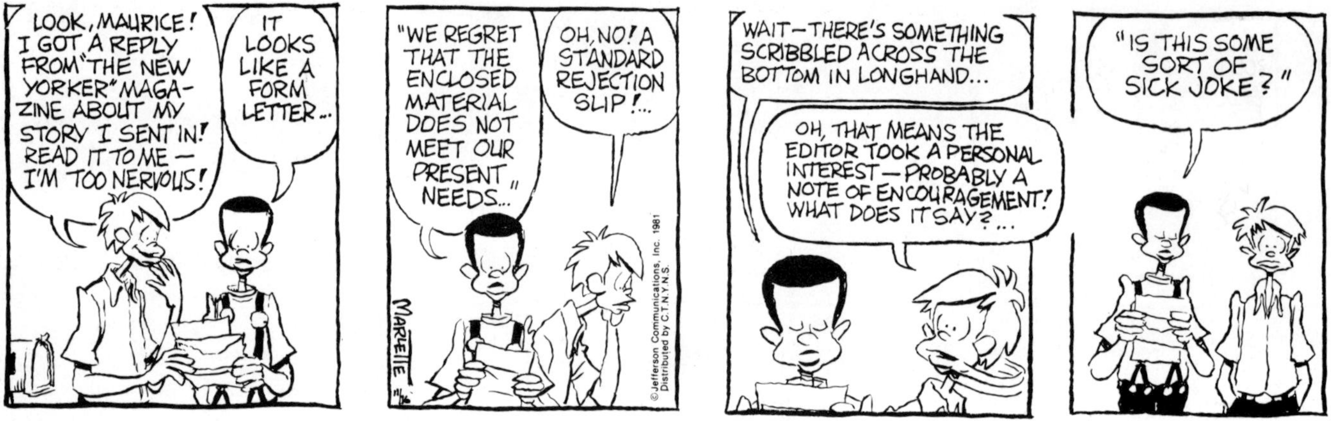
LOOK, MAURICE! I GOT A REPLY FROM "THE NEW YORKER" MAGAZINE ABOUT MY STORY I SENT IN! READ IT TO ME — I'M TOO NERVOUS!
IT LOOKS LIKE A FORM LETTER...
"WE REGRET THAT THE ENCLOSED MATERIAL DOES NOT MEET OUR PRESENT NEEDS..."
OH, NO! A STANDARD REJECTION SLIP!...
MARLETTE 11/16
© Jefferson Communications, Inc. 1981
Distributed by C.T.N.Y.N.S.
WAIT—THERE'S SOMETHING SCRIBBLED ACROSS THE BOTTOM IN LONGHAND...
OH, THAT MEANS THE EDITOR TOOK A PERSONAL INTEREST—PROBABLY A NOTE OF ENCOURAGEMENT! WHAT DOES IT SAY?...
"IS THIS SOME SORT OF SICK JOKE?"

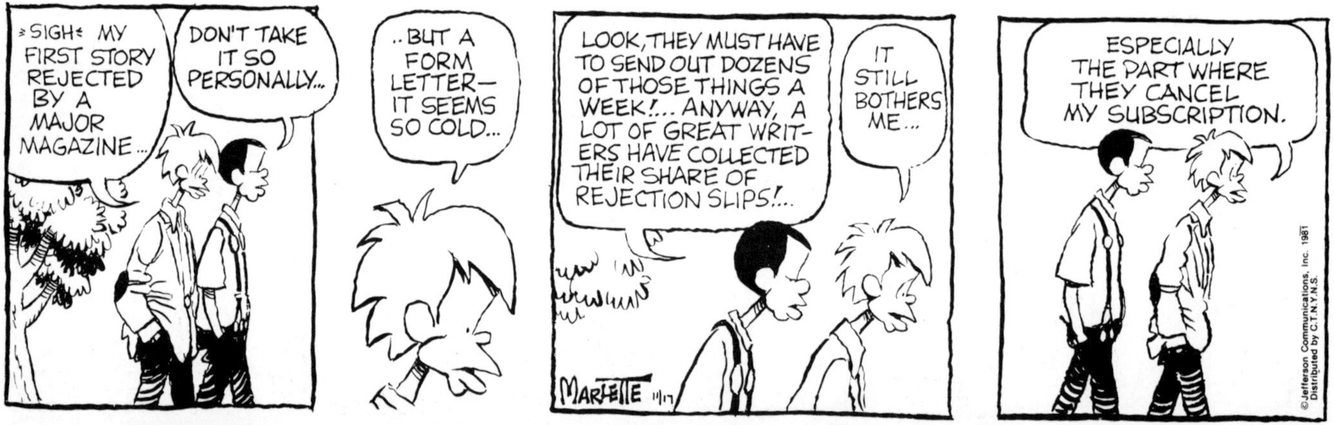
≥SIGH≤ MY FIRST STORY REJECTED BY A MAJOR MAGAZINE...
DON'T TAKE IT SO PERSONALLY...
..BUT A FORM LETTER—IT SEEMS SO COLD...
LOOK, THEY MUST HAVE TO SEND OUT DOZENS OF THOSE THINGS A WEEK!... ANYWAY, A LOT OF GREAT WRITERS HAVE COLLECTED THEIR SHARE OF REJECTION SLIPS!...
IT STILL BOTHERS ME...
MARLETTE 11/17
ESPECIALLY THE PART WHERE THEY CANCEL MY SUBSCRIPTION.
© Jefferson Communications, Inc. 1981
Distributed by C.T.N.Y.N.S.

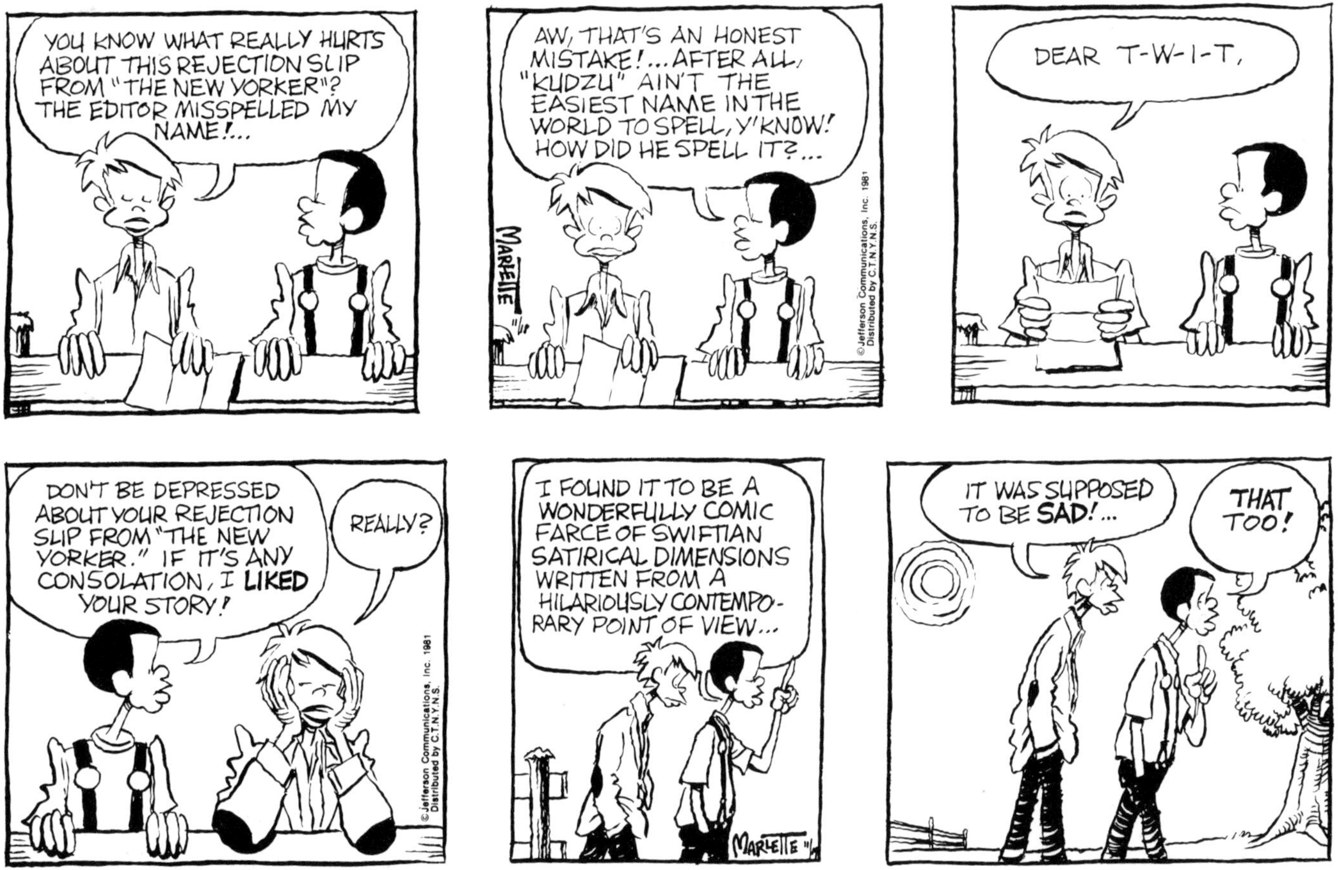
YOU KNOW WHAT REALLY HURTS ABOUT THIS REJECTION SLIP FROM "THE NEW YORKER"? THE EDITOR MISSPELLED MY NAME!...
AW, THAT'S AN HONEST MISTAKE!... AFTER ALL, "KUDZU" AIN'T THE EASIEST NAME IN THE WORLD TO SPELL, Y'KNOW! HOW DID HE SPELL IT?...
MARLETTE
© Jefferson Communications, Inc. 1981 Distributed by C.T.N.Y.N.S.
DEAR T-W-I-T,
DON'T BE DEPRESSED ABOUT YOUR REJECTION SLIP FROM "THE NEW YORKER." IF IT'S ANY CONSOLATION, I **LIKED** YOUR STORY!
REALLY?
© Jefferson Communications, Inc. 1981 Distributed by C.T.N.Y.N.S.
I FOUND IT TO BE A WONDERFULLY COMIC FARCE OF SWIFTIAN SATIRICAL DIMENSIONS WRITTEN FROM A HILARIOUSLY CONTEMPORARY POINT OF VIEW...
MARLETTE
IT WAS SUPPOSED TO BE **SAD**!...
THAT TOO!

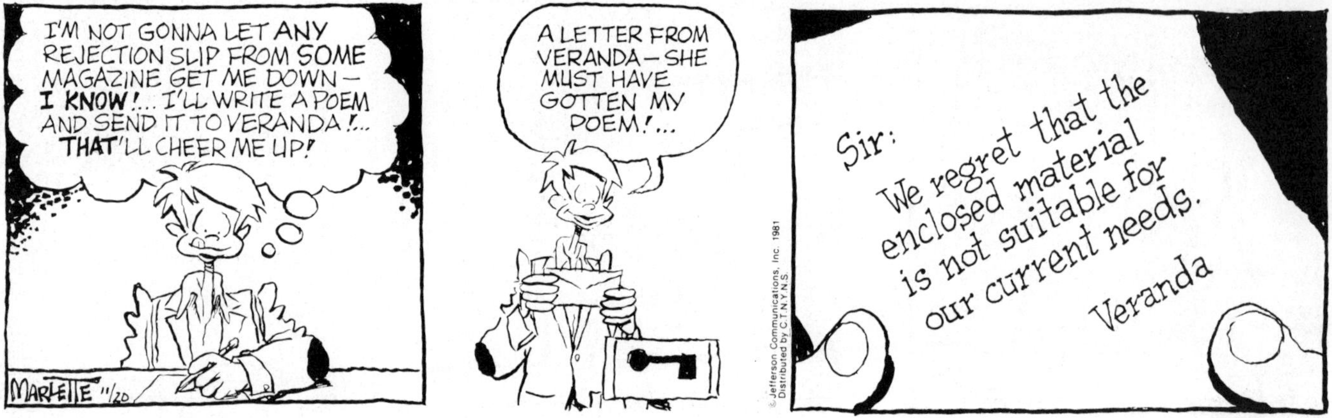
I'M NOT GONNA LET ANY REJECTION SLIP FROM SOME MAGAZINE GET ME DOWN— I KNOW!... I'LL WRITE A POEM AND SEND IT TO VERANDA!... THAT'LL CHEER ME UP!
MARLETTE 11/20
A LETTER FROM VERANDA—SHE MUST HAVE GOTTEN MY POEM!...
Sir:
We regret that the enclosed material is not suitable for our current needs.
Veranda

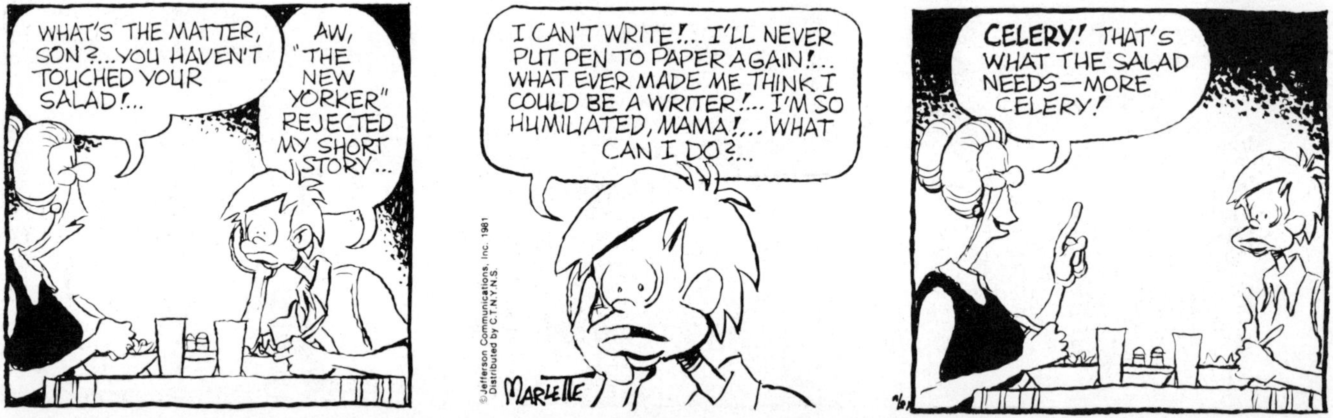
WHAT'S THE MATTER, SON?...YOU HAVEN'T TOUCHED YOUR SALAD!...
AW, "THE NEW YORKER" REJECTED MY SHORT STORY...
I CAN'T WRITE!... I'LL NEVER PUT PEN TO PAPER AGAIN!... WHAT EVER MADE ME THINK I COULD BE A WRITER!... I'M SO HUMILIATED, MAMA!... WHAT CAN I DO?...
MARLETTE
CELERY! THAT'S WHAT THE SALAD NEEDS—MORE CELERY!

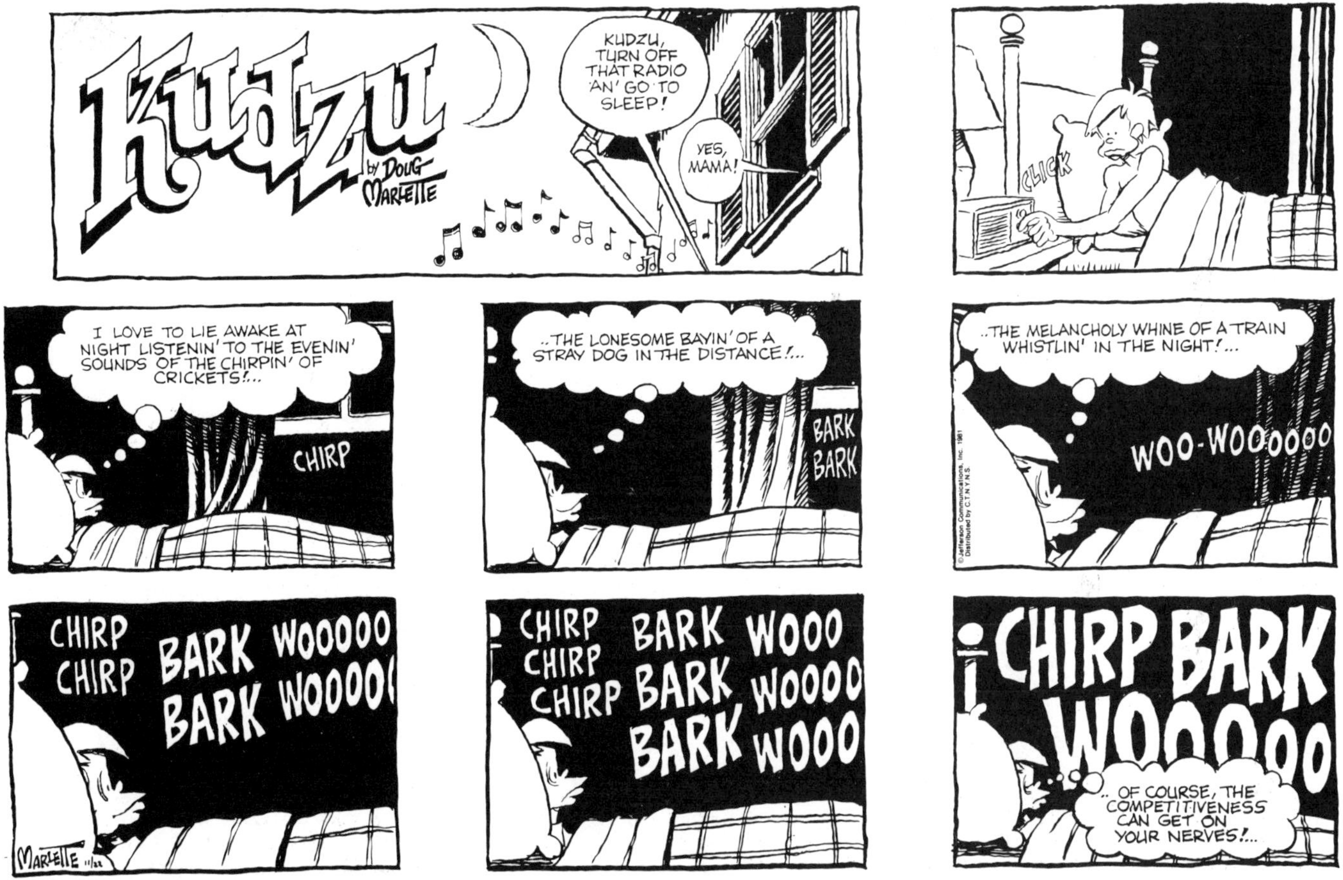
KUDZU
by DOUG MARLETTE
KUDZU, TURN OFF THAT RADIO AN' GO TO SLEEP!
YES, MAMA!
CLICK
I LOVE TO LIE AWAKE AT NIGHT LISTENIN' TO THE EVENIN' SOUNDS OF THE CHIRPIN' OF CRICKETS!...
CHIRP
..THE LONESOME BAYIN' OF A STRAY DOG IN THE DISTANCE!...
BARK BARK
..THE MELANCHOLY WHINE OF A TRAIN WHISTLIN' IN THE NIGHT!...
WOO-WOOOOOO
©Jefferson Communications, Inc. 1981
Distributed by C.T.N.Y.N.S.
CHIRP CHIRP
BARK BARK
WOOOOO WOOOO
MARLETTE 11/22
CHIRP CHIRP CHIRP
BARK BARK BARK
WOOO WOOOO WOOO
CHIRP BARK WOOOOO
..OF COURSE, THE COMPETITIVENESS CAN GET ON YOUR NERVES!...

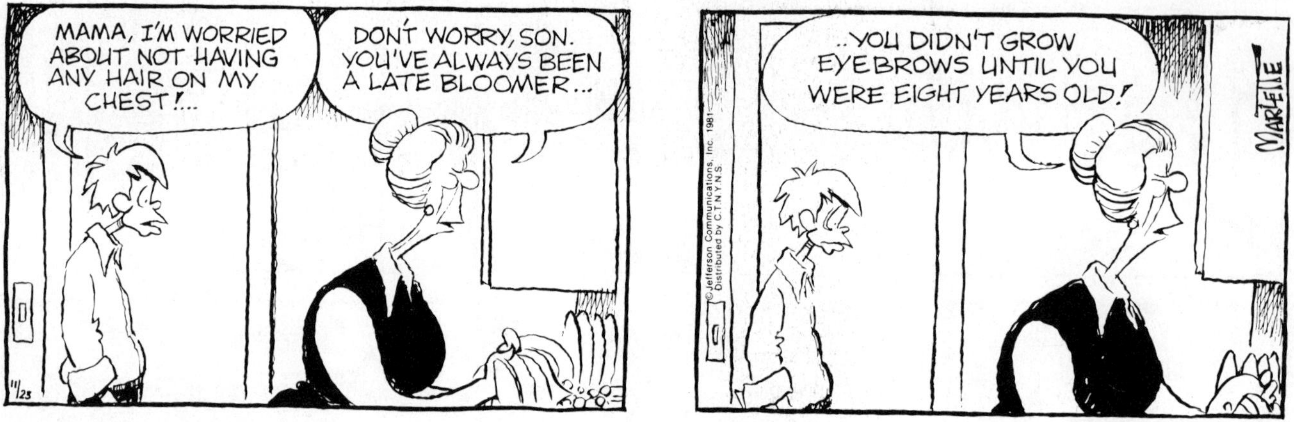
MAMA, I'M WORRIED ABOUT NOT HAVING ANY HAIR ON MY CHEST!...
DON'T WORRY, SON. YOU'VE ALWAYS BEEN A LATE BLOOMER...
..YOU DIDN'T GROW EYEBROWS UNTIL YOU WERE EIGHT YEARS OLD!
11/23
MARLETTE
© Jefferson Communications, Inc. 1981
Distributed by C.T.N.Y.N.S.

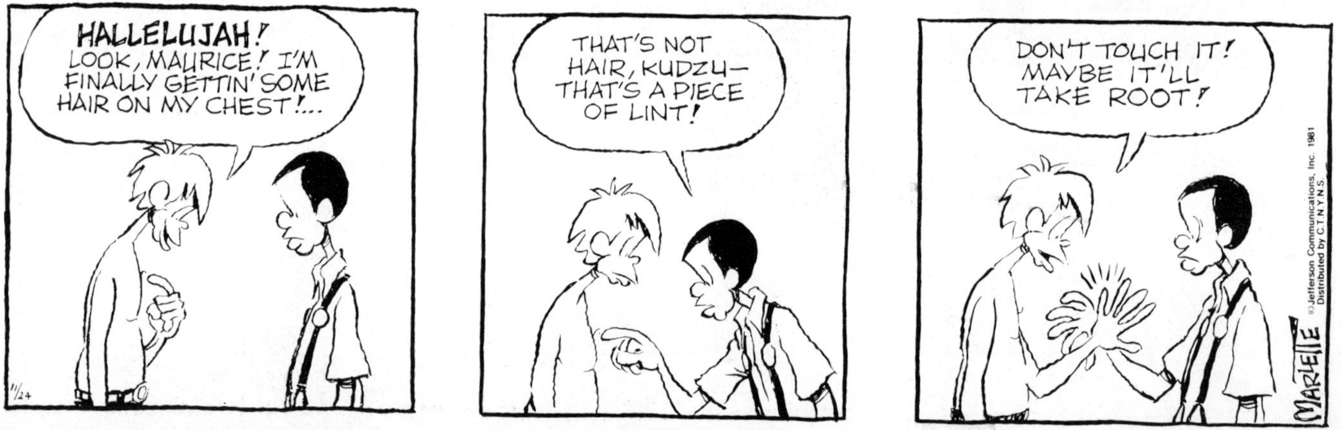
HALLELUJAH! LOOK, MAURICE! I'M FINALLY GETTIN' SOME HAIR ON MY CHEST!...
THAT'S NOT HAIR, KUDZU— THAT'S A PIECE OF LINT!
DON'T TOUCH IT! MAYBE IT'LL TAKE ROOT!
11/24
MARLETTE
© Jefferson Communications, Inc. 1981
Distributed by C.T.N.Y.N.S.

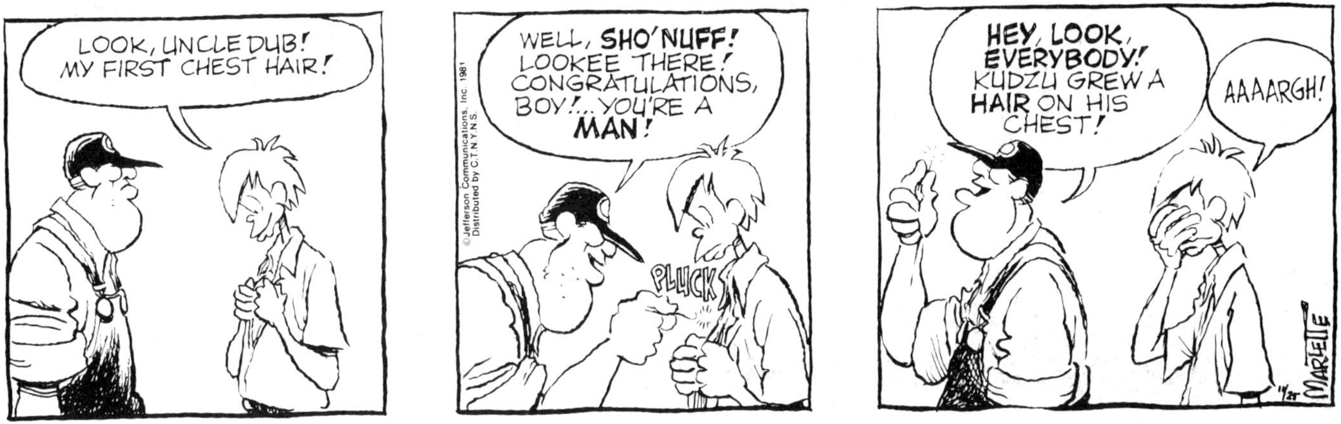
LOOK, UNCLE DUB! MY FIRST CHEST HAIR!
WELL, SHO' NUFF! LOOKEE THERE! CONGRATULATIONS, BOY!... YOU'RE A MAN!
PLUCK
©Jefferson Communications, Inc. 1981
Distributed by C.T.N.Y.N.S.
HEY, LOOK, EVERYBODY! KUDZU GREW A HAIR ON HIS CHEST!
AAAARGH!
MARLETTE
11/25

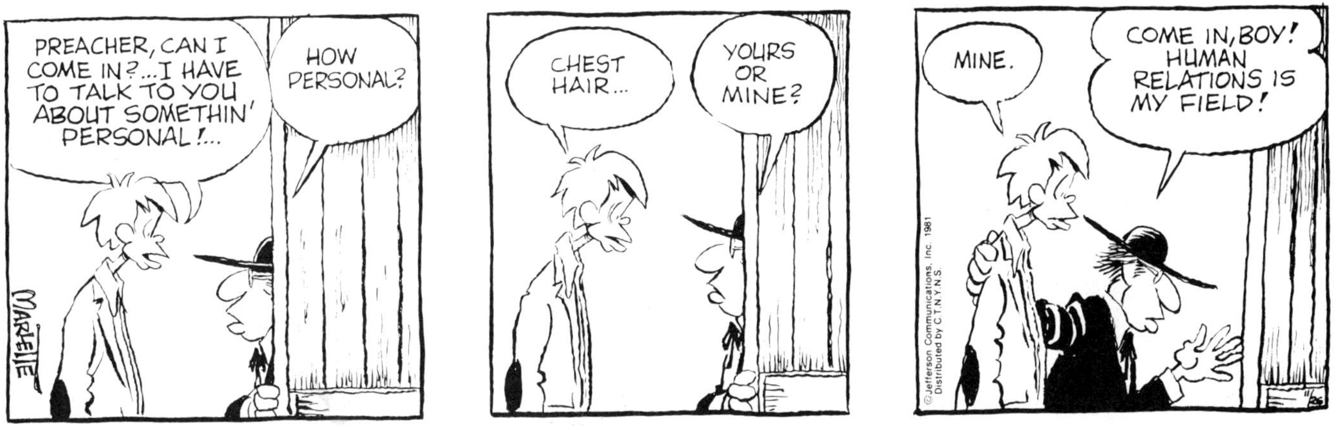
PREACHER, CAN I COME IN?... I HAVE TO TALK TO YOU ABOUT SOMETHIN' PERSONAL!...
HOW PERSONAL?
MARLETTE
CHEST HAIR...
YOURS OR MINE?
MINE.
COME IN, BOY! HUMAN RELATIONS IS MY FIELD!
©Jefferson Communications, Inc. 1981
Distributed by C.T.N.Y.N.S.
11/26

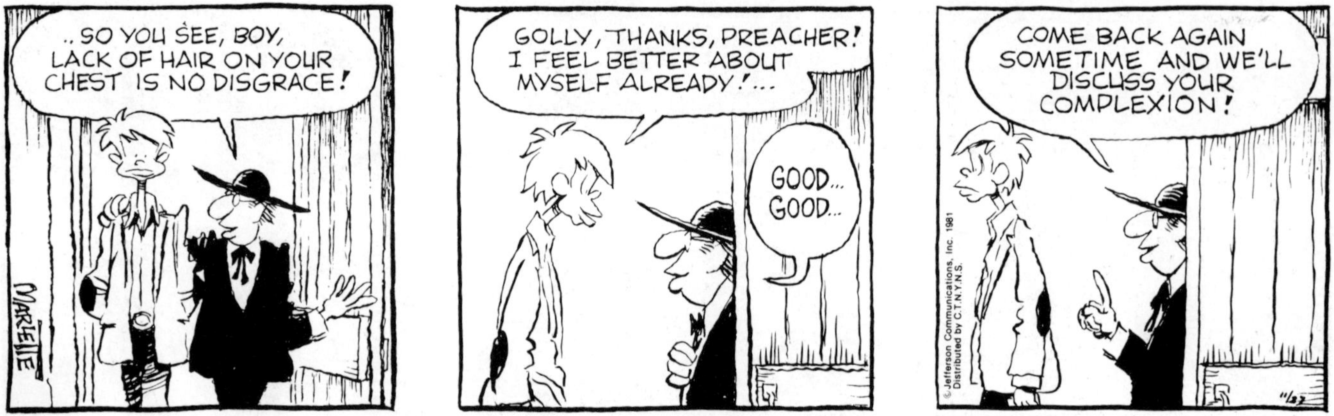
..SO YOU SEE, BOY, LACK OF HAIR ON YOUR CHEST IS NO DISGRACE!
MARLETTE
GOLLY, THANKS, PREACHER! I FEEL BETTER ABOUT MYSELF ALREADY!...
GOOD... GOOD...
COME BACK AGAIN SOMETIME AND WE'LL DISCUSS YOUR COMPLEXION!
© Jefferson Communications, Inc. 1981
Distributed by C.T.N.Y.N.S.
11/27

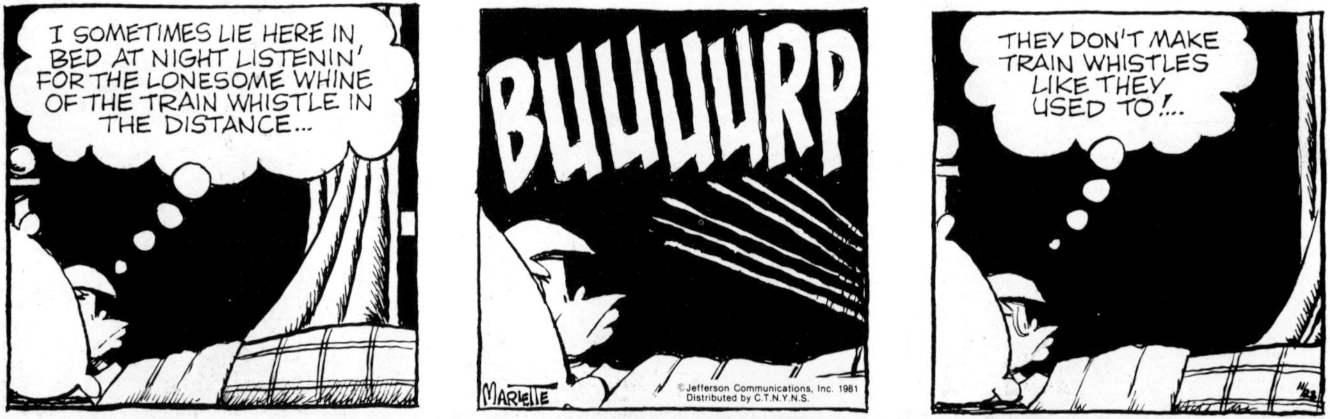
I SOMETIMES LIE HERE IN BED AT NIGHT LISTENIN' FOR THE LONESOME WHINE OF THE TRAIN WHISTLE IN THE DISTANCE...
BUUUURP
MARLETTE
© Jefferson Communications, Inc. 1981
Distributed by C.T.N.Y.N.S.
THEY DON'T MAKE TRAIN WHISTLES LIKE THEY USED TO!...

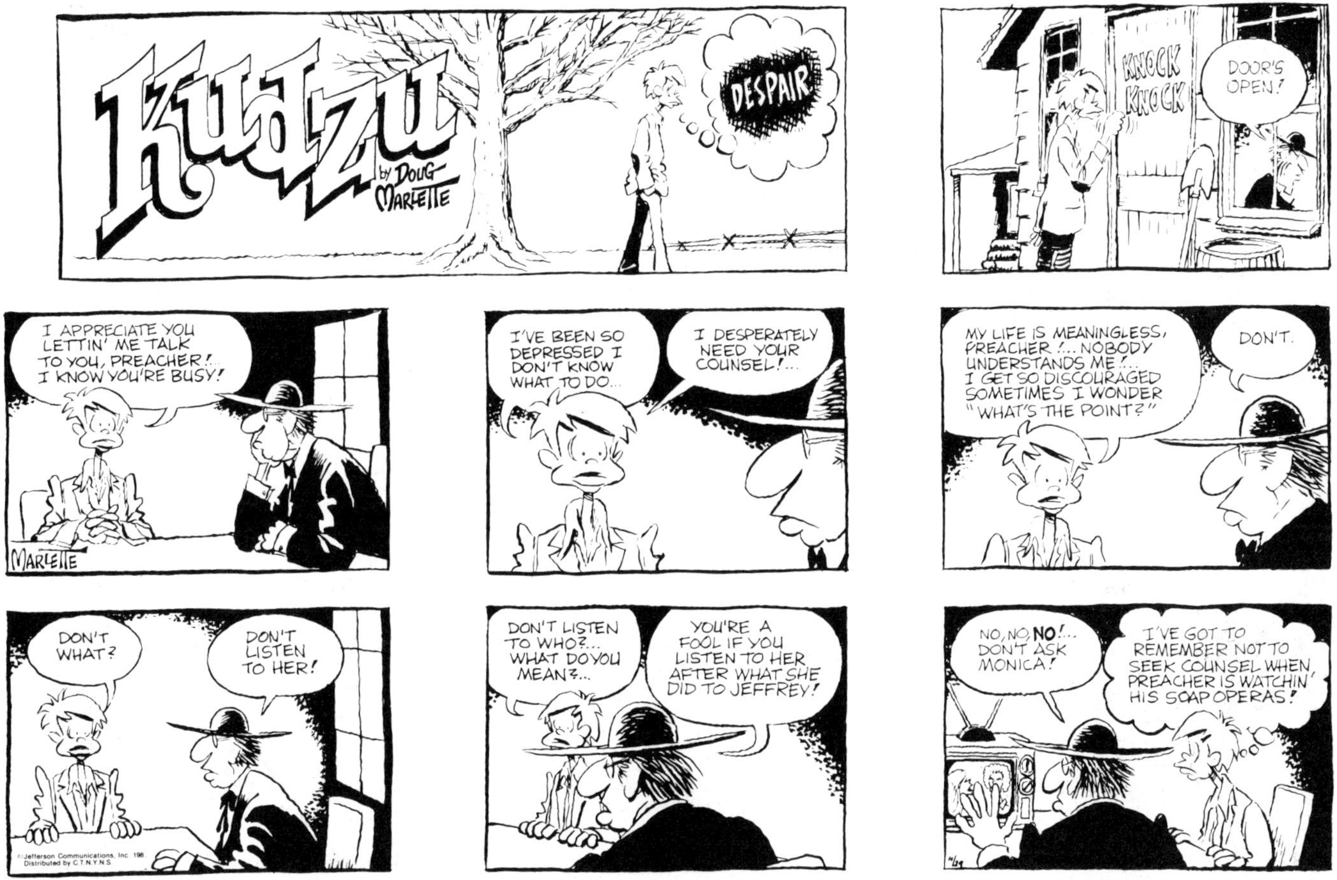
Kudzu
by Doug Marlette
DESPAIR
KNOCK KNOCK
DOOR'S OPEN!
I APPRECIATE YOU LETTIN' ME TALK TO YOU, PREACHER!... I KNOW YOU'RE BUSY!
MARLETTE
I'VE BEEN SO DEPRESSED I DON'T KNOW WHAT TO DO...
I DESPERATELY NEED YOUR COUNSEL!...
MY LIFE IS MEANINGLESS, PREACHER!... NOBODY UNDERSTANDS ME!... I GET SO DISCOURAGED SOMETIMES I WONDER "WHAT'S THE POINT?"
DON'T.
DON'T WHAT?
DON'T LISTEN TO HER!
DON'T LISTEN TO WHO?... WHAT DO YOU MEAN?...
YOU'RE A FOOL IF YOU LISTEN TO HER AFTER WHAT SHE DID TO JEFFREY!
NO, NO, NO!... DON'T ASK MONICA!
I'VE GOT TO REMEMBER NOT TO SEEK COUNSEL WHEN PREACHER IS WATCHIN' HIS SOAP OPERAS!
© Jefferson Communications, Inc. 198
Distributed by C.T.N.Y.N.S.

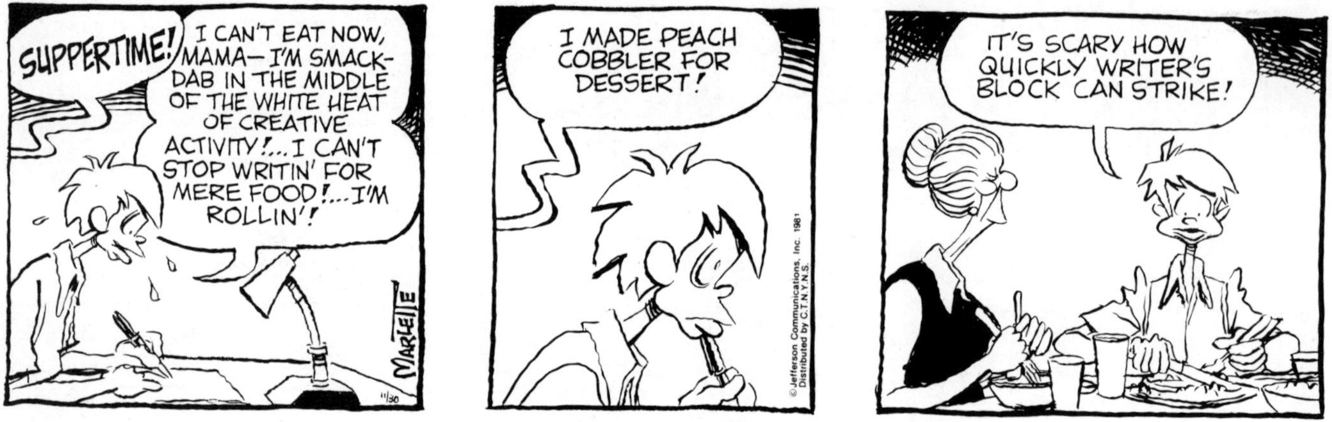
SUPPERTIME!
I CAN'T EAT NOW, MAMA— I'M SMACK-DAB IN THE MIDDLE OF THE WHITE HEAT OF CREATIVE ACTIVITY!... I CAN'T STOP WRITIN' FOR MERE FOOD!... I'M ROLLIN'!
MARLETTE
11/30
I MADE PEACH COBBLER FOR DESSERT!
© Jefferson Communications, Inc. 1981
Distributed by C.T.N.Y.N.S.
IT'S SCARY HOW QUICKLY WRITER'S BLOCK CAN STRIKE!

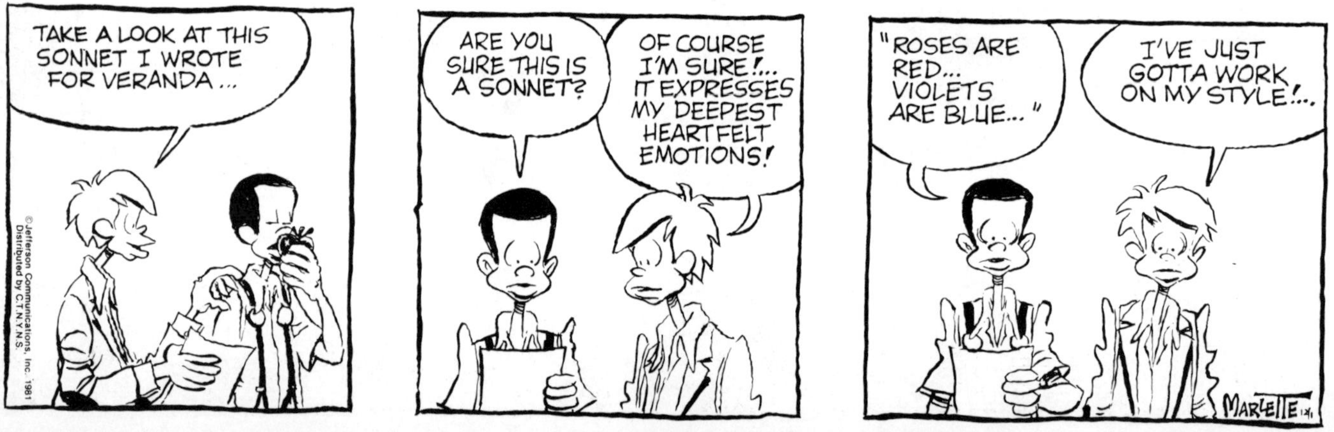
TAKE A LOOK AT THIS SONNET I WROTE FOR VERANDA ...
© Jefferson Communications, Inc. 1981
Distributed by C.T.N.Y.N.S.
ARE YOU SURE THIS IS A SONNET?
OF COURSE I'M SURE!... IT EXPRESSES MY DEEPEST HEARTFELT EMOTIONS!
"ROSES ARE RED... VIOLETS ARE BLUE..."
I'VE JUST GOTTA WORK ON MY STYLE!...
MARLETTE 12/1

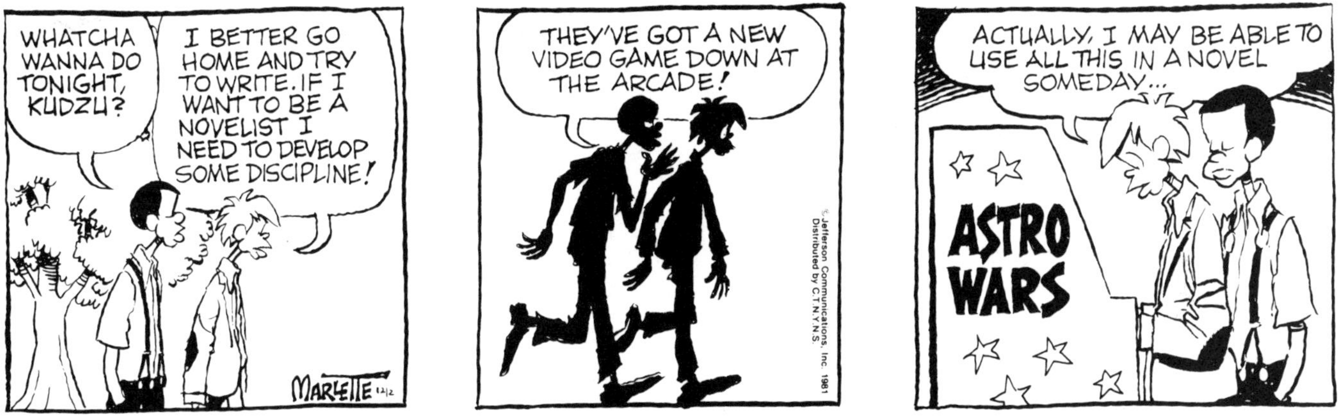
WHATCHA WANNA DO TONIGHT, KUDZU?
I BETTER GO HOME AND TRY TO WRITE. IF I WANT TO BE A NOVELIST I NEED TO DEVELOP SOME DISCIPLINE!
MARLETTE 12/2
THEY'VE GOT A NEW VIDEO GAME DOWN AT THE ARCADE!
©Jefferson Communications, Inc. 1981 Distributed by C.T.N.Y.N.S.
ACTUALLY, I MAY BE ABLE TO USE ALL THIS IN A NOVEL SOMEDAY...
ASTRO WARS

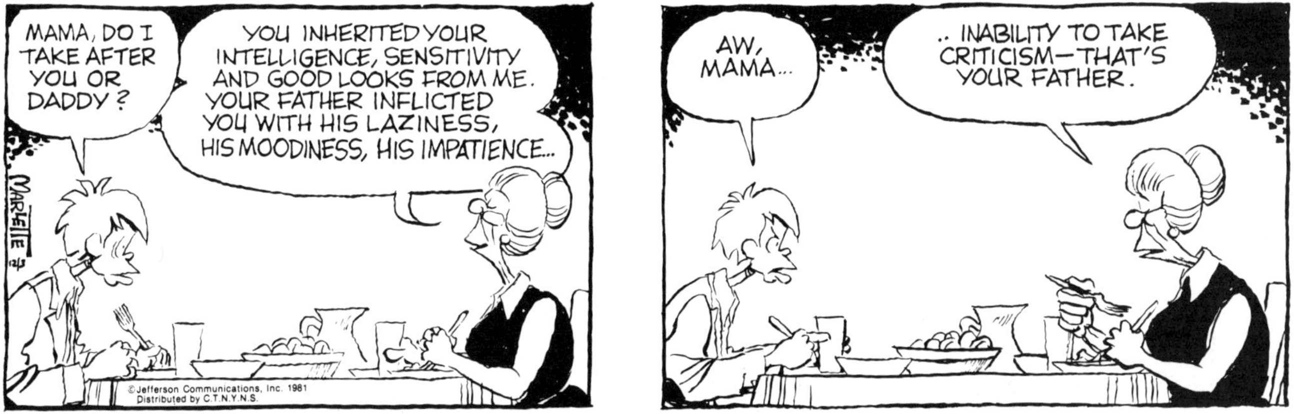
MAMA, DO I TAKE AFTER YOU OR DADDY?
YOU INHERITED YOUR INTELLIGENCE, SENSITIVITY AND GOOD LOOKS FROM ME. YOUR FATHER INFLICTED YOU WITH HIS LAZINESS, HIS MOODINESS, HIS IMPATIENCE...
MARLETTE 12/3
©Jefferson Communications, Inc. 1981 Distributed by C.T.N.Y.N.S.
AW, MAMA...
.. INABILITY TO TAKE CRITICISM—THAT'S YOUR FATHER.

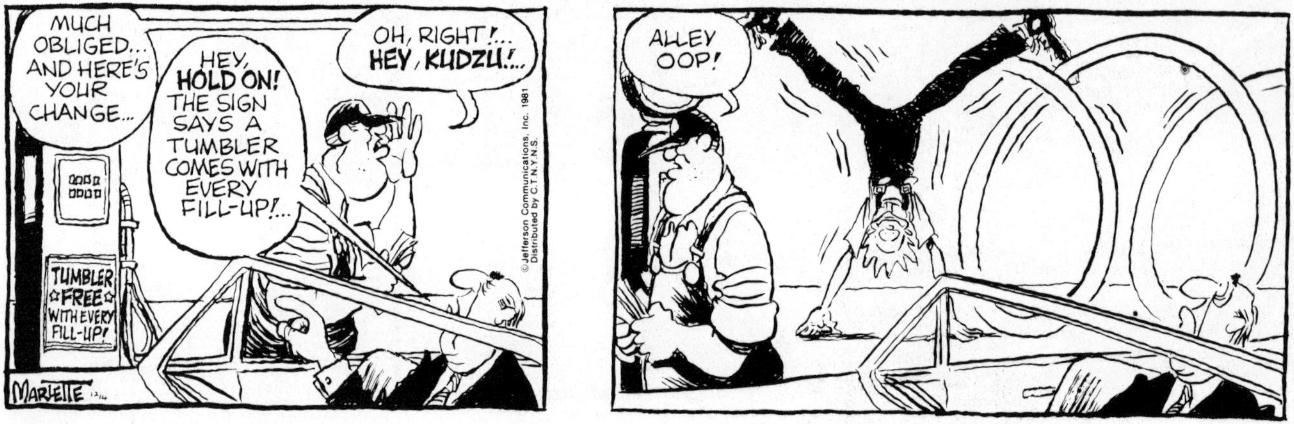
MUCH OBLIGED... AND HERE'S YOUR CHANGE...
HEY, **HOLD ON!** THE SIGN SAYS A TUMBLER COMES WITH EVERY FILL-UP!...
OH, RIGHT!... **HEY, KUDZU!...**
TUMBLER FREE WITH EVERY FILL-UP!
ALLEY OOP!
MARLETTE 12/14
©Jefferson Communications, Inc. 1981
Distributed by C.T.N.Y.N.S.

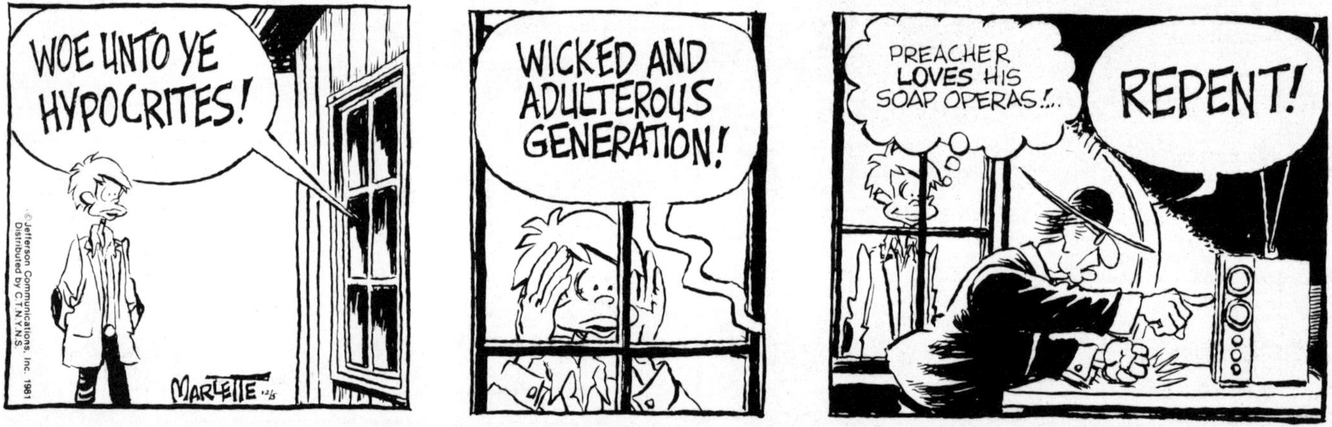
WOE UNTO YE HYPOCRITES!
WICKED AND ADULTEROUS GENERATION!
PREACHER **LOVES** HIS SOAP OPERAS!...
REPENT!
MARLETTE 12/15
©Jefferson Communications, Inc. 1981
Distributed by C.T.N.Y.N.S.

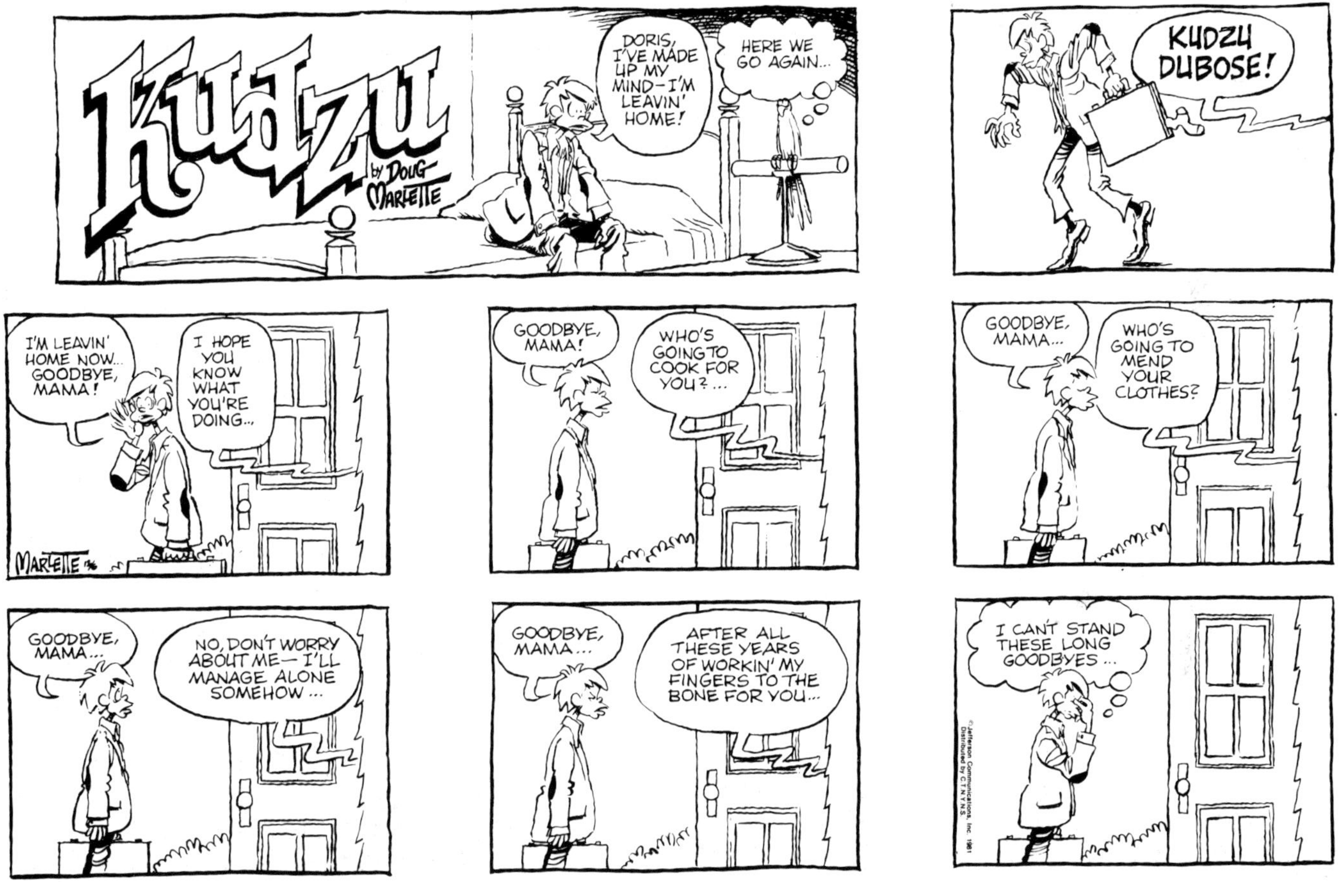
Kudzu
by DOUG MARLETTE
DORIS, I'VE MADE UP MY MIND—I'M LEAVIN' HOME!
HERE WE GO AGAIN...
KUDZU DUBOSE!
I'M LEAVIN' HOME NOW... GOODBYE, MAMA!
I HOPE YOU KNOW WHAT YOU'RE DOING...
MARLETTE
GOODBYE, MAMA!
WHO'S GOING TO COOK FOR YOU?...
GOODBYE, MAMA...
WHO'S GOING TO MEND YOUR CLOTHES?
GOODBYE, MAMA...
NO, DON'T WORRY ABOUT ME— I'LL MANAGE ALONE SOMEHOW...
GOODBYE, MAMA...
AFTER ALL THESE YEARS OF WORKIN' MY FINGERS TO THE BONE FOR YOU...
I CAN'T STAND THESE LONG GOODBYES...
©Jefferson Communications, Inc. 1981
Distributed by C.T.N.Y.N.S.

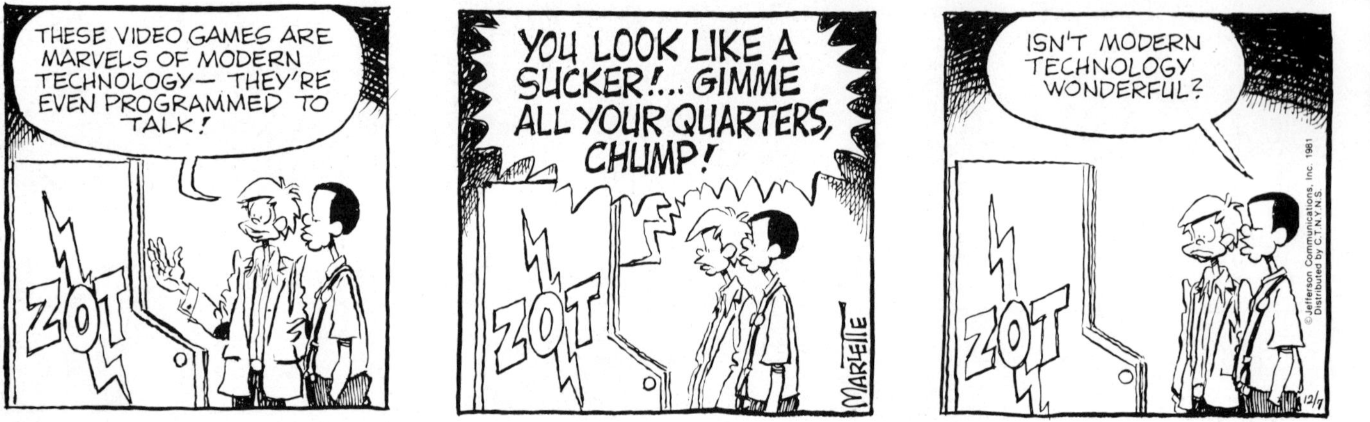
THESE VIDEO GAMES ARE MARVELS OF MODERN TECHNOLOGY— THEY'RE EVEN PROGRAMMED TO TALK!
ZOT
YOU LOOK LIKE A SUCKER!... GIMME ALL YOUR QUARTERS, CHUMP!
ZOT
MARLETTE
ISN'T MODERN TECHNOLOGY WONDERFUL?
ZOT
© Jefferson Communications, Inc. 1981
Distributed by C.T.N.Y.N.S.
12/7

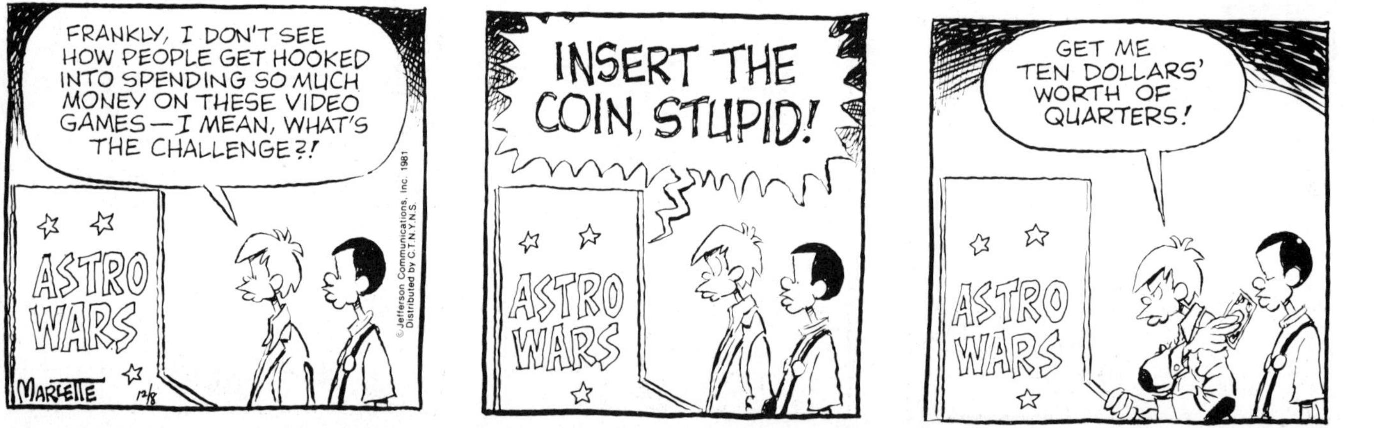
FRANKLY, I DON'T SEE HOW PEOPLE GET HOOKED INTO SPENDING SO MUCH MONEY ON THESE VIDEO GAMES—I MEAN, WHAT'S THE CHALLENGE?!
ASTRO WARS
MARLETTE
12/8
© Jefferson Communications, Inc. 1981
Distributed by C.T.N.Y.N.S.
INSERT THE COIN, STUPID!
ASTRO WARS
GET ME TEN DOLLARS' WORTH OF QUARTERS!
ASTRO WARS

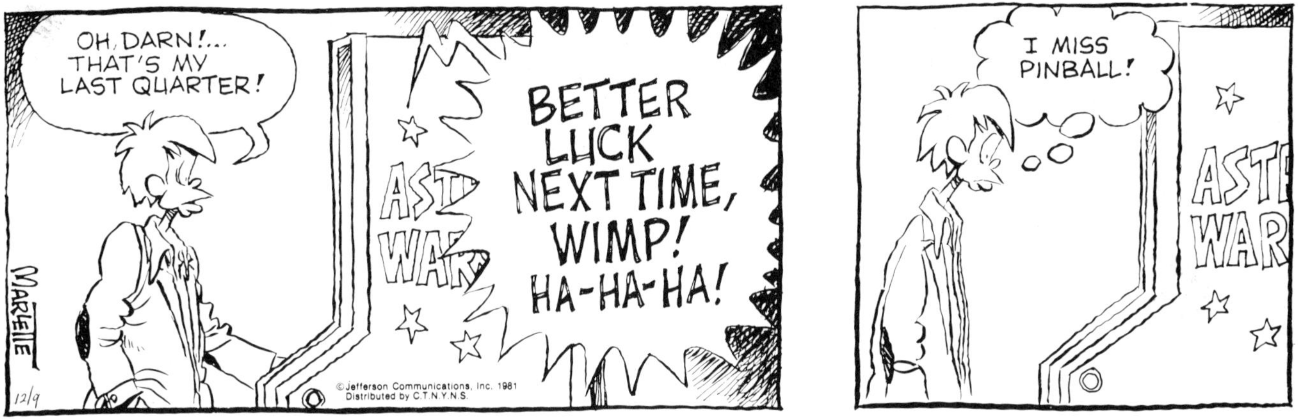

OH, DARN!... THAT'S MY LAST QUARTER!
BETTER LUCK NEXT TIME, WIMP! HA-HA-HA!
ASTE WAR
MARLETTE
12/9
©Jefferson Communications, Inc. 1981 Distributed by C.T.N.Y.N.S.
I MISS PINBALL!

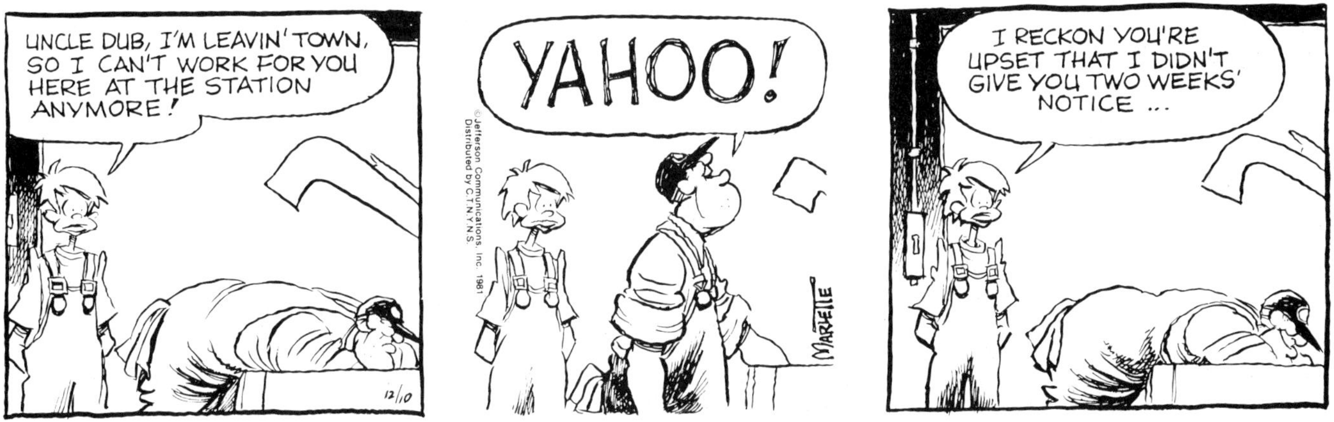

UNCLE DUB, I'M LEAVIN' TOWN, SO I CAN'T WORK FOR YOU HERE AT THE STATION ANYMORE!
12/10
YAHOO!
©Jefferson Communications, Inc. 1981 Distributed by C.T.N.Y.N.S.
MARLETTE
I RECKON YOU'RE UPSET THAT I DIDN'T GIVE YOU TWO WEEKS' NOTICE ...

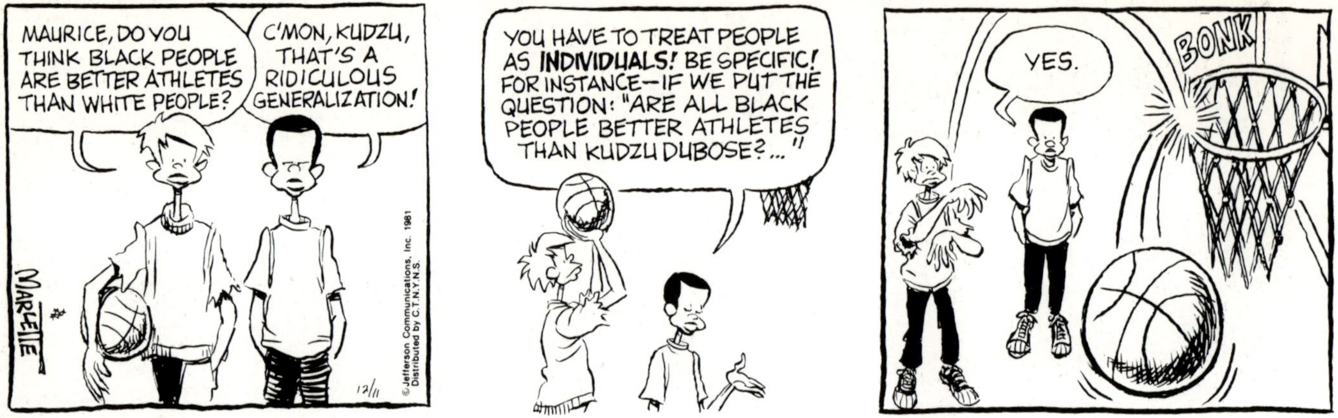
MAURICE, DO YOU THINK BLACK PEOPLE ARE BETTER ATHLETES THAN WHITE PEOPLE?
C'MON, KUDZU, THAT'S A RIDICULOUS GENERALIZATION!
MARLETTE
12/11
©Jefferson Communications, Inc. 1981 Distributed by C.T.N.Y.N.S.
YOU HAVE TO TREAT PEOPLE AS **INDIVIDUALS!** BE SPECIFIC! FOR INSTANCE—IF WE PUT THE QUESTION: "ARE ALL BLACK PEOPLE BETTER ATHLETES THAN KUDZU DUBOSE?..."
YES.
BONK

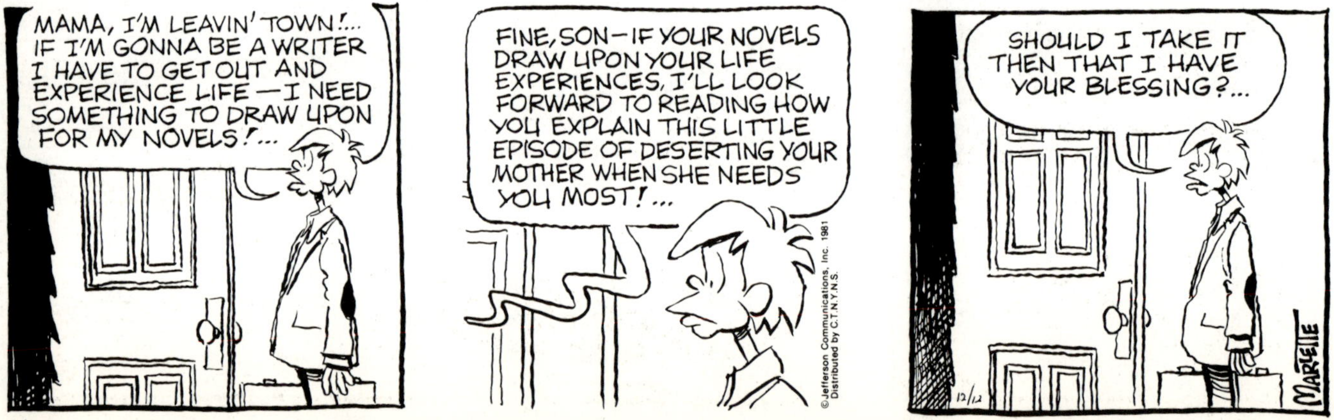
MAMA, I'M LEAVIN' TOWN!... IF I'M GONNA BE A WRITER I HAVE TO GET OUT AND EXPERIENCE LIFE—I NEED SOMETHING TO DRAW UPON FOR MY NOVELS!...
FINE, SON—IF YOUR NOVELS DRAW UPON YOUR LIFE EXPERIENCES, I'LL LOOK FORWARD TO READING HOW YOU EXPLAIN THIS LITTLE EPISODE OF DESERTING YOUR MOTHER WHEN SHE NEEDS YOU MOST!...
©Jefferson Communications, Inc. 1981 Distributed by C.T.N.Y.N.S.
SHOULD I TAKE IT THEN THAT I HAVE YOUR BLESSING?...
12/12
MARLETTE

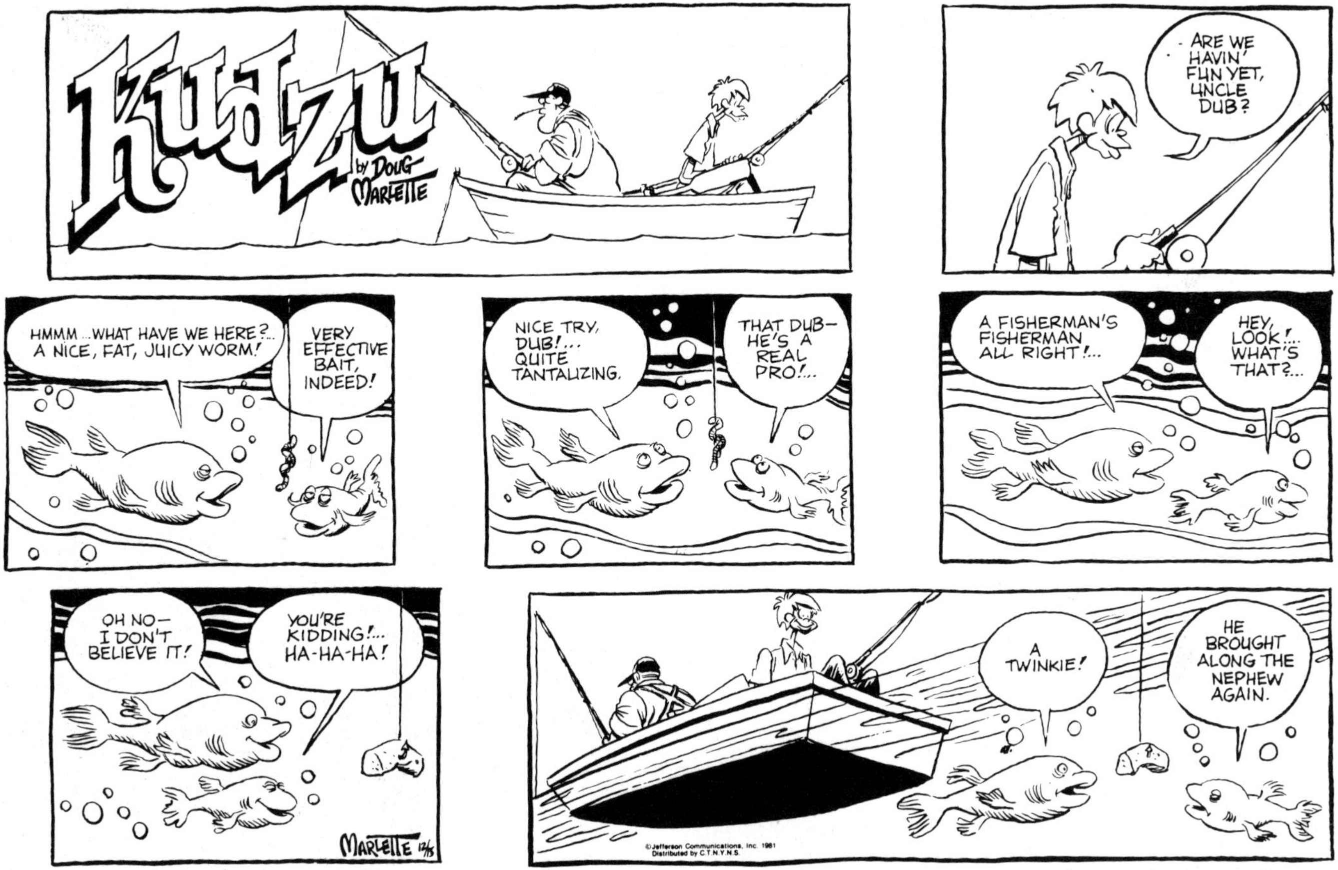
Kudzu
by Doug Marlette
ARE WE HAVIN' FUN YET, UNCLE DUB?
HMMM...WHAT HAVE WE HERE?... A NICE, FAT, JUICY WORM!
VERY EFFECTIVE BAIT, INDEED!
NICE TRY, DUB!... QUITE TANTALIZING.
THAT DUB— HE'S A REAL PRO!...
A FISHERMAN'S FISHERMAN ALL RIGHT!...
HEY, LOOK!... WHAT'S THAT?...
OH NO— I DON'T BELIEVE IT!
YOU'RE KIDDING!... HA-HA-HA!
MARLETTE 12/13
A TWINKIE!
HE BROUGHT ALONG THE NEPHEW AGAIN.
© Jefferson Communications, Inc. 1981
Distributed by C.T.N.Y.N.S.

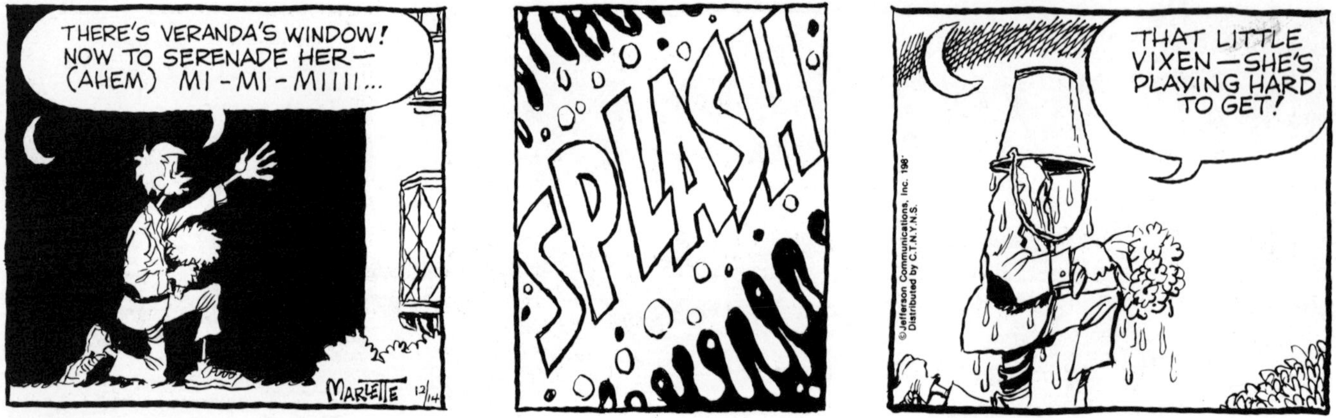
THERE'S VERANDA'S WINDOW! NOW TO SERENADE HER— (AHEM) MI-MI-MIIIII...
MARLETTE 12/14
SPLASH
THAT LITTLE VIXEN—SHE'S PLAYING HARD TO GET!
© Jefferson Communications, Inc. 198
Distributed by C.T.N.Y.N.S.

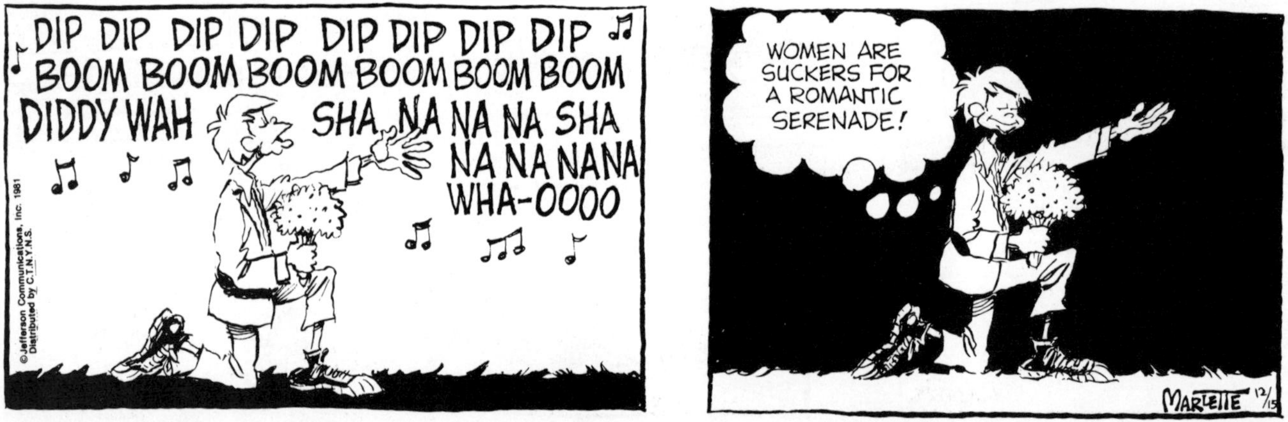
DIP DIP DIP DIP DIP DIP DIP DIP
BOOM BOOM BOOM BOOM BOOM BOOM
DIDDY WAH
SHA NA NA NA SHA NA NA NANA WHA-OOOO
© Jefferson Communications, Inc. 1981
Distributed by C.T.N.Y.N.S.
WOMEN ARE SUCKERS FOR A ROMANTIC SERENADE!
MARLETTE 12/15

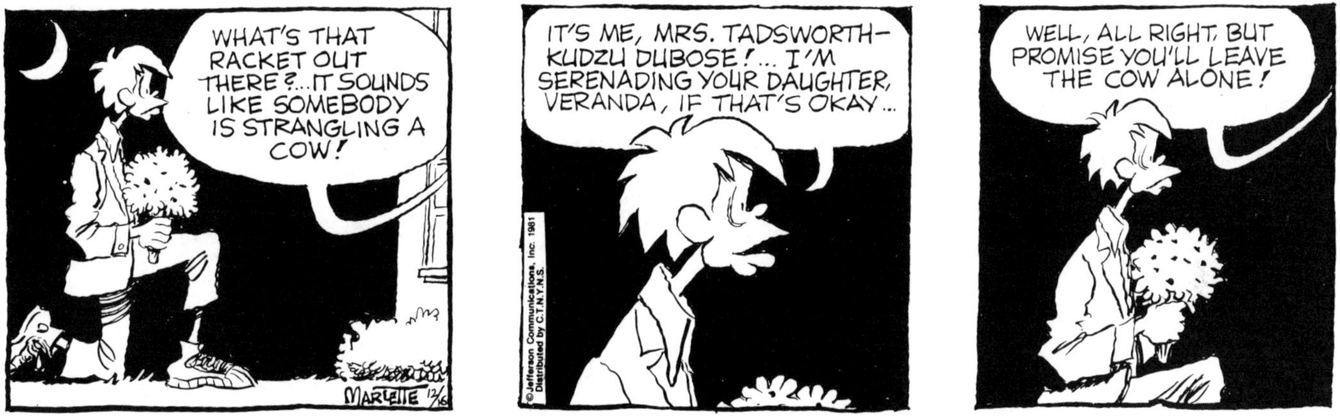
WHAT'S THAT RACKET OUT THERE?...IT SOUNDS LIKE SOMEBODY IS STRANGLING A COW!
MARLETTE 12/16
IT'S ME, MRS. TADSWORTH-KUDZU DUBOSE!... I'M SERENADING YOUR DAUGHTER, VERANDA, IF THAT'S OKAY...
©Jefferson Communications, Inc. 1981
Distributed by C.T.N.Y.N.S.
WELL, ALL RIGHT, BUT PROMISE YOU'LL LEAVE THE COW ALONE!

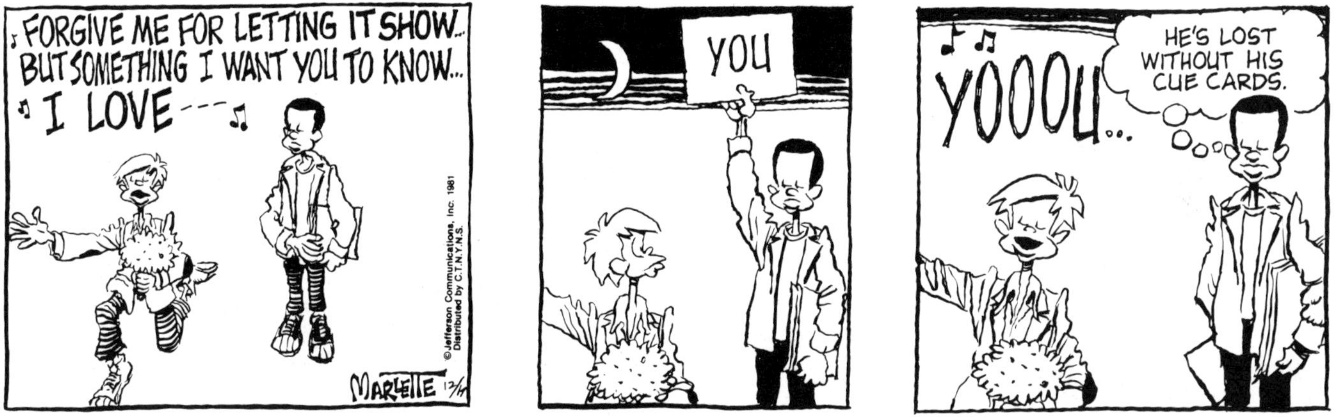
FORGIVE ME FOR LETTING IT SHOW...
BUT SOMETHING I WANT YOU TO KNOW...
I LOVE---
©Jefferson Communications, Inc. 1981
Distributed by C.T.N.Y.N.S.
MARLETTE 12/17
YOU
YOOOU...
HE'S LOST WITHOUT HIS CUE CARDS.

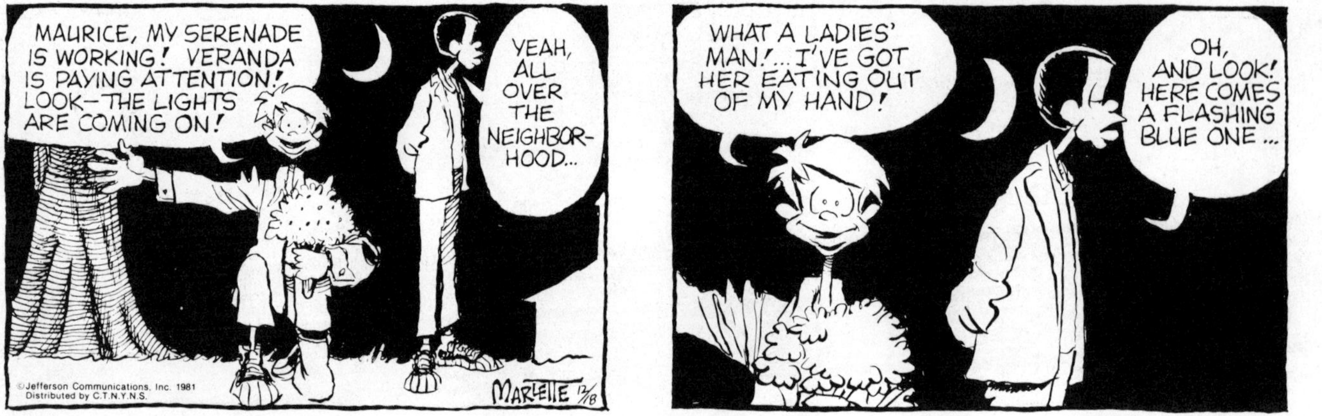
MAURICE, MY SERENADE IS WORKING! VERANDA IS PAYING ATTENTION! LOOK—THE LIGHTS ARE COMING ON!
YEAH, ALL OVER THE NEIGHBOR-HOOD...
©Jefferson Communications, Inc. 1981 Distributed by C.T.N.Y.N.S.
MARLETTE 12/8
WHAT A LADIES' MAN!... I'VE GOT HER EATING OUT OF MY HAND!
OH, AND LOOK! HERE COMES A FLASHING BLUE ONE ...

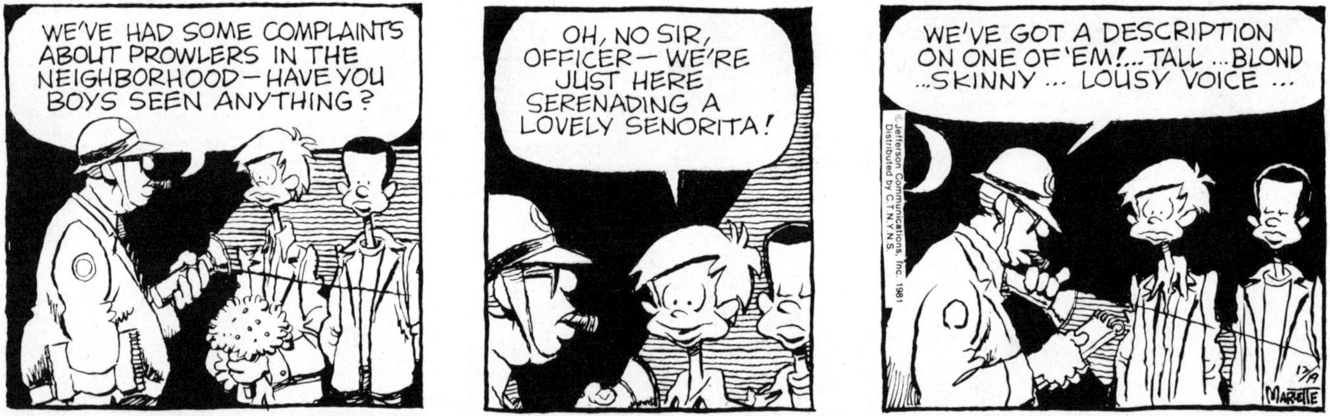
WE'VE HAD SOME COMPLAINTS ABOUT PROWLERS IN THE NEIGHBORHOOD—HAVE YOU BOYS SEEN ANYTHING?
OH, NO SIR, OFFICER— WE'RE JUST HERE SERENADING A LOVELY SENORITA!
WE'VE GOT A DESCRIPTION ON ONE OF 'EM!... TALL ... BLOND ...SKINNY ... LOUSY VOICE ...
© Jefferson Communications, Inc. 1981 Distributed by C.T.N.Y.N.S.
12/9
MARLETTE

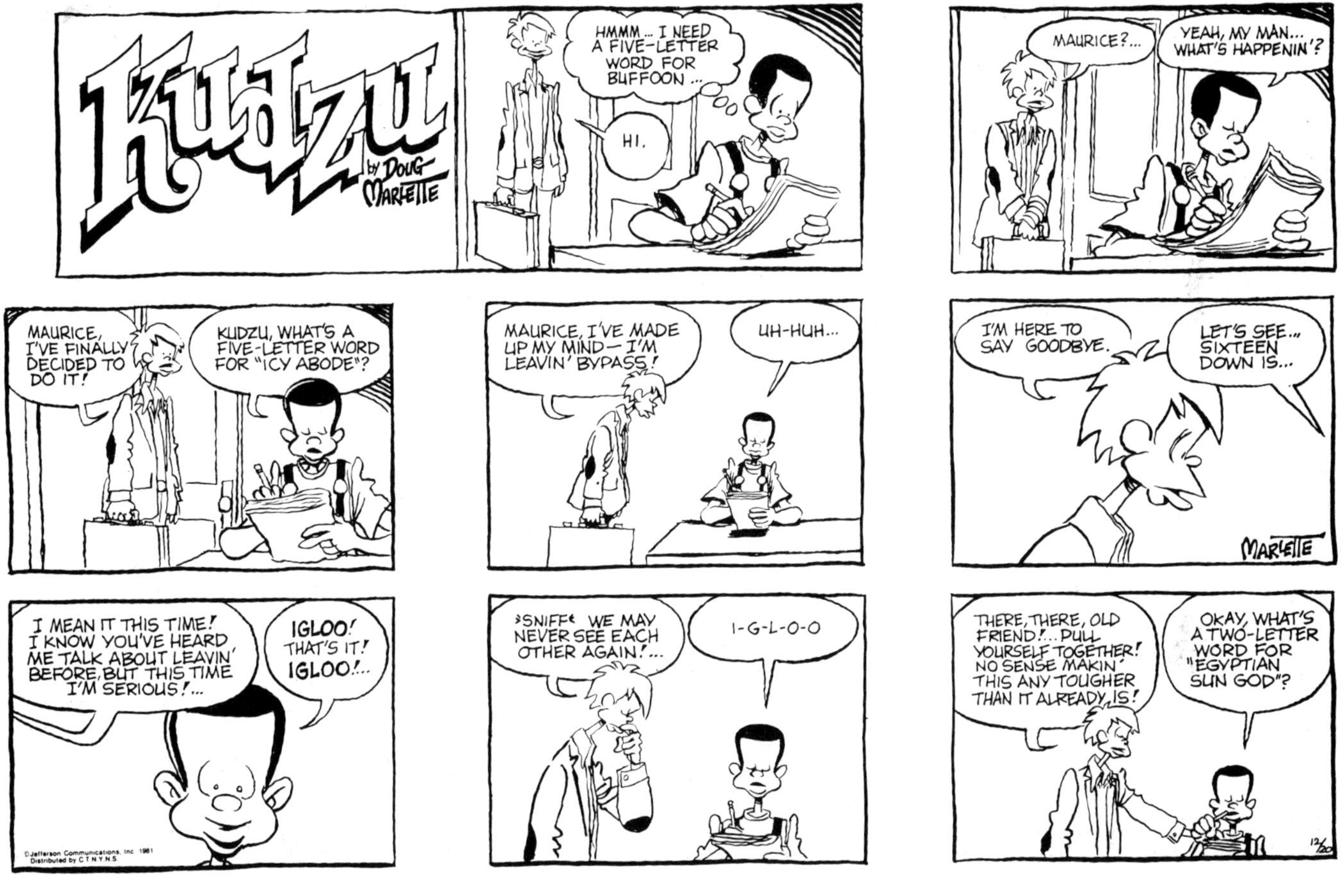
KUDZU
by DOUG MARLETTE
HMMM ... I NEED A FIVE-LETTER WORD FOR BUFFOON ...
HI.
MAURICE?...
YEAH, MY MAN... WHAT'S HAPPENIN'?
MAURICE, I'VE FINALLY DECIDED TO DO IT!
KUDZU, WHAT'S A FIVE-LETTER WORD FOR "ICY ABODE"?
MAURICE, I'VE MADE UP MY MIND— I'M LEAVIN' BYPASS!
UH-HUH...
I'M HERE TO SAY GOODBYE.
LET'S SEE... SIXTEEN DOWN IS...
MARLETTE
I MEAN IT THIS TIME! I KNOW YOU'VE HEARD ME TALK ABOUT LEAVIN' BEFORE, BUT THIS TIME I'M SERIOUS!...
IGLOO! THAT'S IT! IGLOO!...
©Jefferson Communications, Inc 1981 Distributed by C.T.N.Y.N.S.
SNIFF WE MAY NEVER SEE EACH OTHER AGAIN!...
I-G-L-O-O
THERE, THERE, OLD FRIEND!... PULL YOURSELF TOGETHER! NO SENSE MAKIN' THIS ANY TOUGHER THAN IT ALREADY IS!
OKAY, WHAT'S A TWO-LETTER WORD FOR "EGYPTIAN SUN GOD"?
12/20

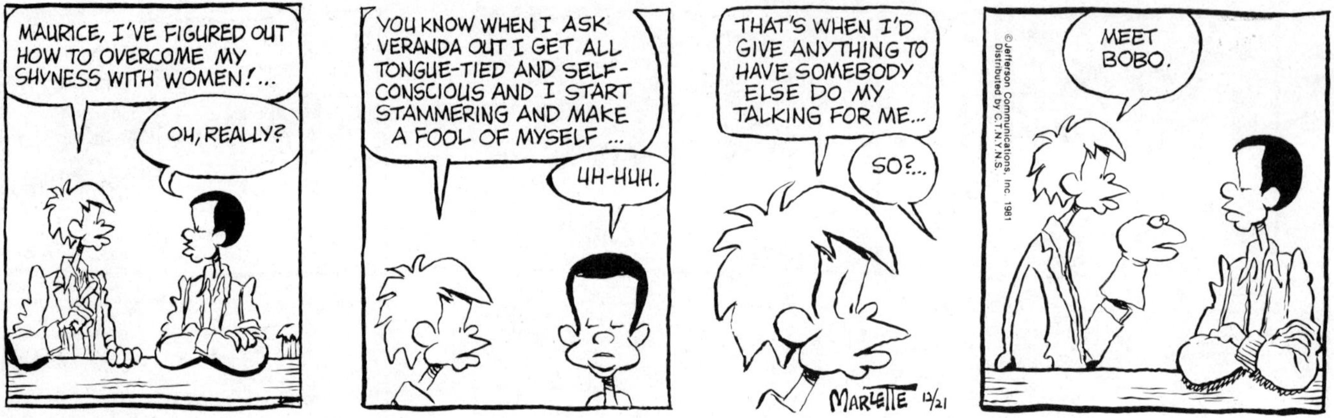
MAURICE, I'VE FIGURED OUT HOW TO OVERCOME MY SHYNESS WITH WOMEN!...
OH, REALLY?
YOU KNOW WHEN I ASK VERANDA OUT I GET ALL TONGUE-TIED AND SELF-CONSCIOUS AND I START STAMMERING AND MAKE A FOOL OF MYSELF ...
UH-HUH.
THAT'S WHEN I'D GIVE ANYTHING TO HAVE SOMEBODY ELSE DO MY TALKING FOR ME...
SO?...
MARLETTE 12/21
©Jefferson Communications, Inc. 1981
Distributed by C.T.N.Y.N.S.
MEET BOBO.

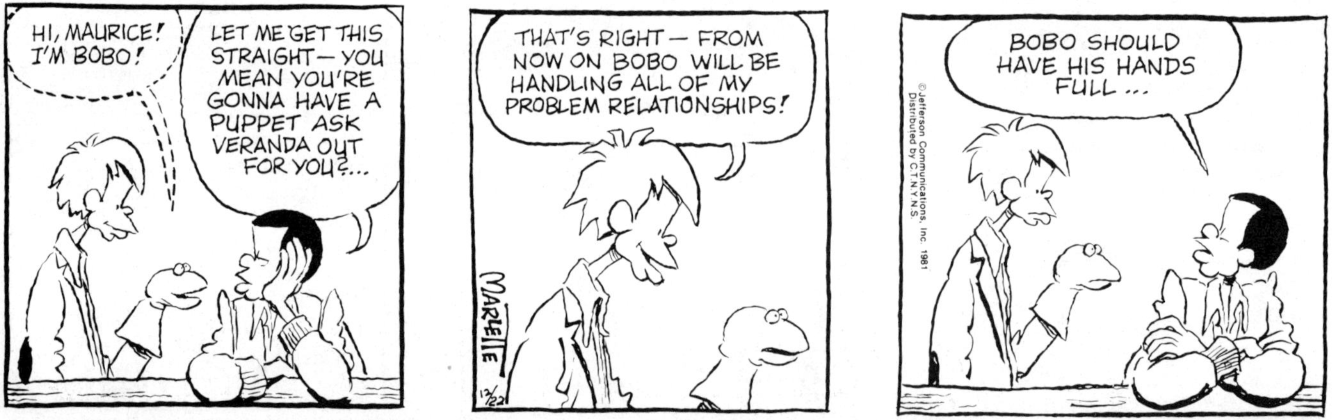
HI, MAURICE! I'M BOBO!
LET ME GET THIS STRAIGHT— YOU MEAN YOU'RE GONNA HAVE A PUPPET ASK VERANDA OUT FOR YOU?...
THAT'S RIGHT — FROM NOW ON BOBO WILL BE HANDLING ALL OF MY PROBLEM RELATIONSHIPS!
MARLETTE 12/22
©Jefferson Communications, Inc. 1981
Distributed by C.T.N.Y.N.S.
BOBO SHOULD HAVE HIS HANDS FULL ...

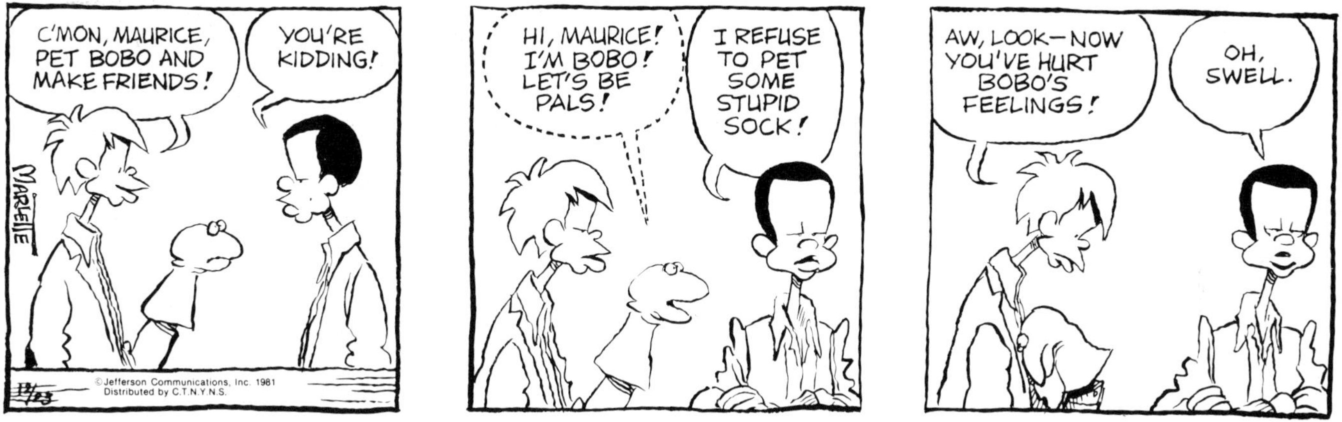
C'MON, MAURICE, PET BOBO AND MAKE FRIENDS!
YOU'RE KIDDING!
MARLETTE
© Jefferson Communications, Inc. 1981
Distributed by C.T.N.Y.N.S.
HI, MAURICE! I'M BOBO! LET'S BE PALS!
I REFUSE TO PET SOME STUPID SOCK!
AW, LOOK—NOW YOU'VE HURT BOBO'S FEELINGS!
OH, SWELL.

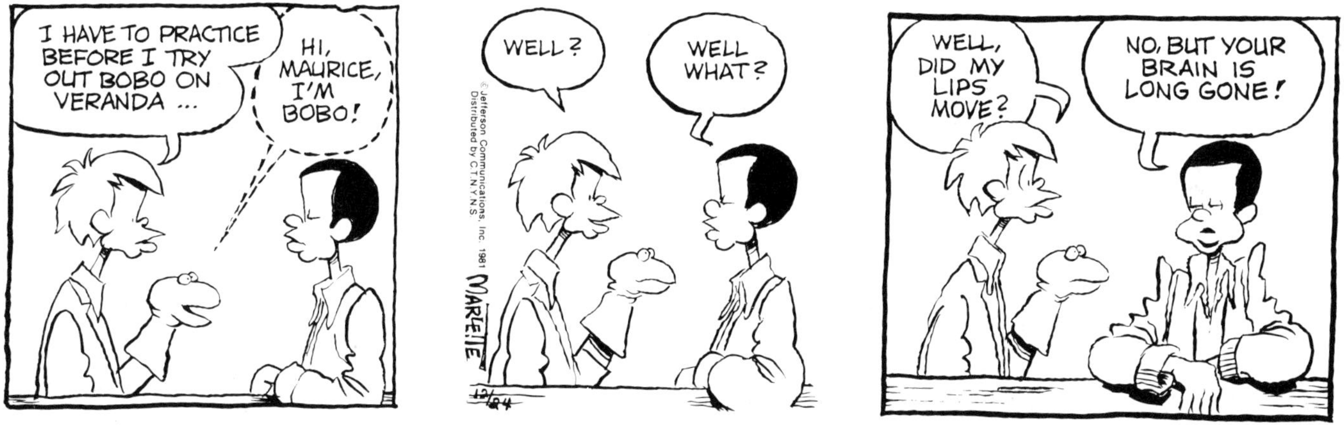
I HAVE TO PRACTICE BEFORE I TRY OUT BOBO ON VERANDA ...
HI, MAURICE, I'M BOBO!
WELL?
WELL WHAT?
© Jefferson Communications, Inc. 1981
Distributed by C.T.N.Y.N.S.
MARLETTE
WELL, DID MY LIPS MOVE?
NO, BUT YOUR BRAIN IS LONG GONE!

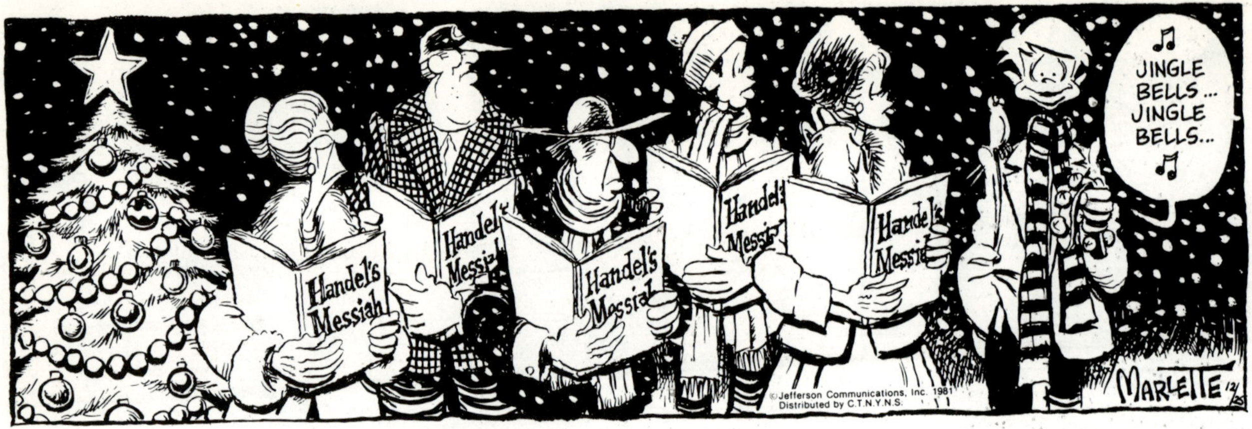

Handel's Messiah
JINGLE BELLS... JINGLE BELLS...
©Jefferson Communications, Inc. 1981 Distributed by C.T.N.Y.N.S.
MARLETTE

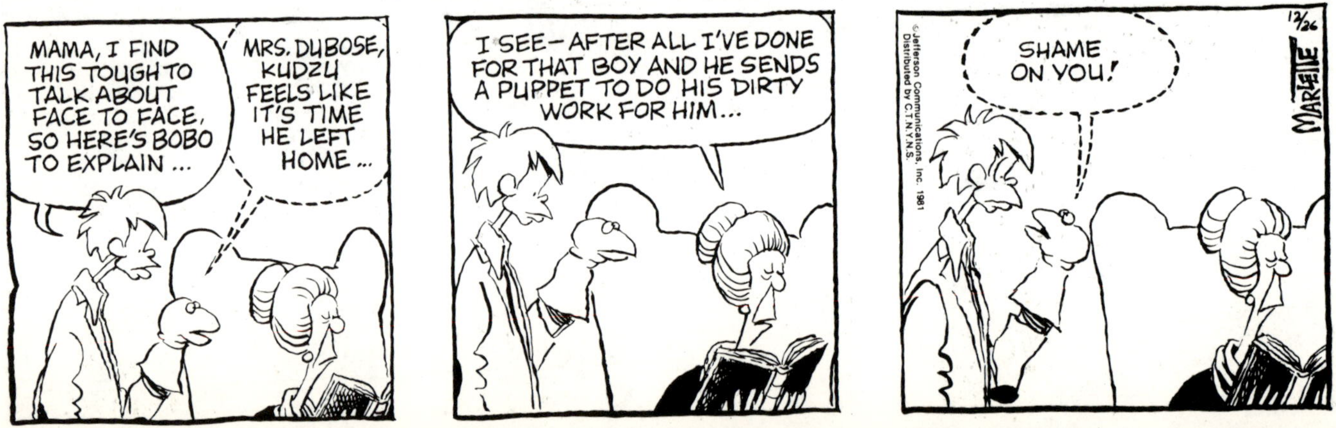

MAMA, I FIND THIS TOUGH TO TALK ABOUT FACE TO FACE, SO HERE'S BOBO TO EXPLAIN ...
MRS. DUBOSE, KUDZU FEELS LIKE IT'S TIME HE LEFT HOME ...
I SEE—AFTER ALL I'VE DONE FOR THAT BOY AND HE SENDS A PUPPET TO DO HIS DIRTY WORK FOR HIM ...
SHAME ON YOU!
©Jefferson Communications, Inc. 1981 Distributed by C.T.N.Y.N.S.
MARLETTE 12/26

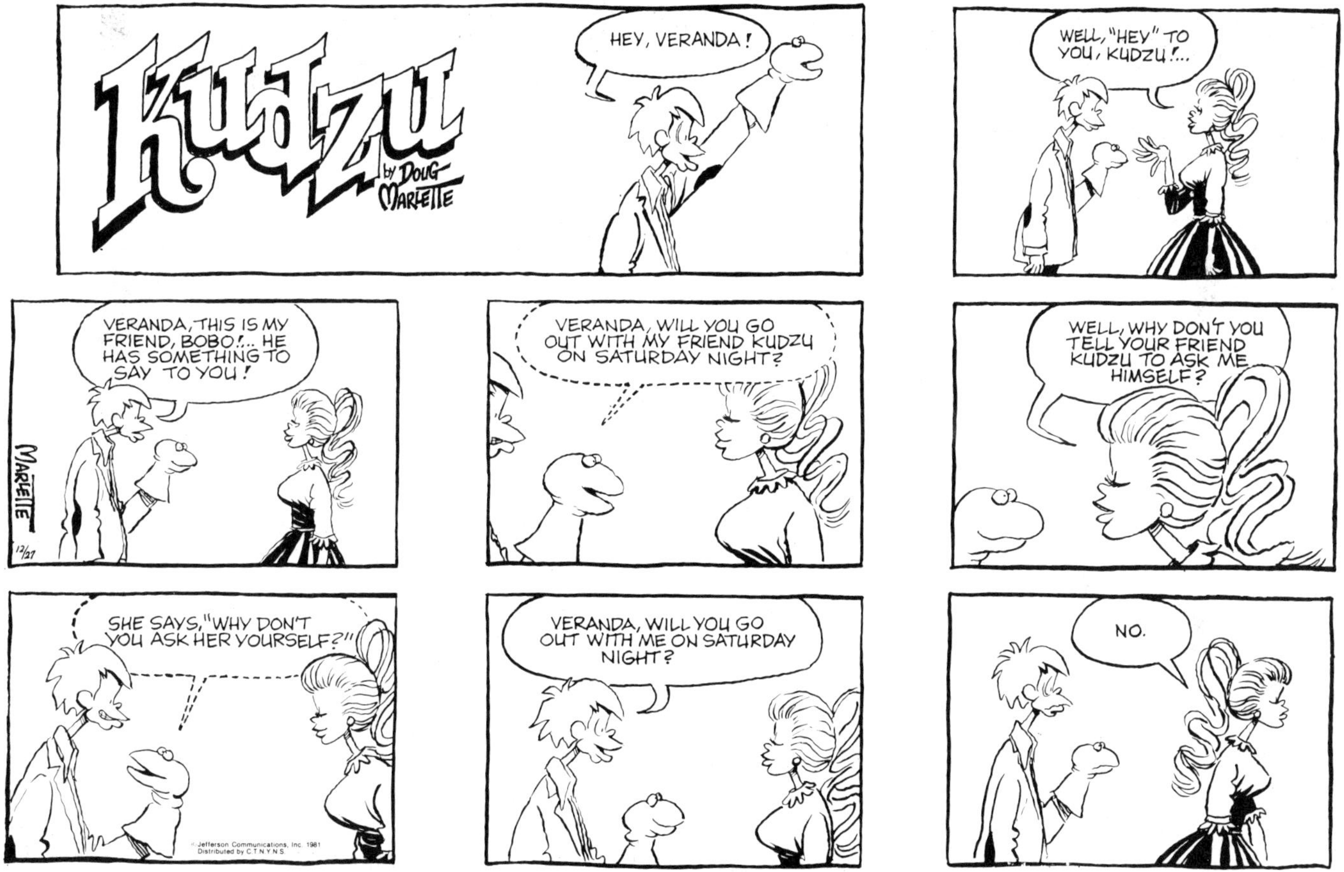
Kudzu
by Doug Marlette
HEY, VERANDA!
WELL, "HEY" TO YOU, KUDZU!...
VERANDA, THIS IS MY FRIEND, BOBO!... HE HAS SOMETHING TO SAY TO YOU!
MARLETTE
12/27
VERANDA, WILL YOU GO OUT WITH MY FRIEND KUDZU ON SATURDAY NIGHT?
WELL, WHY DON'T YOU TELL YOUR FRIEND KUDZU TO ASK ME HIMSELF?
SHE SAYS, "WHY DON'T YOU ASK HER YOURSELF?"
© Jefferson Communications, Inc. 1981
Distributed by C.T.N.Y.N.S.
VERANDA, WILL YOU GO OUT WITH ME ON SATURDAY NIGHT?
NO.

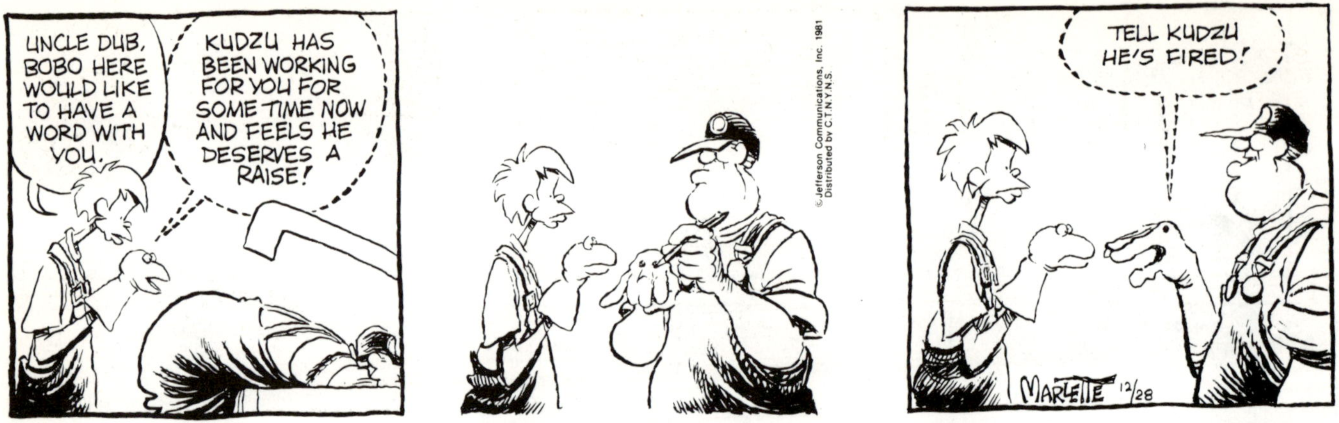

UNCLE DUB, BOBO HERE WOULD LIKE TO HAVE A WORD WITH YOU.
KUDZU HAS BEEN WORKING FOR YOU FOR SOME TIME NOW AND FEELS HE DESERVES A RAISE!
TELL KUDZU HE'S FIRED!
MARLETTE 12/28
© Jefferson Communications, Inc. 1981
Distributed by C.T.N.Y.N.S.

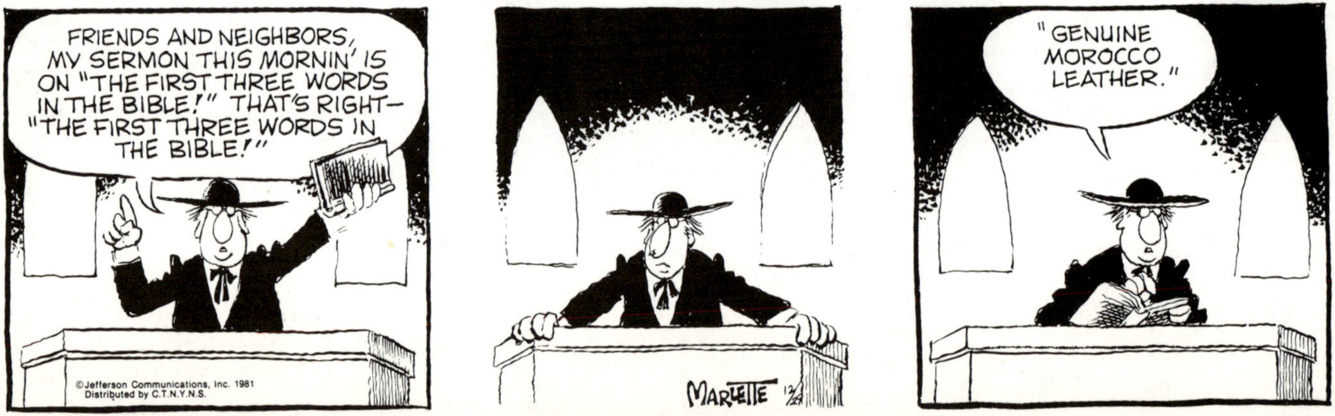

FRIENDS AND NEIGHBORS, MY SERMON THIS MORNIN' IS ON "THE FIRST THREE WORDS IN THE BIBLE!" THAT'S RIGHT— "THE FIRST THREE WORDS IN THE BIBLE!"
© Jefferson Communications, Inc. 1981
Distributed by C.T.N.Y.N.S.
MARLETTE 12/27
"GENUINE MOROCCO LEATHER."

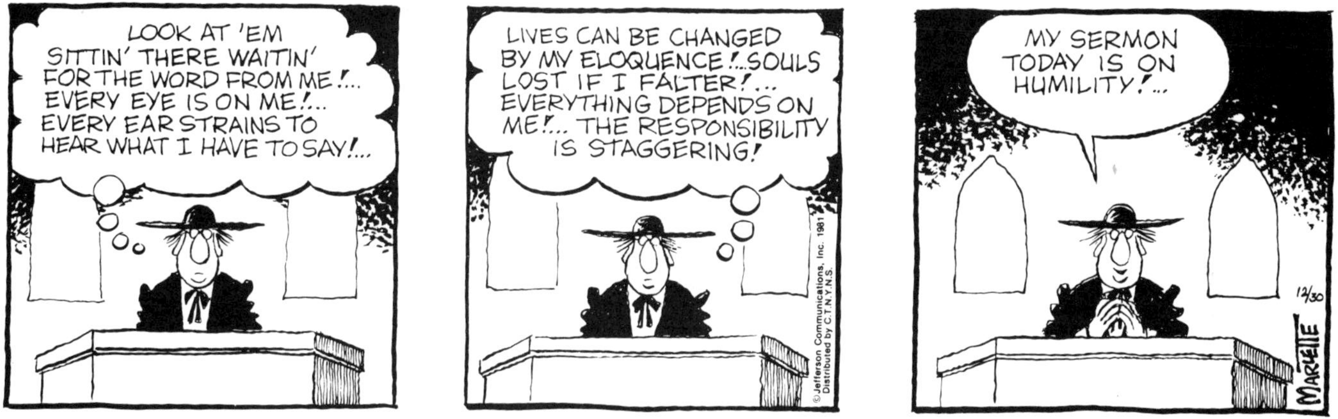
LOOK AT 'EM SITTIN' THERE WAITIN' FOR THE WORD FROM ME!... EVERY EYE IS ON ME!... EVERY EAR STRAINS TO HEAR WHAT I HAVE TO SAY!...
LIVES CAN BE CHANGED BY MY ELOQUENCE!...SOULS LOST IF I FALTER!... EVERYTHING DEPENDS ON ME!... THE RESPONSIBILITY IS STAGGERING!
© Jefferson Communications, Inc. 1981
Distributed by C.T.N.Y.N.S.
MY SERMON TODAY IS ON HUMILITY!...
12/30
MARLETTE

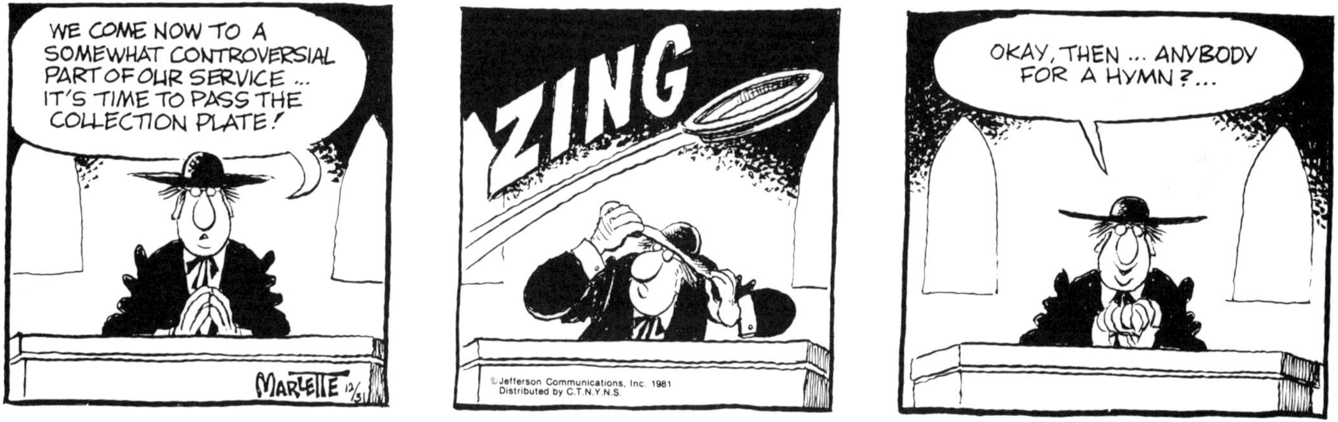
WE COME NOW TO A SOMEWHAT CONTROVERSIAL PART OF OUR SERVICE ... IT'S TIME TO PASS THE COLLECTION PLATE!
MARLETTE 12/31
ZING
© Jefferson Communications, Inc. 1981
Distributed by C.T.N.Y.N.S.
OKAY, THEN ... ANYBODY FOR A HYMN?...

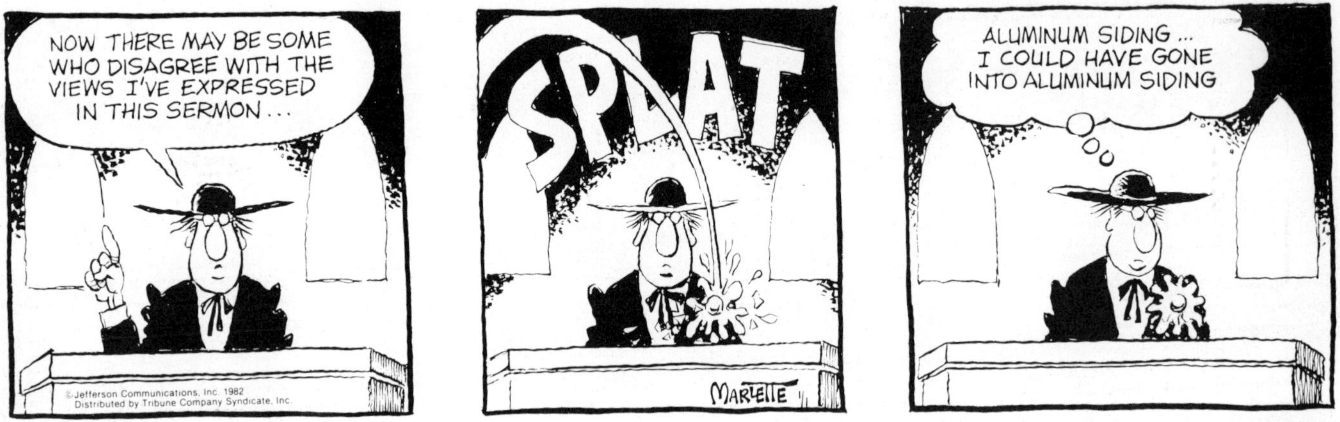
NOW THERE MAY BE SOME WHO DISAGREE WITH THE VIEWS I'VE EXPRESSED IN THIS SERMON . . .
©Jefferson Communications, Inc. 1982
Distributed by Tribune Company Syndicate, Inc.
SPLAT
MARLETTE 1/1
ALUMINUM SIDING ... I COULD HAVE GONE INTO ALUMINUM SIDING

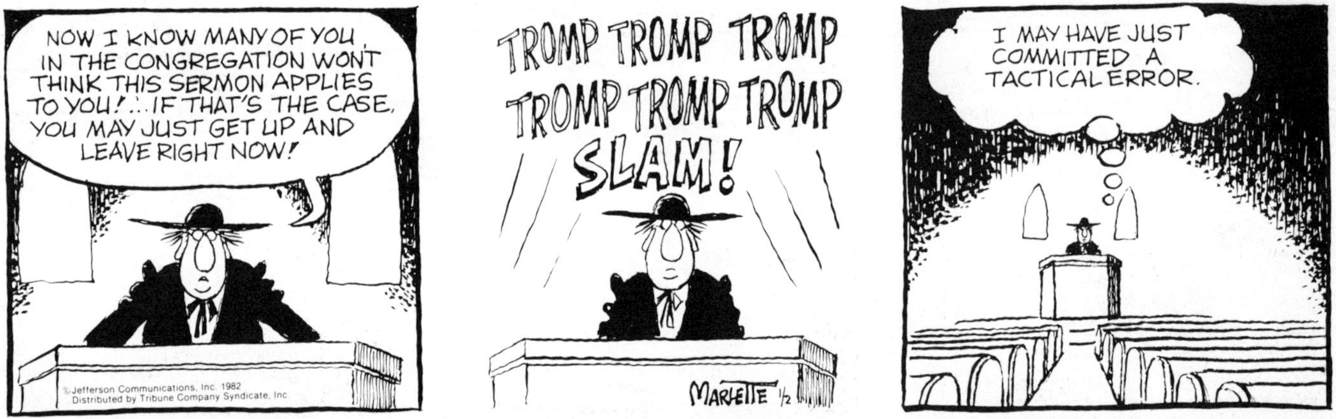
NOW I KNOW MANY OF YOU IN THE CONGREGATION WON'T THINK THIS SERMON APPLIES TO YOU! ... IF THAT'S THE CASE, YOU MAY JUST GET UP AND LEAVE RIGHT NOW!
©Jefferson Communications, Inc. 1982
Distributed by Tribune Company Syndicate, Inc.
TROMP TROMP TROMP
TROMP TROMP TROMP
SLAM!
MARLETTE 1/2
I MAY HAVE JUST COMMITTED A TACTICAL ERROR.

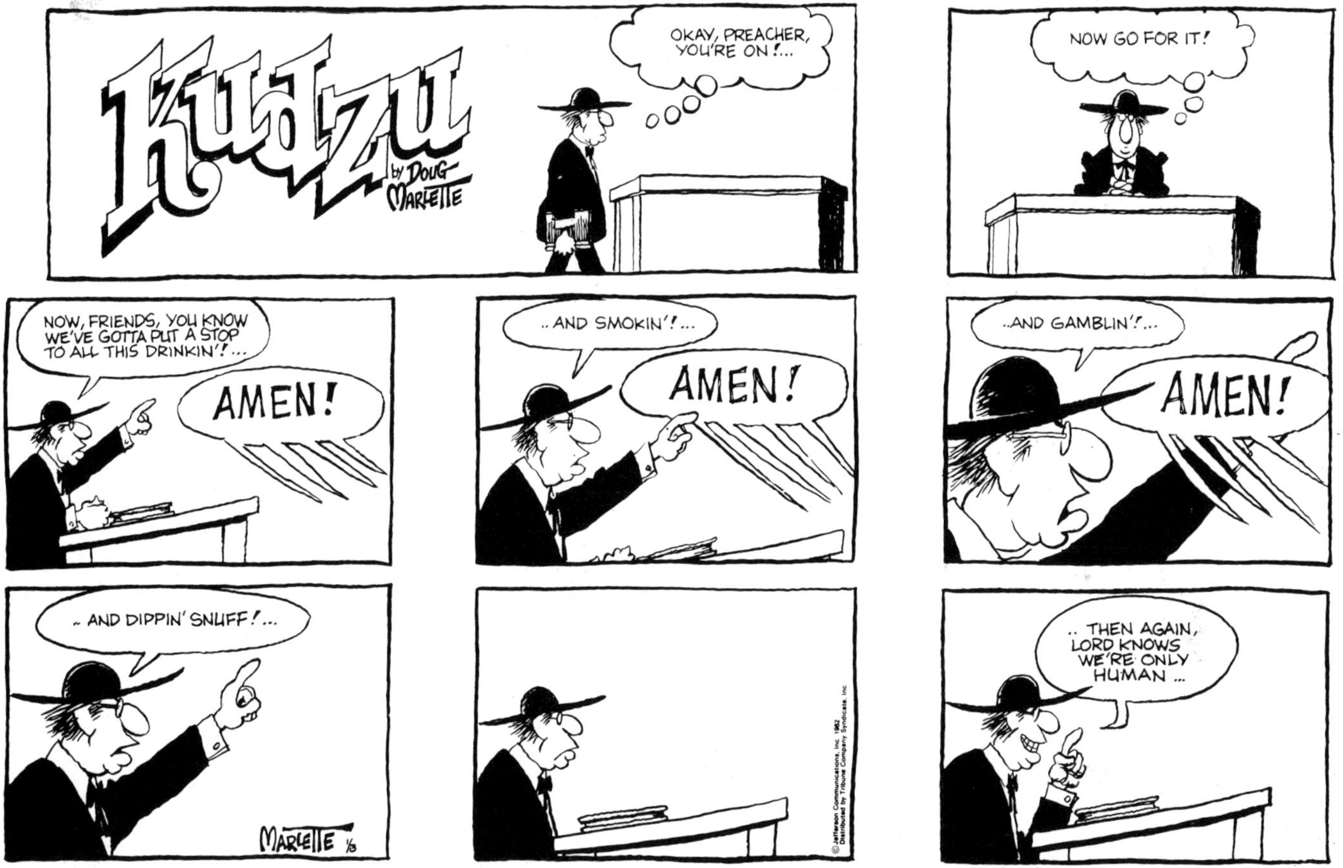
Kudzu
by Doug Marlette
OKAY, PREACHER, YOU'RE ON!...
NOW GO FOR IT!
NOW, FRIENDS, YOU KNOW WE'VE GOTTA PUT A STOP TO ALL THIS DRINKIN'!...
AMEN!
..AND SMOKIN'!...
AMEN!
..AND GAMBLIN'!...
AMEN!
.. AND DIPPIN' SNUFF!...
MARLETTE 1/3
© Jefferson Communications, Inc. 1982 Distributed by Tribune Company Syndicate, Inc
.. THEN AGAIN, LORD KNOWS WE'RE ONLY HUMAN ...

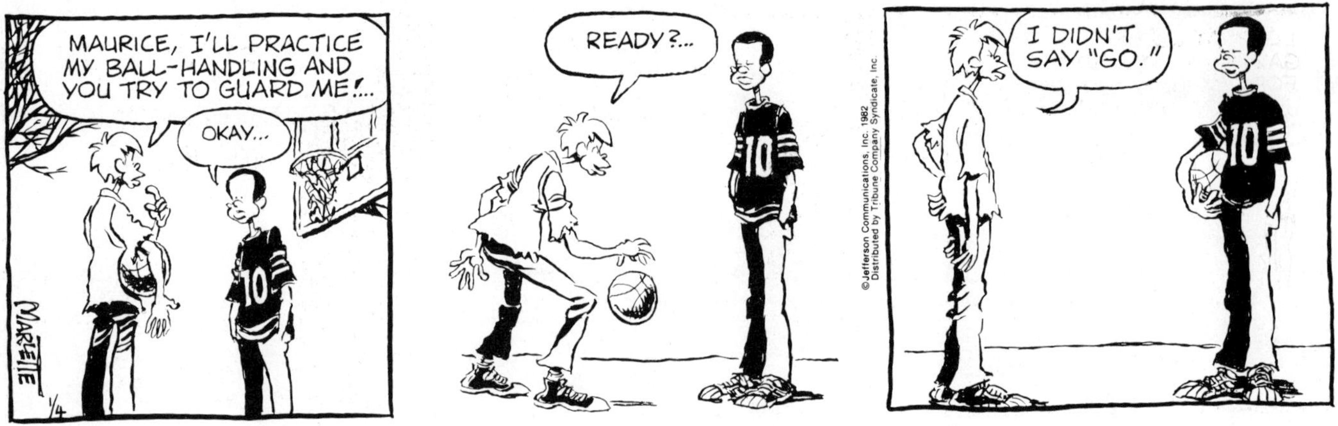
MAURICE, I'LL PRACTICE MY BALL-HANDLING AND YOU TRY TO GUARD ME!...
OKAY...
READY?...
I DIDN'T SAY "GO."
1/4
©Jefferson Communications, Inc. 1982
Distributed by Tribune Company Syndicate, Inc.

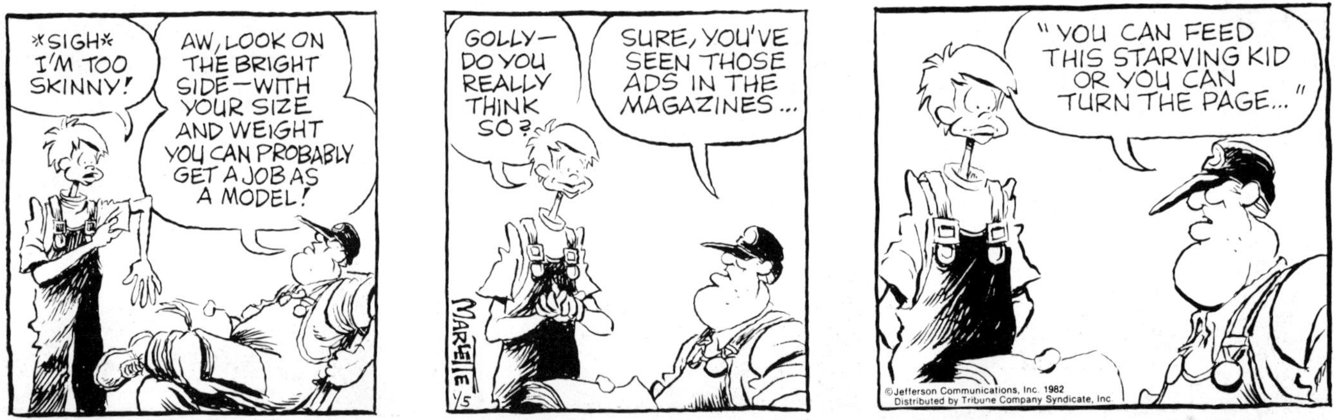
SIGH I'M TOO SKINNY!
AW, LOOK ON THE BRIGHT SIDE—WITH YOUR SIZE AND WEIGHT YOU CAN PROBABLY GET A JOB AS A MODEL!
GOLLY— DO YOU REALLY THINK SO?
SURE, YOU'VE SEEN THOSE ADS IN THE MAGAZINES...
"YOU CAN FEED THIS STARVING KID OR YOU CAN TURN THE PAGE..."
1/5
©Jefferson Communications, Inc. 1982
Distributed by Tribune Company Syndicate, Inc.

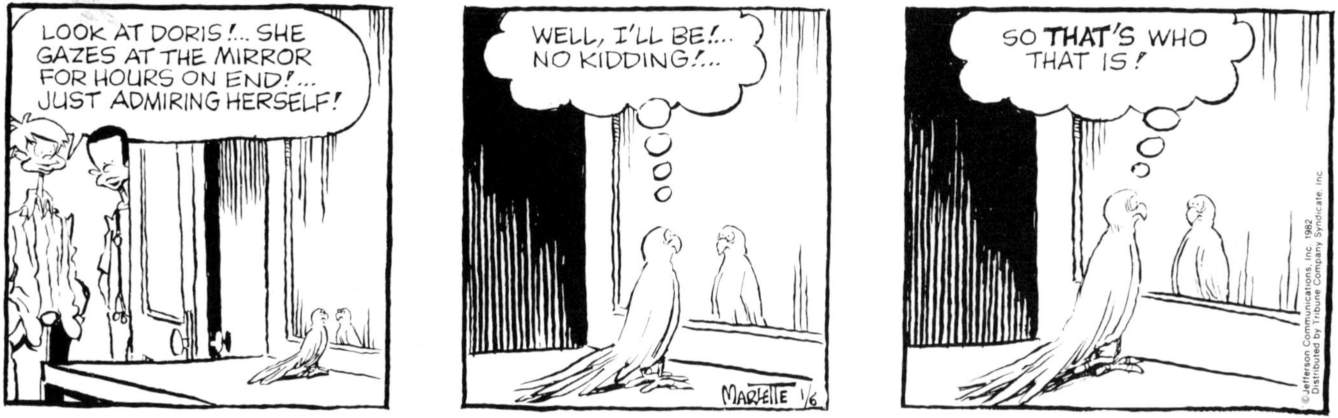
LOOK AT DORIS!... SHE GAZES AT THE MIRROR FOR HOURS ON END!... JUST ADMIRING HERSELF!
WELL, I'LL BE!... NO KIDDING!...
MARLETTE 1/6
SO **THAT'S** WHO THAT IS!
© Jefferson Communications, Inc. 1982 Distributed by Tribune Company Syndicate, Inc.

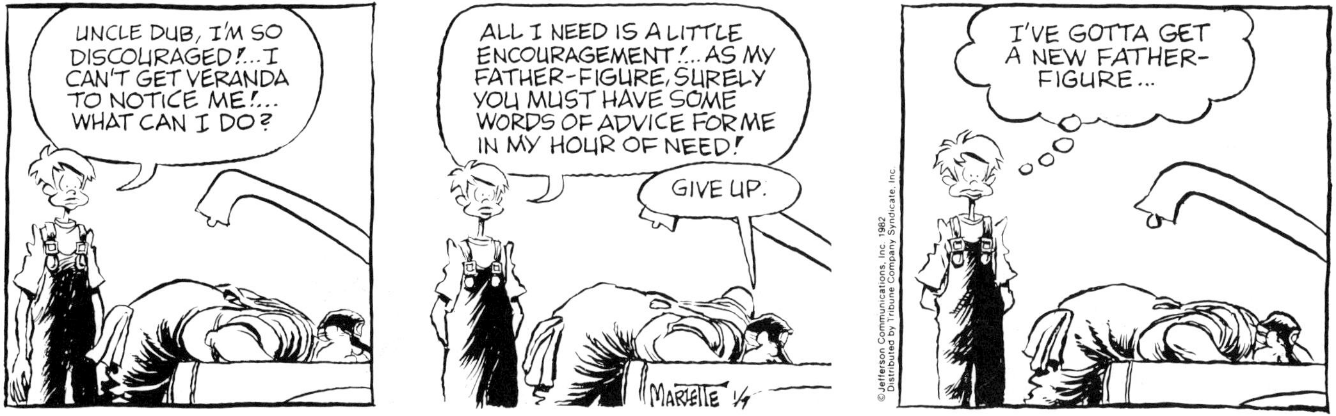
UNCLE DUB, I'M SO DISCOURAGED!... I CAN'T GET VERANDA TO NOTICE ME!... WHAT CAN I DO?
ALL I NEED IS A LITTLE ENCOURAGEMENT!... AS MY FATHER-FIGURE, SURELY YOU MUST HAVE SOME WORDS OF ADVICE FOR ME IN MY HOUR OF NEED!
GIVE UP.
MARLETTE 1/7
© Jefferson Communications, Inc. 1982 Distributed by Tribune Company Syndicate, Inc.
I'VE GOTTA GET A NEW FATHER-FIGURE...

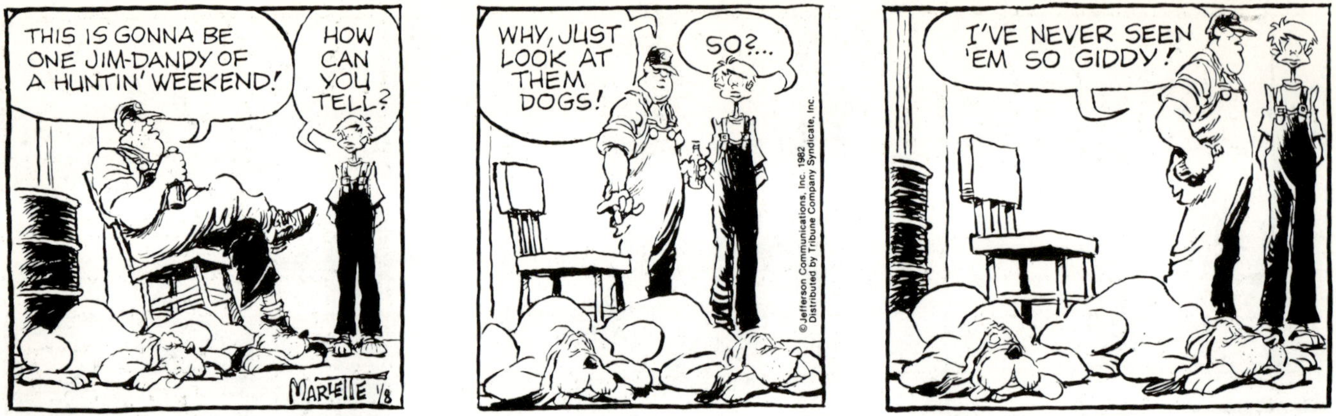
THIS IS GONNA BE ONE JIM-DANDY OF A HUNTIN' WEEKEND!
HOW CAN YOU TELL?
WHY, JUST LOOK AT THEM DOGS!
SO?...
I'VE NEVER SEEN 'EM SO GIDDY!
MARLETTE 1/8
© Jefferson Communications, Inc. 1982 Distributed by Tribune Company Syndicate, Inc.

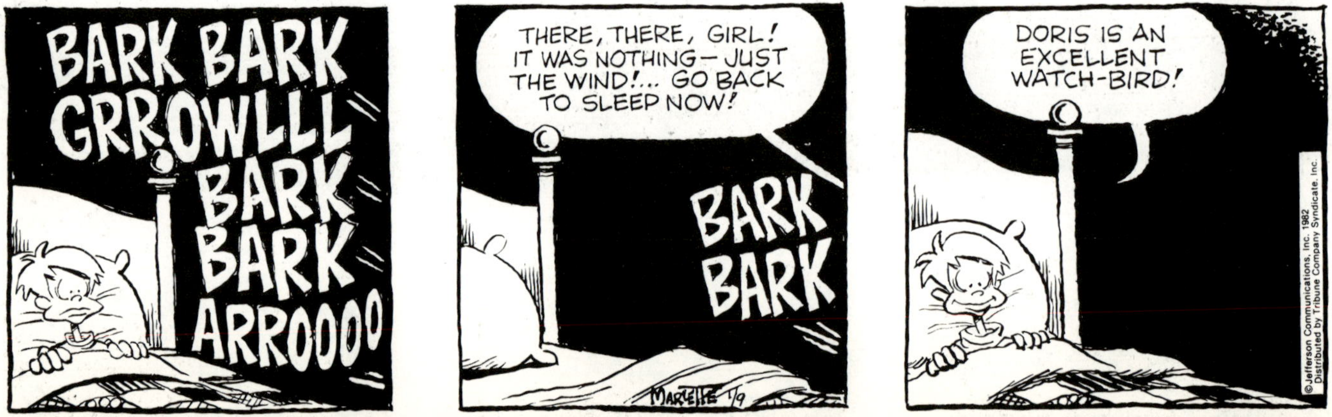
BARK BARK GRROWLLL BARK BARK ARROOOO
THERE, THERE, GIRL! IT WAS NOTHING— JUST THE WIND!... GO BACK TO SLEEP NOW!
BARK BARK
DORIS IS AN EXCELLENT WATCH-BIRD!
MARLETTE 1/9
© Jefferson Communications, Inc. 1982 Distributed by Tribune Company Syndicate, Inc.

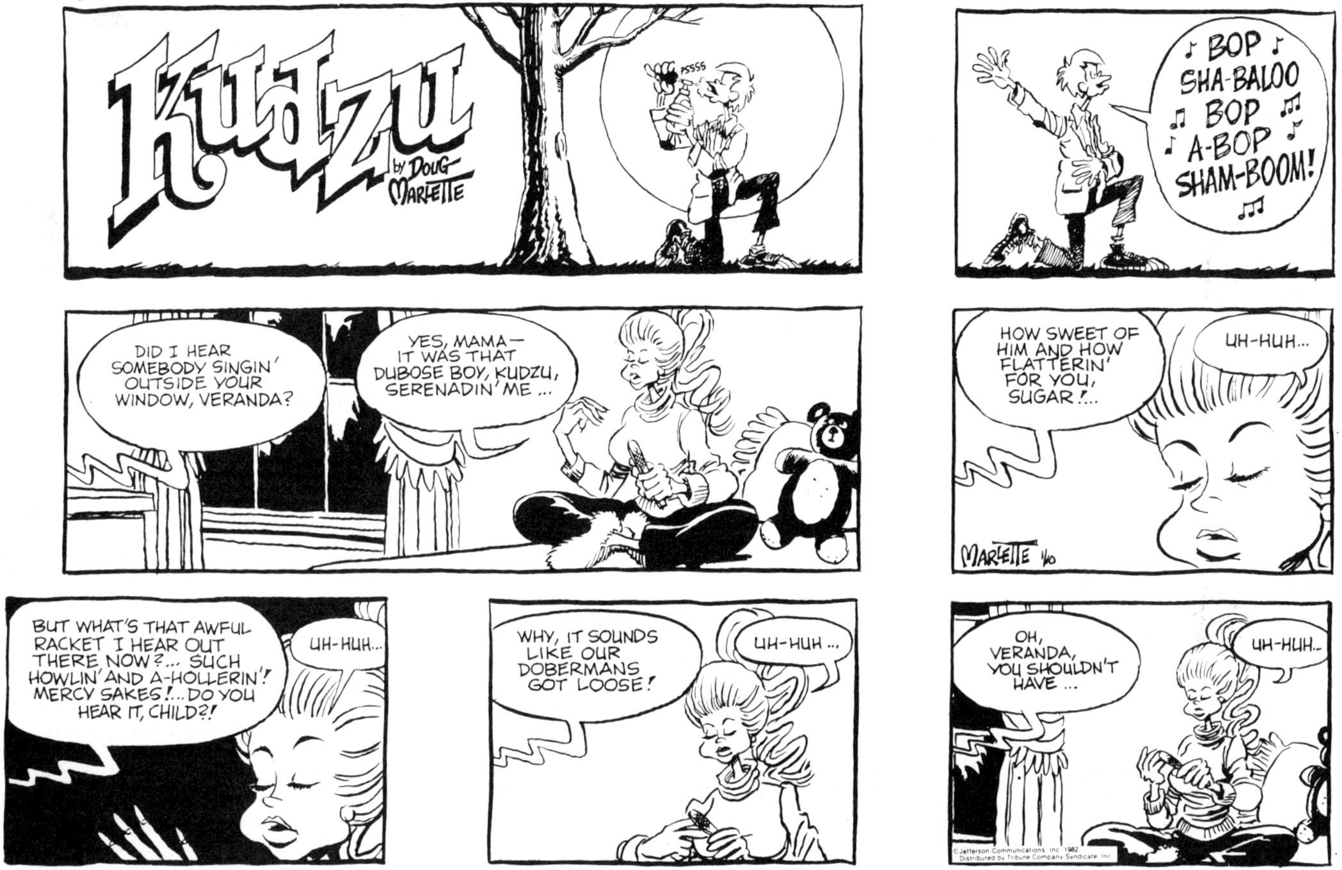
KUDZU
by DOUG MARLETTE
PSSSS
BOP SHA-BALOO BOP A-BOP SHAM-BOOM!
DID I HEAR SOMEBODY SINGIN' OUTSIDE YOUR WINDOW, VERANDA?
YES, MAMA— IT WAS THAT DUBOSE BOY, KUDZU, SERENADIN' ME ...
HOW SWEET OF HIM AND HOW FLATTERIN' FOR YOU, SUGAR!...
UH-HUH...
MARLETTE 1/10
BUT WHAT'S THAT AWFUL RACKET I HEAR OUT THERE NOW?... SUCH HOWLIN' AND A-HOLLERIN'! MERCY SAKES!... DO YOU HEAR IT, CHILD?!
UH-HUH...
WHY, IT SOUNDS LIKE OUR DOBERMANS GOT LOOSE!
UH-HUH ...
OH, VERANDA, YOU SHOULDN'T HAVE ...
UH-HUH...
© Jefferson Communications Inc. 1982
Distributed by Tribune Company Syndicate Inc.

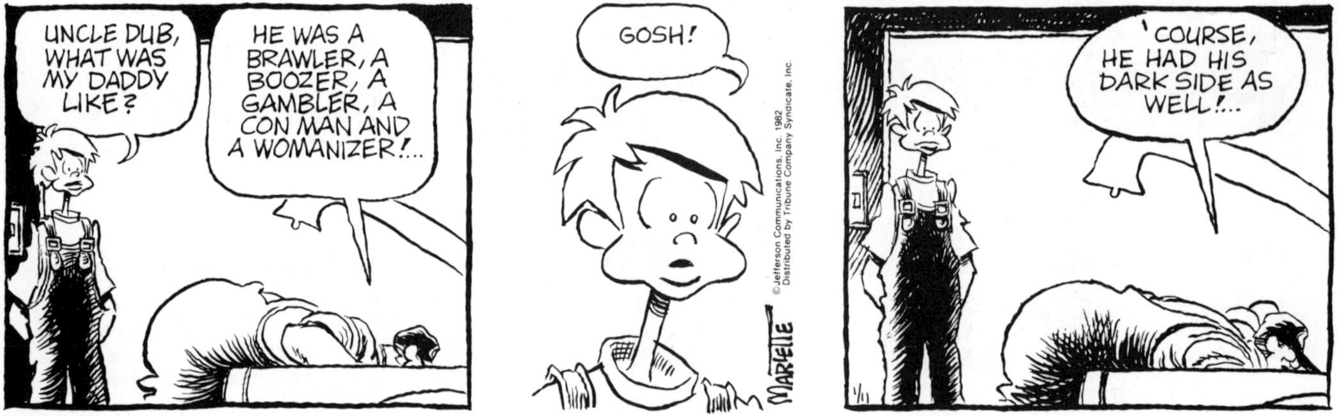
UNCLE DUB, WHAT WAS MY DADDY LIKE?
HE WAS A BRAWLER, A BOOZER, A GAMBLER, A CON MAN AND A WOMANIZER!...
GOSH!
©Jefferson Communications, Inc. 1982
Distributed by Tribune Company Syndicate, Inc.
MARLETTE
'COURSE, HE HAD HIS DARK SIDE AS WELL!...
1/11

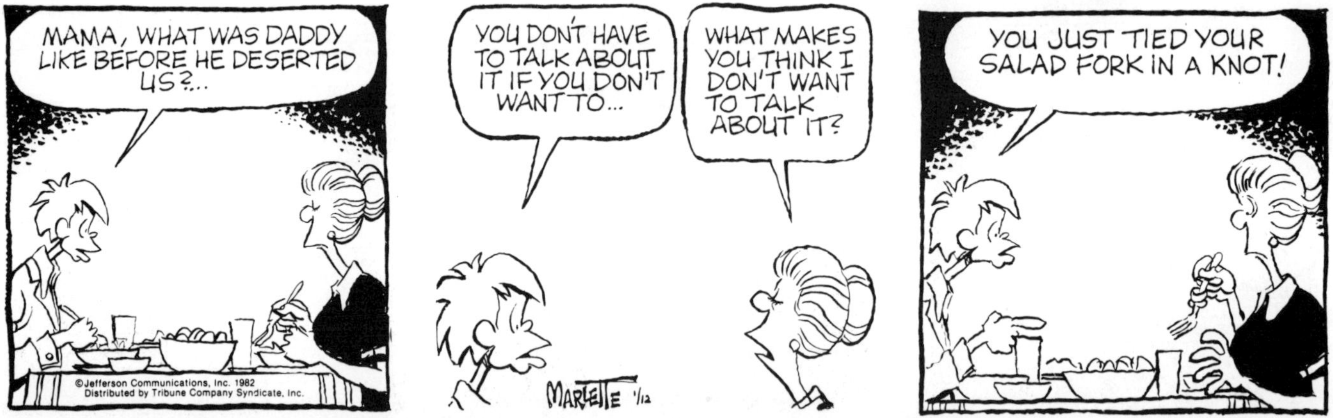
MAMA, WHAT WAS DADDY LIKE BEFORE HE DESERTED US?...
©Jefferson Communications, Inc. 1982
Distributed by Tribune Company Syndicate, Inc.
YOU DON'T HAVE TO TALK ABOUT IT IF YOU DON'T WANT TO...
WHAT MAKES YOU THINK I DON'T WANT TO TALK ABOUT IT?
MARLETTE 1/12
YOU JUST TIED YOUR SALAD FORK IN A KNOT!

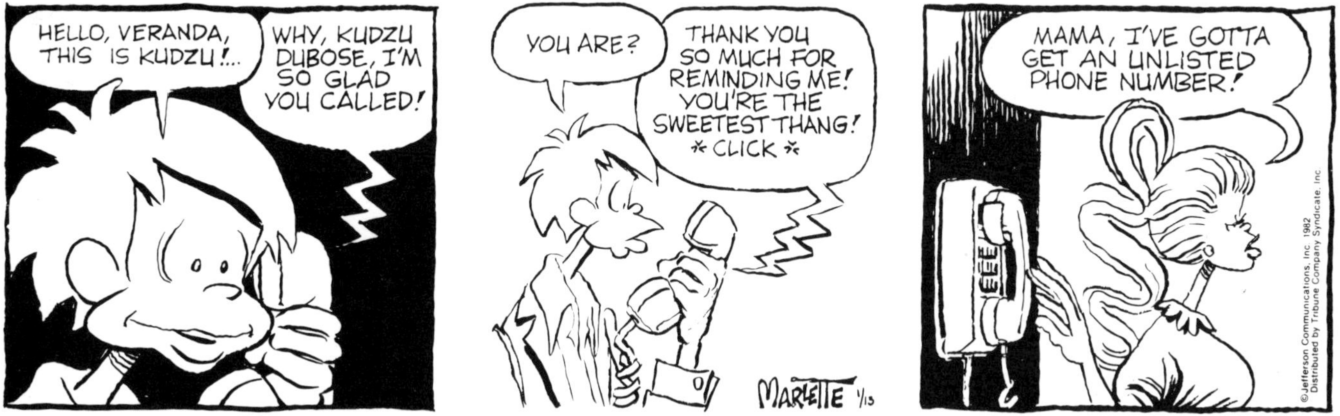
HELLO, VERANDA, THIS IS KUDZU!...
WHY, KUDZU DUBOSE, I'M SO GLAD YOU CALLED!
YOU ARE?
THANK YOU SO MUCH FOR REMINDING ME! YOU'RE THE SWEETEST THANG!
* CLICK *
MARLETTE 1/13
MAMA, I'VE GOTTA GET AN UNLISTED PHONE NUMBER!
©Jefferson Communications, Inc. 1982
Distributed by Tribune Company Syndicate, Inc.

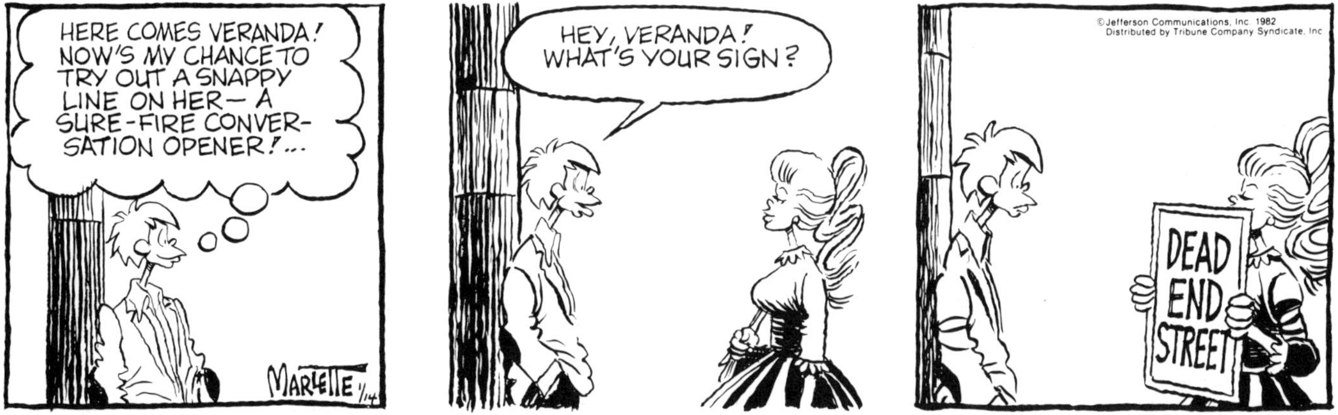
HERE COMES VERANDA! NOW'S MY CHANCE TO TRY OUT A SNAPPY LINE ON HER— A SURE-FIRE CONVERSATION OPENER!...
MARLETTE 1/14
HEY, VERANDA! WHAT'S YOUR SIGN?
©Jefferson Communications, Inc. 1982
Distributed by Tribune Company Syndicate, Inc
DEAD END STREET

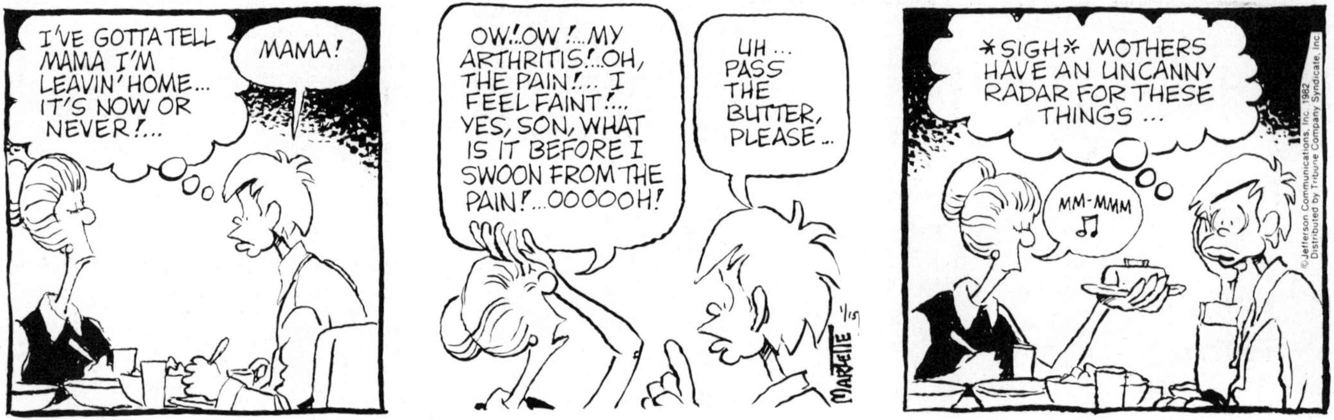
I'VE GOTTA TELL MAMA I'M LEAVIN' HOME... IT'S NOW OR NEVER!...
MAMA!
OW!..OW!...MY ARTHRITIS!...OH, THE PAIN!... I FEEL FAINT!... YES, SON, WHAT IS IT BEFORE I SWOON FROM THE PAIN!...OOOOOH!
UH ... PASS THE BUTTER, PLEASE...
1/15
MARLETTE
SIGH MOTHERS HAVE AN UNCANNY RADAR FOR THESE THINGS ...
MM-MMM ♫
© Jefferson Communications, Inc. 1982
Distributed by Tribune Company Syndicate, Inc.

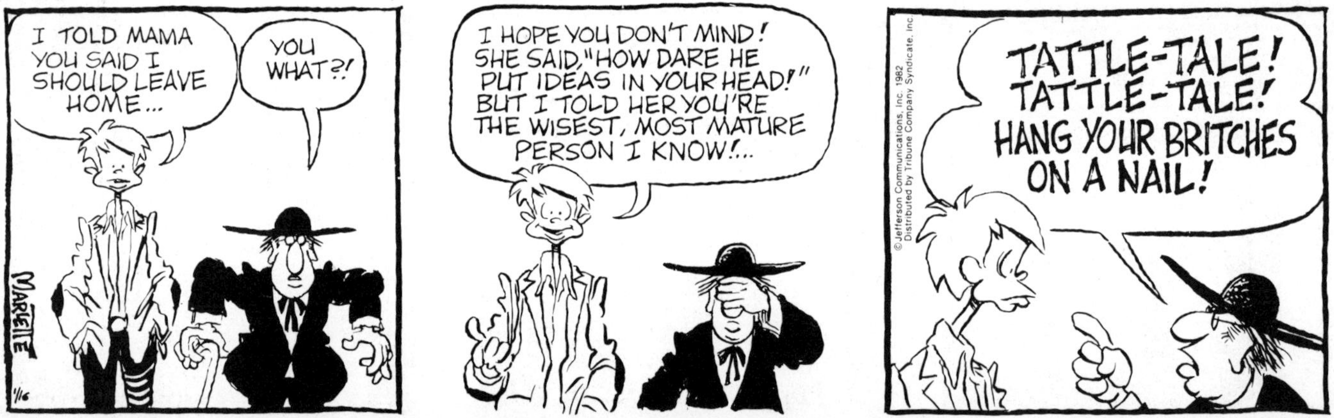
I TOLD MAMA YOU SAID I SHOULD LEAVE HOME...
YOU WHAT?!
MARLETTE
1/16
I HOPE YOU DON'T MIND! SHE SAID, "HOW DARE HE PUT IDEAS IN YOUR HEAD!" BUT I TOLD HER YOU'RE THE WISEST, MOST MATURE PERSON I KNOW!...
© Jefferson Communications, Inc. 1982
Distributed by Tribune Company Syndicate, Inc.
TATTLE-TALE! TATTLE-TALE! HANG YOUR BRITCHES ON A NAIL!

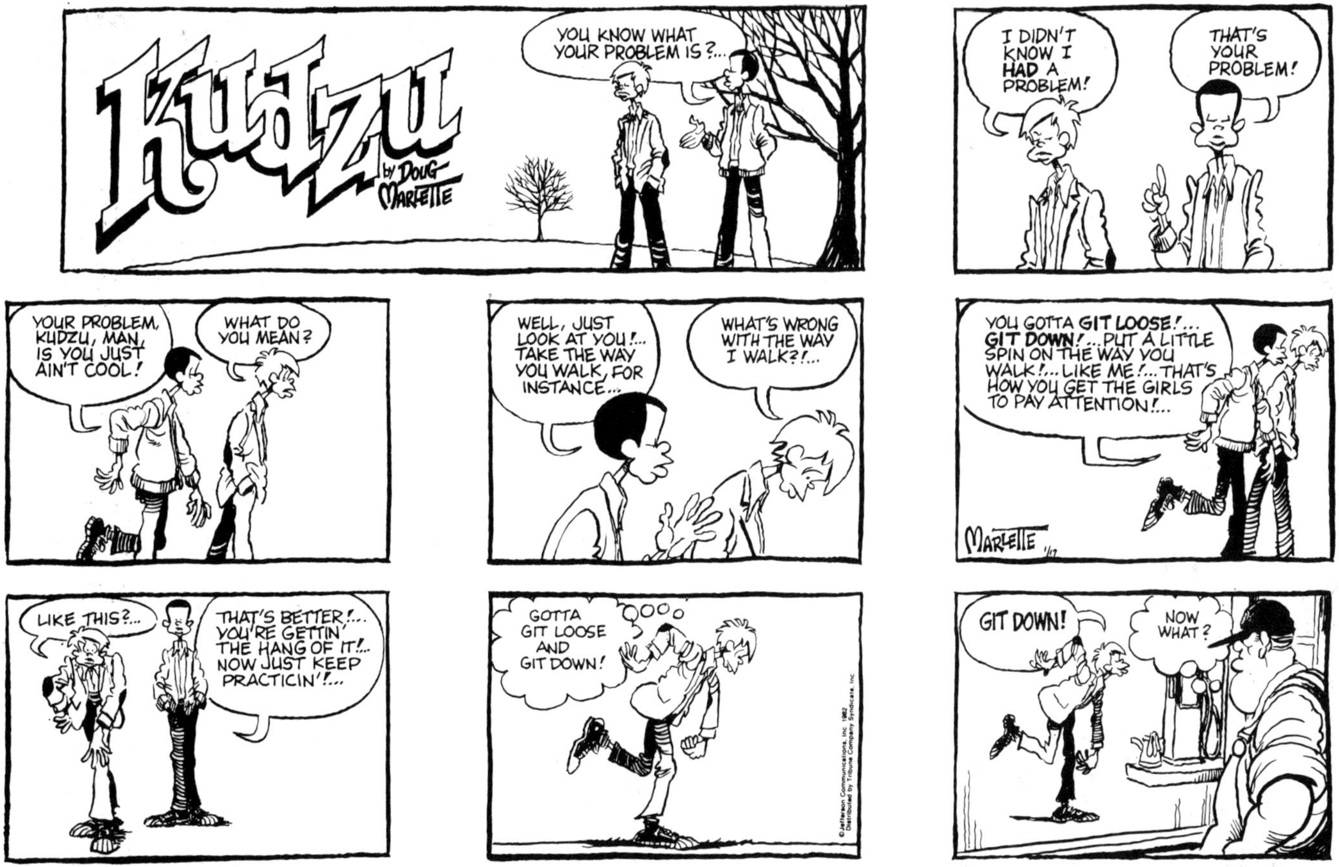
Kudzu
by DOUG MARLETTE
YOU KNOW WHAT YOUR PROBLEM IS?...
I DIDN'T KNOW I **HAD** A PROBLEM!
THAT'S YOUR PROBLEM!
YOUR PROBLEM, KUDZU, MAN, IS YOU JUST AIN'T COOL!
WHAT DO YOU MEAN?
WELL, JUST LOOK AT YOU!... TAKE THE WAY YOU WALK, FOR INSTANCE...
WHAT'S WRONG WITH THE WAY I WALK?!...
YOU GOTTA **GIT LOOSE!**... **GIT DOWN!**... PUT A LITTLE SPIN ON THE WAY YOU WALK!... LIKE ME!... THAT'S HOW YOU GET THE GIRLS TO PAY ATTENTION!...
MARLETTE 1/17
LIKE THIS?...
THAT'S BETTER!... YOU'RE GETTIN' THE HANG OF IT!... NOW JUST KEEP PRACTICIN'!...
GOTTA GIT LOOSE AND GIT DOWN!
© Jefferson Communications, Inc 1982 Distributed by Tribune Company Syndicate, Inc
GIT DOWN!
NOW WHAT?

About Doug Marlette, creator of KUDZU

Born in Greensboro, N.C. in 1949, Doug Marlette grew up in Durham, N.C., Laurel, Miss., and Sanford, Fla., the son of a naval chief petty officer. "There's a good deal of me in my principal character, Kudzu," he says, "and a good deal of Laurel and Sanford in Bypass. I located it in North Carolina because I was born there, but it could be anywhere."

Doug began drawing from the time he was old enough to hold a pencil. "The first indication I was on a downhill slide to a career in cartooning," he says, "came when I received my first report card at the age of five. My teacher notified my parents that although I excelled in art, I had a tendency to visit with my neighbors during naptime."

"By this time," he explains, "I was reproducing Mickey Mouse, Donald Duck, and Popeye with Xerox-like accuracy for my classmates, who rewarded me with marbles and extra desserts. Needless to say, I began to perceive that the cartoon business could be lucrative. But my real lucky break came in the ninth grade after the Beatles appeared on the Ed Sullivan Show one Sunday night. That Monday morning I began selling drawings of Paul McCartney to girls in my algebra class at fifty cents a shot."

As he came of age in the sixties, Doug's talent for drawing combined with an interest in politics. Fresh out of college, he landed a job on the *Charlotte Observer*, where, he says, "I have drawn more or less outrageous political cartoons ever since." In 1980-81 Doug took a year off to study at Harvard as the first cartoonist ever to receive a Nieman Fellowship in journalism. He is married to Melinda Hartley, a film producer in Charlotte, N.C.

Why the name KUDZU for the strip? "Kudzu is a fast-growing oriental creeper," Doug explains. "It was introduced years ago in the South to control soil erosion and is now a menace that covers millions of acres. My Kudzu is something of a menace, too, or at least his blunderings are."

Does he enjoy drawing the strip? "It's the fulfillment of my childhood ambition to make up my very own funny characters — without having to copy Mickey Mouse or Popeye. The only problem," Doug says, "is that I don't get the marbles or extra desserts anymore."